P9-DWU-812

OKANAGAN UNIV/COLLEGE LIBRARY

02458826

K

SEXUALLY AGGRESSIVE CHILDREN

BOOKS UNDER THE GENERAL EDITORSHIP OF JON R. CONTE, Ph.D.

Hate Crimes: Confronting Violence Against Lesbians and Gay Men
edited by Gregory M. Herek and Kevin T. Berrill

Legal Responses to Wife Assault: Current Trends and Evaluation
edited by N. Zoe Hilton

The Male Survivor: The Impact of Sexual Abuse
by Matthew Parynik Mendel

The Child Sexual Abuse Custody Dispute: Annotated Bibliography
by Wendy Deaton, Suzanne Long, Holly A. Magaña, and Julie Robbins

The Survivor's Guide
by Sharice A. Lee

Sexual Abuse in Nine North American Cultures: Treatment and Prevention
edited by Lisa Aronson Fontes

The Impact of Mandated Reporting on the Therapeutic Process:
Picking Up the Pieces
by Murray Levine, Howard J. Doueck, and Associates

Intimate Betrayal: Understanding and Responding to the Trauma
of Acquaintance Rape
by Vernon R. Wiehe and Ann L. Richards

Preventing Child Maltreatment Through Social Support: A Critical Analysis
by Ross A. Thompson

Researching Sexual Violence Against Women: Methodological and
Personal Perspectives
edited by Martin D. Schwartz

Sibling Abuse: Hidden Physical, Emotional, and Sexual Trauma
by Vernon R. Wiehe

Sexually Aggressive Children: Coming to Understand Them
by Sharon K. Araji

OKANAGAN UNIVERSITY COLLEGE
LIBRARY
BRITISH COLUMBIA

SEXUALLY AGGRESSIVE CHILDREN

Coming to Understand Them

Foreword by William N. Friedrich

Sharon K. Araji

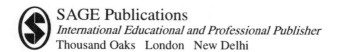

SAGE Publications
International Educational and Professional Publisher
Thousand Oaks   London   New Delhi

Copyright © 1997 by Sage Publications, Inc.

All rights reserved. No part of this book may be reproduced or utilized in any form or by any means, electronic or mechanical, including photocopying, recording, or by any information storage and retrieval system, without permission in writing from the publisher.

For information:

SAGE Publications, Inc.
2455 Teller Road
Thousand Oaks, California 91320
E-mail: order@sagepub.com

SAGE Publications Ltd.
6 Bonhill Street
London EC2A 4PU
United Kingdom

SAGE Publications India Pvt. Ltd.
M-32 Market
Greater Kailash I
New Delhi 110 048 India

Printed in the United States of America

Library of Congress Cataloging-in-Publication Data

Main entry under title:

Sexually aggressive children: Coming to understand them /
    edited by Sharon K. Araji.
        p. cm.
    Includes bibliographical references and index.
    ISBN 0-8039-5175-2 (cloth: acid-free paper). — ISBN
    0-8039-5176-0 (pbk.: acid-free paper)
        1. Psychosexual disorders in children. 2. Children and sex.
    3. Sexually abused children. 4. Children—Sexual behavior.
    I. Araji, Sharon.
    RJ506.P72S49 1997
    618.92′8583—dc21   97-4819

97 98 99 00 01 02 03   10 9 8 7 6 5 4 3 2 1

Acquiring Editor:	C. Terry Hendrix
Editorial Assistant:	Dale Mary Grenfell
Production Editor:	Michele Lingre
Production Assistant:	Denise Santoyo
Typesetter/Designer:	Marion Warren
Indexer:	Cristina Haley
Cover Designer:	Candice Harman
Print Buyer:	Anna Chin

To My Mother,
Who still lives in Nebraska,

and to My Father,
who is polishing stars in the sky,

thank you for providing a home free from the problems
described in this book. When we were children,
growing up at home, we probably did not
appreciate how lucky we were.

Your daughter,
Sharon Kay (Kropp) Araji

Contents

1. Identifying, Labeling, and Explaining Children's Sexually Aggressive Behaviors   1

Sharon K. Araji

5. Redirecting Children's Sexually Abusive and Sexually Aggressive Behaviors: Programs and Practices 161

Elizabeth A. Sirles, Sharon K. Araji, and Rebecca L. Bosek

Foreword

I want the readers of this book to appreciate that they are reading a work in progress, so to speak. Dr. Araji has assembled all the literature in a nascent field, one that is just now receiving a significant research focus. Two federally funded projects on sexually aggressive children are currently coming to fruition. One is sited in Vermont and directed by Allison Gray and Bill Pithers. The other is an Oklahoma City–Seattle project that involves Barbara Bonner, Gene Walker, and Lucy Berliner. As a consultant to both of these studies, it has been intriguing to watch conceptualizations be created, shattered, and then reformed, based on experiences with clinical referrals. I expect that publications from these two studies during the next 2 or 3 years will greatly enhance our understanding not only of who these children are but also of precursors to their behavior and the effectiveness of treatment.

I speak to eight key issues in the remainder of this foreword. I think it is very important that we have an accurate appreciation of the diversity of sexually aggressive children, that we appreciate them as more than a newly discovered phenomenon, that we debate seriously how much we can learn from adult sex offenders in understanding sexually aggressive children, and that a developmentally sound theoretical framework be articulated to understand these children better. Other issues include the role of the family in the emergence of sexual aggression, the similarity of sexual aggression to other externalizing behaviors, the influence of sexual abuse in the emergence of sexual aggression, and, based on these considerations, who is the best qualified to treat sexually aggressive children.

Sexually Aggressive
Children as Heterogeneous

Although the label *sexually aggressive children* is used throughout this book, it masks a considerable underlying diversity. It is very important to realize that there are many types of children who are labeled as sexually aggressive. Some children who are called sexually aggressive may not even be intrusive with other children but are simply reacting to their own victimization in a compulsive, self-stimulating manner. Other sexually aggressive children may engage in a very extensive but largely mutual interaction with other children, typically other sexually abused children. Finally, there are sexually aggressive children who truly are intrusive and coercive, but they are quite different from children who are simply reactive to their sexual abuse.

In addition, it is very important that we not lose sight of the normalcy of sexual behavior in children. Because sexual behavior is the best marker of sexual abuse (Kendall-Tackett, Williams, & Finkelhor, 1993), it becomes an easy step to pathologize all sexual behavior in children. The more researchers and clinicians appreciate that sexual aggression is an aberration of an underlying, universal behavior and do not view it as a totally deviant behavior, the more accurately we can understand how sexually aggressive behavior might emerge.

Sexual Aggression as a "New" Behavior
That Has Always Been in Existence

Sexually aggressive children most likely have been around as long as trauma and children have existed. It is very interesting to watch the evolution of knowledge in this field. In 1962, we discovered physical abuse with the publication of an article on the battered child (Kempe, Silverman, Steele, Droegmueller, & Silver, 1962). My personal introduction to the literature on sexual abuse came with the publication of Karen Meiselman's book *Incest* (1978). In 1988, along with the separate but simultaneous publication of a paper by Toni Johnson (1988), I helped to introduce the phenomenon of sexually aggressive children (Friedrich &

Luecke, 1988). Each of these publications illustrates how our inhumanity to each other comes into focus but only in stages that are tolerable to the viewer. The "discovery" of sexually aggressive children does not mean that our society is deteriorating; rather, it reflects in large part that we have not allowed ourselves to appreciate what is a universal.

Contribution From
Adult Offenders

There is also something very universal about the kernel of meanness that exists in people. This kernel has expanded in adult offenders. Our field also has a history of borrowing from adults to understand children. I believe, however, it is an error to borrow too heavily from adult offenders in understanding sexually aggressive children.

For example, the temptation in dealing with aberrant adult behavior is to either criminalize or pathologize the behavior. Sometimes, we do both. Adult sexual aggression becomes politicized and the only way we can understand sexual aggression is if we have victims. This then creates the potential for a rift between victim therapists and offender therapists. That rift is counterproductive with sexually aggressive children.

It is much more useful to think about sexually aggressive children as being in close proximity to their own victimization, whether that be sexual abuse, physical abuse, psychological rejection, emotional neglect, or a combination of the four. The more we appreciate that sexual aggression reflects aberrations in parenting, the more we accurately understand that the focus of treatment must be on the child within the context of the family relationship.

No doubt some researcher will find a gene for sexual aggression. It is unlikely, however, that this finding will be replicated, that this finding will help us treat these children, and that genetic contributions to complex behavioral sequences explain more than a few percentage points of the variance. The most important influence will be contextual in nature.

Only a very small subset of the children who qualify for a label of sexually aggressive children carry with them some of the features that I have seen in adolescent and adult offenders. These are typically 11-or 12-year-old boys who have a very planful and focused approach to creating new victims, and some will even report a fairly well-developed fantasy system that involves child victims. I believe, however, they represent the minority of sexually aggressive children.

Developmental Psychopathology
as the Appropriate Framework

In this book, Dr. Araji points to developmental psychopathology as an appropriate perspective to understand the emergence of sexual aggression in children. I underscore her suggestion. Considerable progress has been made in our understanding of the etiology and consequences of child abuse and neglect (Cicchetti & Toth, 1995). The framework provided by developmental psychopathology allows one to look at a broad range of issues that are related to consequences of child maltreatment. These include problems with the regulation of affect, impairment of attachment, how the self system is formed, and the nature and extent of peer relationships. Cicchetti and Toth describe the transaction of risk factors, with risk factors divided into two broad categories: potentiating factors, which increase the probability of a negative consequence, and compensatory factors, which decrease the risk for a negative consequence.

A developmental perspective also helps us appreciate the differences between a 6-year-old sexually aggressive child and a 10-year-old sexually aggressive child. Although the act may be the same, each child may attribute different meaning to his or her behavior, may be more or less immediate to his or her trauma, and each will have had different amounts of time in which the behavior can become entrenched. In addition, a 6-year-old will have a different range of interaction with peers than will a 10-year-old. The behavior becomes much better understood with a developmental perspective.

The more our current and future knowledge can be placed within an integrated theoretical framework, the more knowledge can be advanced and treatment interventions created. Clearly, the most appropriate framework is that of developmental psychopathology.

Family Contribution

According to developmental psychopathology, the family is one of several ecological contexts for the child. The family is a microsystem that is embedded within a community and also the larger culture. For example, in addition to the role of the family, a very interesting question would be the degree to which community violence is related to the risk for sexual aggression.

Families contribute a sexual climate. In fact, family sexuality is a risk factor that seems to potentiate the persistence of sexual aggression (Gray & Friedrich, 1996). Exposure to pornography has been shown to be related to sexual behavior in children (D. Elliott, personal communication, December 2, 1996). Predictors of sexual behavior in a sample of nonsexually abused preteen boys included sexual socialization in the family and, to a lesser degree, parent-child conflict (Meyer-Bahlberg, Wasserman, Dolesal, & Bueno, 1996).

The quality of attachment between parent and child is probably the most critical family contribution. Not only does it provide a map of relating but also it is the relationship from which empathy is modeled and the kernel of meanness becomes diminished.

Generalizations
From Dysregulation

Dr. Araji correctly identifies fire-setting as a behavior problem that shares a number of similarities with sexual aggression in young children. Fire-setting is secretive, usually outside the purview of parents, it seems to have multiple origins, and it primarily involves boys.

Fire-setting and sexual aggression are behaviors that reflect dysregulation, or difficulties with the modulation of affect and behavior. In fact, affect regulation has increasingly come to be viewed as a primary developmental task with wide-ranging implications for children's development (Cicchetti & Toth, 1995). Affect-regulatory processes emerge within the context of the parent-child relationship. Disruptions in the development of affect regulation most likely occur in children who have experienced one or another form of maltreatment. For example, physically abused children are routinely found to be more aggressive, both in their behavior and in their cognition (Cicchetti & Toth, 1995). Aggression reflects dysregulation and a breakdown in the child's ability to regulate behavior. Aggression, fire-setting, stealing, and posttraumatic stress disorder are some manifestations of dysregulation, whether it is problems regulating affect, behavior, cognition, or a combination.

Viewing sexual aggression as a disorder of regulation allows the clinician to generalize to other syndromes that have developed their own interventions. Research by Patterson (1982) illustrates how poor parental monitoring is related to the emergence of stealing. Increasing parental monitoring, particularly if it is paired with increasing positive parent involvement, can have a very positive effect on both stealing and sexual aggression (Friedrich, 1995).

Influence of Sexual Abuse

Developmental psychopathology reports that there is no single pathway to maltreatment, and there is no single pathway to behavioral consequence of maltreatment (Cicchetti & Toth, 1995). Sexual aggression is a consequence of one or another form of maltreatment, usually sexual abuse is one of them. Dr. Araji notes this fact, and early findings from the Vermont-based project illustrate this (Gray & Friedrich, 1996).

In her recent presentation at the Association for Treatment of Sexual Aggression conference in Chicago, Allison Gray reported on five clusters of sexually aggressive children. One of those clusters, which was populated primarily by children who had a conduct disorder or oppositional defiant disorder diagnosis, also happened to be the cluster of children who had the lowest incidence of prior sexual abuse. Her findings suggest the following: Sexual abuse is not the only cause of sexual aggression, and we may never know the true extent of sexual abuse in some of these children's backgrounds. Aggression is a disorder reflecting dysregulation, and sexual aggression seems to exist right next door to aggression, particularly when family sexuality has gone awry.

Although sexual abuse is not a universal predictor of sexual aggression in children, it is more likely to be a predictor in female children because females have fewer opportunities to behave in aggressive ways. In addition, Gil and Johnson (1993a) write that sexual abuse in families can be either overt or covert. We will never know the nature and extent of covert sexual abuse within families, and children are unable to accurately report it.

In a curious way, and one that is explained best by the field of developmental psychopathology, posttraumatic stress disorder (PTSD) in the sexually abused child may actually inhibit their behaving in a sexually aggressive way. PTSD predisposes the child to avoid sexual behavior and thoughts because they are retraumatizing. Although a large number of sexually abused children exhibit increased behavior, those children with PTSD may actually exhibit less overt sexual behavior overall.

Qualities of Treatment Providers

There are features of treatment programs that can counter the fragmented nature of maltreating families (Cicchetti & Toth, 1995). Although the field of child maltreatment is far from a consensus regarding the most effective treatment approach, families that are struggling with basic survival needs have difficulty engaging in complex psychological and behavioral change. Therapists working with sexually aggressive children must be capable of developing a trusting relationship with both parents and children. Clinical interventions need to be sensitive to the developmental stage of the child. Service provision to parents and children should occur within a single site to counter preexisting family fragmentation. Home visitation is an important program component, particularly for families that have difficulty connecting with needed services because of very realistic constraints regarding transportation and child care (Friedrich, 1995).

In addition to these features, I am suggesting that therapists of sexually aggressive children be well versed in both victim issues and how violence and aggression emerge. For example, many sexually aggressive children will decrease and even eliminate their behaviors in response to increased parental monitoring and behavioral interventions. For lasting change, however, a focus on the underlying trauma is extremely important and cannot be denied.

—W. N. Friedrich
Mayo Clinic
Department of Psychology
Rochester, Minnesota

Preface

Dr. Araji's work on children with sexual behavior problems provides a very useful snapshot of the past 15 years of clinical treatment and research. No previous volume has summarized the clinical conceptions of pioneering treatment providers and researchers in this area of work. The therapeutic practices reviewed in this volume were entirely dependent on the observations of astute clinicians because, until recently, very little solid research has been performed with these children and families. Among the themes you will find in these approaches are the need to address directly a child's altered development, to educate and collaborate across natural divisions of agencies, to respond compassionately to a child's trauma, and to assist children to acquire greater skills in impulse control and self-management.

We encourage practitioners to read carefully the therapeutic approaches reviewed here, to exercise critical thought in examining their relative merits, and to identify what we know and, most important, what we do not yet know. Clearly, the things we do not know about children with sexual behavior problems dwarf the things we know.

Research on children with sexual behavior problems is in its infancy. Debate about whether children can have sexual behavior problems has only recently begun. Treatment for children who appear to have problems with sexual behaviors has existed for several years, but little research exists to document its efficacy. The parental characteristics that contribute to, or deter, the development of childhood sexual behavior problems remain largely unspecified and we eagerly await the next generation of concepts, which are just now coming into view.

In 1990, we were fortunate to be one of two recipients of major demonstration grants awarded by the National Center on Child Abuse and Neglect (NCCAN). Since that time, we have been actively engaged in research that proposed to define the characteristics of families of children with sexual behavior problems, to determine whether subtypes of children with sexual behavior problems can be identified, and to evaluate the relative efficacy of two treatment models for families with children who had engaged in problematic sexual behaviors. We currently are preparing manuscripts that we hope will provide an empirical foundation that might contribute to the evolution of this critically important field. We take this opportunity to express our deep gratitude to NCCAN for its support of research on families of children with sexual behavior problems.

What no one knows is whether children with sexual behavior problems continue to engage in such behaviors into adolescence. Within the current social climate, it sometimes seems that once an individual has engaged in a sexually abusive behavior, he or she is permanently branded a perpetrator and considered less than human. We seem to have lost sight of the fact that even though some adult sex offenders have engaged in inhumane acts, they possess all the qualities and potential found among people who have not engaged in sex offenses: hatred and love, cowardice and courage, and compassion and coldness. In some American states, the social misperception of sex offenders has led to the imposition of some criminal sanctions that appear, at least to us, to be quite inhumane themselves (e.g., mandatory castration and "one-strike" legislation).

We are particularly concerned that the tendency to dehumanize adult sexual offenders not be extended to children with sexual behavior problems. Regardless of whether you are a researcher, treatment provider, or a child's caregiver, always remember that childhood is a time of boundless potential. It is the responsibility of adults who care for children to take measures to ensure that the potential of childhood is nurtured into a strong sense of personal ethics and social responsibility of adulthood. When we identify children who are engaging in behaviors destructive to themselves or others, we must fulfill our own social contract to provide interventions that will inspire them to become adults with a strong sense of personal ethics. Although everyone will not agree with us, labeling these children in a manner that even remotely implies that they have lifelong problems with sexual assaultiveness (e.g., child sex offenders), and that denies their potential to change, is simply wrong and should not be done.

In an era when we have recognized the importance of conserving precious natural resources, we all must recognize that children are the most precious resource in the world. We all must accept the challenge of demonstrating respect for the preciousness of children, place value in protecting their boundless potential, and work to alter conditions that impair it. When harm has already been done, we must dedicate our own resources to reclaim the hope for a better future offered by every child's life. The loss of one child's ability to nurture unlimited dreams for his or her future limits all of us.

You are reading this book because you are dedicated to a goal greater than child "welfare"—you probably are more invested in child prosperity. Although vitally important, it is insufficient for individuals alone to acknowledge the importance of children to our collective future. Professionals dedicated to preventing child maltreatment must strive to nurture respect for the preciousness of children in every citizen, among all families, within every school, inside the medical community, among law enforcement professionals, inside the therapeutic milieu, within social service agencies, and throughout the continuum of care. This principle of respect for the wondrous potential of children must resonate loudly enough within the hearts of healers that those with whom they interact can hear the sound and feel its rhythm. Our belief in the potential of children must endure, indeed must grow stronger, when we encounter the numb face of extensive maltreatment within families, the ravaging effects of poverty on the spirit, the haunting memories of domestic violence, the soul-chilling coldness of parental rejection, or the crushing silence of parental absence. Our recognition of the preciousness of children must be modeled again and again in each act of social service, no matter how objective or administrative it might appear. Compassion for the whole person, whether overwhelmed or resilient, must win the day. The spirit with which we conduct our work affects our effectiveness, particularly when the spirits of the people with whom we work have been deeply wounded and trust in others poses an ultimate challenge.

We know you can make a significant difference in many children's lives. Continue to seek information about children with sexual behavior problems. In coming years, much more will be available to assist your dedicated efforts. Never give up hope that people, most of all children, can make dramatic changes in their lives.

—Alison Gray and Bill Pithers
STEP Program, Center for Prevention Services
Underhill Center, Williston, Vermont

Acknowledgments

Many individuals contributed to this project as it moved toward fruition. Now that it is complete, I want to acknowledge those who assisted. First, the invaluable contributions of Ann Jache, Karl Pfeiffer, and Bruce Smith, who were integrally involved in the initial development of this book, are recognized. All three spent many hours developing a survey that was used to gather data reported in Chapter 2 (Araji, Jache, Pfeiffer, & Smith, 1993). Ann Jache also helped supervise students as we gathered agency data that are reported in the Araji, Jache, Tyrrell, and Field (1992) study (Chapter 2). Additionally, she located information used in the Introduction and Chapter 1. Bruce Smith was helpful in identifying important information about providers and treatment programs. Some of his contributions and ideas are reflected in Chapter 5. Along with sharing ideas in the initial phase of this project, Karl Pfeiffer served as a "sounding board" and provided assistance with program development and data analysis for the Araji et al. (1993) study noted previously. Second, I am indebted to Rebecca Bosek who is coauthor of Chapters 3 and 5. Her contributions, support, and assistance throughout this project are very much appreciated. Also, my deepest appreciation is extended to Beth Sirles, who is coauthor of Chapter 5. Her contributions were invaluable. Third, I thank all the University of Alaska, Anchorage students who assisted with data collection and data entry as well as library research. These include Colleen Tyrrell, Corinne Field, Donna Malone, Kathy Coprivnicar, Marla Mosher, Steve Schwartz, Beverli Thomas, Tom Rutledge, Lisa Pajot, Michael Ray, and Kristina Glover. They assisted with many of the time-consuming but necessary research tasks. Fourth, the following individuals provided valuable feedback on drafts of chapter material or exchanges of ideas or both. At the top of the list are Alison Gray and William (Bill) Friedrich. Not only did Alison Gray take time to explore ideas with me and review material but also Gray, Pithers, and Friedrich authored the Preface and Foreword to this book. Similarly, I am indebted to the following individuals for their cooperation, review of materials, exchange of ideas, or all three: Eliana Gil, Toni Johnson, Lucy Berliner, Gail Ryan, Jan Hindman, Lucinda Rasmussen, Jan Burton, Barbara Christopherson, Arthur Brown, Julie Bradshaw, Vicki M. Jean, Barbara Bonner, Dave Fowers, and Utah's Network on Juveniles Offending Sexually. I also thank Doug Kennedy, Mike Gonzalez, and Kylie Gardner, who completed the practitioners survey and shared their time and experiences. Early in the project, they helped focus my thinking about the characteristics of sexually aggressive children and their environment. Others who completed the practitioners survey are too numerous to mention, although I do thank all of them and want to acknowledge two with whom I had additional extensive conversations: Richard Sandafur and Andrew Klamser. To several others whose names cannot be mentioned because of the sensitive nature of information provided from case files, I say "Thank you." Fifth, I recognize Dee Foster and the Anchorage (Alaska) Center for Families for their cooperation. They sponsored several workshops at which I presented material from the book and important feedback was obtained from participants. Rob Freeman-Longo and the Safer Society Program are acknowledged for their cooperation and sharing of materials. Thanks go to Fay Honey-Knopp (posthumously). I am also indebted to Bryon Matsuda, Carrie Longoria, Jeff Burger, Jim Heafner, Elly Lane, and Margo Knuth for information or support or both of this project. Also, to the Anchorage (Alaska) Sexual Assault Task Force, I say "Thank you." It was discussions in one of our meetings several years ago that planted the seed for this project. Sixth, but of significant importance because this book could not have been completed without the tireless typing and retyping of draft manuscripts during the past several years, I extend my sincere appreciation to Carlette Ivory. Without her computer services and skills, and patience, this book would still be "in progress." A "thank you" goes to Jon Conte, who encouraged me to pursue the idea of this book and who reviewed several drafts. Also, I extend my appreciation to Sage Publications for accepting the original book proposal. Special thanks go to Dale Grenfell for her assistance throughout the project. Finally, I extend my appreciation to family members and friends whose social requests were frequently put on the "back burner" while the manuscript was being researched and written. Fortunately, when they now ask if the book is finished, I can say yes. In closing, my apologies are sent to anyone I failed to recognize in this Acknowledgment. Please be assured any omissions are unintentional.

Introduction

Sharon K. Araji

Book Focus and Objectives

This book is about children 12 years of age and younger who are engaged in sexually aggressive behaviors. *Sexually aggressive* is used to describe abusive behaviors that have both a sexual and an aggressive component. The targets of children who act sexually aggressive tend to be children who are similar or younger in age, who are viewed as weaker or vulnerable, or both.

The book has two objectives. The first is to collect in one place the available published and unpublished information about sexually aggressive children 12 years of age and younger, including a review of practices and programs that attempt to intervene and treat these children. In addition, social and legal services that are instrumental to identification of and intervention with youthful sexual aggressors will be discussed, including system gaps. Obviously, some information will overlap with publications such as Gil and Johnson's (1993a) book, but this is unavoidable in a comprehensive literature review. There will be information about sexually aggressive children, however, that will not be included in this book because it is embedded in literature on sexual abuse in general and not easily identified in a library search. Other information will be excluded because it resides with practitioners and providers who do not have time to publish or share information.

The second objective is to expand current publications that are primarily descriptive. This is accomplished by offering a synthesis and critical analysis of information reviewed in each chapter.

Development of the book is guided by psychological, social psychological, and sociological perspectives. All three of these perspectives are essential for a comprehensive explanation of children's sexually aggressive behaviors. That is, we must understand interactions between factors that (a) focus on the individual (psychological); (b) explain individuals' thoughts, feelings, and behaviors in terms of how they are influenced by the real, imagined, or implied presence of others (social psychological); and (c) demonstrate social and cultural impacts on the development, maintenance, or changes in patterns of thinking, feeling, and acting (sociological).

Recognizing Sexual Abuse

Sexual abuse of children was first documented by Tardieu in 1860 (Radbill, 1968), but it took more than 100 years before it became widely recognized as a social problem in the United States. This recognition, partly because of the work of Kempe and Kempe (1978), led to increased reporting and estimates of the prevalence of sexual abuse. Mass media attention to the molestation of children in day care settings (e.g., the McMartin case in Los Angeles) opened Pandora's box and raised public awareness. Professionals became increasingly vocal about the extent of child sexual abuse, and, as more government funds became available, the scientific community increased its level of inquiry and research. During the mid-1970s to mid-1980s, publications developed at a rapid rate.

In the mid-1980s, therapists working with adults who molested children discovered that some offenders had begun their perpetrating behaviors when they were adolescents (Fehrenback, Smith, Monastersky, & Deisher, 1986; Lane, 1991a; Longo & Groth, 1983). Prior to this discovery, many clinicians, researchers, and parents tended to view sexually aggressive behavior by adolescents as "reactive" or "acting out." They denied, rationalized, or minimized the offending nature of the acts with explanations such as "boys will be boys" (Cantwell, 1988, 1995; Groth & Loredo, 1981; National Adolescent Perpetrator Network, 1988; Ryan, 1989) or "they were just playing doctor" or "they were just curious" (Kikuchi, 1995).

Once there was acceptance that adolescents could be involved in sexually abusive behaviors, however, research on these offenders and their victims and the development of related treatment programs grew rapidly (e.g., Ageton, 1983; Becker, Kaplan, Cunningham-Rathner, & Kovoussi, 1986; Longo & Groth, 1983). Johnson and Berry (1989) reported that in 1982, 22 programs were providing services to adolescent offenders. Five years later, there were 470 programs and service providers.

As more information about adolescent sexual offenders became available, the late 1980s ushered in awareness of yet another abusive population: children 12 years of age and younger who were sexually abusing other children or those deemed more vulnerable. Literature around this topic has grown during the past decade (Cantwell, 1988, 1995; Cunningham & MacFarlane, 1991, 1996; Friedrich & Luecke, 1988; Gil & Johnson, 1993a; Gray & Pithers, 1992; Greenwald & Leitenberg, 1989; Groth & Loredo, 1981; Haugaard & Tilly, 1988; Johnson, 1988, 1989, 1991; Johnson & Berry, 1989; Lewis, Shanok, & Pincus, 1979; Rasmussen, Burton, & Christopherson, 1992; Ryan, 1989, 1990; Ryan, Lane, Davis, & Isaac, 1987; Sorrenti-Little, Bagley, & Robertson, 1984; Yates, 1982) and provides telling evidence that preadolescent children's behaviors can be as aggressive and assaultive as those of adolescents or adults. Considering the young ages of preadolescent children, the tendencies to deny, minimize, or rationalize their sexually abusive behaviors have been even greater than when adolescents were the focus of attention (Groth & Loredo, 1981). The preliminary report from the National Taskforce on Juvenile Sex Offending commented on this problem (National Adolescent Perpetrator Network, 1988):

> Identification and reporting of child offending has been almost nonexistent prior to 1985. . . . In a society which denies all sexuality in childhood and attempts to repress sexual behavior in adolescence, it is not surprising that we would minimize and deny sexual offending by children. The histories of adult and adolescent offenders, however, have indicated that sexual offending develops over time (Longo, Groth; Abel); and recent work with children has confirmed that sexual offending may begin in early childhood (Isaac; Cavanaugh-Johnson). (p. 42)

In her 1987 guide for parents of young sex offenders, Eliana Gil described reactions of disbelief that parents experienced when told that their child had committed sexually abusive acts. Typical responses centered around the themes that "there had to be some mistake" or "the person reporting the incident was exaggerating what happened." Parents, she said, continually repeated the phrase "it couldn't be" (Gil, 1987, p. 5). Other parental expressions, such as "Why did my child do that?" "Could this really have happened?" "Did I do something wrong?" or "Not my child!" were reported by Pithers, Gray, Cunningham, and Lane (1993, p. 3). Similar reactions were discussed by Hindman (1989) in her booklet for parents titled, *Just Before Dawn.*

It is not only parents who are reluctant to recognize and label children's behavior as sexually abusive or sexually aggressive. In the Foreword to Gil and Johnson's (1993a) book, William Friedrich, one of the first clinicians to write about sexually aggressive children, described his developing awareness of these children and the reaction of other professionals as follows:

> At conferences when I talk about sexually aggressive children, I still see in fellow clinicians the same look of disbelief I had at one time. It's as if each of us have a level of tolerance of children for the abhorrent, and the thought of children as sexually aggressive exceeds this level for many. (p. ix)

The reluctance to view and label young children as sexual perpetrators is also apparent in the writings of Carolyn Cunningham and Kee MacFarlane, who, like Friedrich, have worked extensively with sexually victimized children. For example, the title to their 1991 book of treatment strategies for these children was *When Children Molest Children.* When the updated version appeared in 1996, however, the title was changed to *When Children Abuse.*

Further ambivalence and confusion about what to call these young sexually aggressive children, as well as how to treat them, is expressed in the prefaces of both Cunningham and MacFarlane's (1991, 1996) treatment manuals:

> To put it in terms that are stark and easily understandable, this book is for and about sex offenders. No, not the ones in trenchcoats who hang out in playgrounds. This book is for the ones who go to playgrounds to play ball and swing on the swings. It is about the young ones, the not-yet-adolescents, the kids whom none of us want to see labeled with pejorative terms like "offender" or "perpetrator." And yet, these are children whose behavior can be defined by these terms.

The fact is, we don't yet know what to call them, how to explain them, or what to do with them. Most are too young for criminal justice solutions, too high risk for foster homes with other kids, and too unsettling to ignore. They make all of us uncomfortable—so uncomfortable we've had to deny their existence and/or minimize their behavior until now. We've called their behavior "exploration" or "curiosity" until they were old enough for us to comfortably call it what it is: sexual abuse of other children. (p. viii)

Cantwell (1995) has also discussed the ambivalence and confusion over what to call these children. She reports that at a 1993 Denver conference, sponsored by Children's World, attendees attempted to label and define sexualized behaviors of children. Only several terms were agreed on. The first was "developmentally appropriate." The second, "worrisome" or "allows for a wait-and-see attitude," was considered most inclusive because the attendees felt there were many children who cannot be categorized with our current level of knowledge. They agreed that if asked to stop, most of these children will. Some children, however, will escalate to more serious offending behavior, and this group made up the third category, in which intervention is deemed necessary because the types of behaviors are serious and require action. As authors of this book, we do not believe these labels are helpful in identifying children whose abusive behaviors contain a "sexual" and an "aggressive" component. They are too ambiguous and inclusive.

Although it may be difficult to think of young children as sexual abusers, particularly as molesters or offenders, further evidence of their abusive behaviors is found in Federal Bureau of Investigation reports (1990), newspaper articles (Barringer, 1989; Kizza, 1993; Price, 1993), television documentaries, and an increasing number of studies and articles. Among adults convicted of sex crimes, approximately 30% said they began offending before they were 9 years old, and some adolescent offenders recalled sexually abusing others when they were 3 or 4 years of age. Children as young as 2 ½ have been referred for sexually abusing other children (Gil, 1987) and, similar to Cunningham and MacFarlane (1991, 1996), other clinicians and researchers have advanced the notion that these young children are similar to adult pedophiles (e.g., Friedrich & Luecke, 1988) or adolescent perpetrators (Lane, 1991a), taking into consideration developmental differences.

Case Study Examples of
Sexually Aggressive Children

Johnson (1993a) reports on a case in Vermont in which a fourth-grade girl was sexually assaulted by several students in the bathroom of a small country school. The perpetrators were two 10-year-old boys from the girl's class who initiated the attempted rape, and three other boys who watched or helped hold the struggling victim while her attackers tried to penetrate her. One of the boys was 8 years old and the other two were 6 years old.

A similar case was reported in an Alaskan newspaper. In this case, three boys ages 11, 12, and 13 years were apprehended by police and charged with first degree sexual assault. The charge related to the boys forcibly raping a 5-year-old girl numerous times. Police indicated that objects were involved, although the specifics were not disclosed. The three boys apparently chased the young girl, caught her, held her on the ground, took off her pants, and took turns raping her. The crime took place in a wooded area near the victim's home and came to light in a therapy session (Kizzia, 1993; Price, 1993).

Although these cases may be hard to believe, an increasing number of similar incidents are gaining media and public attention. The behaviors described represent the extreme end of the sexual abuse continuum and involve children 12 years of age and younger, and the sexually abusive behaviors involve some form of aggression and coercion, among other power-related factors associated with victim compliance. As previously noted, children involved in these behaviors are the focus of this book, and we refer to them as sexually aggressive because our research indicates that this is the concept that best describes their behaviors. Other practitioners and researchers who sometimes use this concept include Friedrich and Luecke (1988), Friedrich (1990), Johnson (1993a, 1993b), and Cantwell (1995).

Research Studies That Help Determine
the Extent of Children Who Act Sexually Aggressive

In addition to case studies, we were able to locate several other published documents that confirm the involvement of preadolescents in sexually aggressive behaviors. Knopp (1982) compiled data from the Uniform

Crime reports for the United States on rape arrests for children under 12. She reported 208 children in this age group were arrested for rape in 1980. Thirty-seven were 10 years of age or younger. In 1979, there were 249 rape arrests of children under age 12, and 66 were for children under 10. The Uniform Crime reports stopped reporting the age of offenders in 1980, but in 1988 the National Center for Juvenile Justice reported a forcible rape rate of .02 cases per 1,000 for 10- and 11-year-olds, respectively.

In 1989, the state of Washington passed legislation to target treatment for sexually aggressive youth (SAY). Sexually aggressive behavior was defined to include "rape, molestation, and non-contact sexual acts such as exposure, public masturbating and peeping" (Washington State Department of Social and Health Services, Office of Children's Administration Research, 1992b). Youth was defined as under the age of 12. According to a report by English and Ray (1991), the state had an active caseload of 691 SAY children in 1990, and these children were responsible for 4,000 acts of suspected sexual aggression and 1,952 acts of known sexual aggression.

Gray and Pithers (1993) reported that between 1984 and 1989 nearly 200 children under the age of 10 had sexually abused other children in the state of Vermont, and in 1991, 100 sexually aggressive children were identified. Because these figures included only forceful or repetitive acts, these authors state that the numbers underestimate the magnitude of sexually abusive behaviors performed by children.

In presenting statistics on sex crimes in New York State, Johnson (1991) reported that juvenile court prosecutors handled 270 cases of sex crimes involving children 12 years old or younger—more cases than in the 13- to 15-year-old range. She indicates that Peter Reinharz, supervisor of the sex crimes prosecution unit, noted that the age drop meant the unit was dealing with "8-, 9-, and 10-year-olds committing rape or sodomy." The identified victims were usually other children.

Lane (1991a, p. 316) reported that since the late 1980s, most states have observed increases in the number of sexual offenders who are 11 or 12 years of age. She indicated that the 1986 Oregon Report on Juvenile Sex Offenders identified approximately 12% of adolescent offenders as being 11 and 12 years old. Although not being specific, she notes that some states have found approximately 10% to 14% of adolescent sex offenders falling in the 11- or 12-year-old age range.

On the basis of interviews with child protective services (CPS) and police officers, Gil and Johnson (1993b, pp. 126-127) reported that CPS workers were seeing sharp increases in cases of preadolescent perpetrators; the average age for referrals of children who molest was 7 or 8, with an age range of 3 to 12. Similar trends were reported by the police officers, although the average ages of children reported for molesting other children were 10 and 12.

Kikuchi (1995) reported that between 1988 and 1991, the Rhode Island Rape Crisis Center presented its Adolescent Assault Awareness program to approximately 18,000 adolescents in Grades 4 to 12. After the presentations, 1,720 adolescents disclosed during a private question time that they had experienced at least one incidence of child sexual assault as defined by Rhode Island laws (physical touching or penetration of the sexual parts of the body without consent; there may or may not be force involved). Of the 1,720 adolescents, 13.3% of the females and 5.8% of the males stated that they had experienced at least one such sexual assault. Eight percent of the reported assaults were by an offender under the age of 13.

The most common assault was a female assaulted by a male offender; 1,169 girls disclosed such an assault. The offender was under the age of 13 in 8% of the incidents. In general, girls reported being abused most commonly by males approximately their own age.

Similar to female victims, male victims (488) reported that their offenders were usually male. The offender was under age 13 in 6% of the assaults. In contrast to females, males indicated that their male abusers were slightly older than themselves.

In 6% of the disclosed assaults, the offender was female. Thirty-three girls and 70 boys described such assaults. In approximately 8% of the assaults on girls, the female offender was less than 13 years of age; this was the case for approximately 11% of the assaults on boys. No cases were reported in which a female assaulted a victim older than herself.

Kikuchi (1995) summarized her findings by noting that young children are sexually assaulting other children; some of these assaults are rapes; and both males and females are victimizing as well as being victims.

Other telling evidence that sexually aggressive children do exist and that there is an increasing recognition of the problem is found in the growing number of treatment programs for this age group. On the basis of statistics gathered by the Safer Society Program, which has been conducting nationwide surveys on adult and juvenile treatment programs and models since 1976, no available programs or models for sexually abusive children were reported until 1994. On the basis of the nationwide 1994 survey data, 390 programs were identified in the United States; 352 were community based and 38 were residential (Freeman-Longo, Bird, Stevenson, & Fiske, 1994).

Finally, in every group presentation I have made to professionals who work with children and families, all participants believed that the number of sexually aggressive children is growing. Whether these observations mean that the number is actually increasing or there is greater awareness or both is hard to say. Practitioners at these presentations also expressed frustration over the lack of public awareness, programs, services, and, especially, the lack of coordinated local and state efforts to acknowledge these children and to intervene—a topic that will be addressed in Chapter 6.

Reasons Preadolescents' Sexually Aggressive Behaviors Are Overlooked

Although the very young ages associated with preadolescents have led to difficulties in conceptualizing them as sexually abusive or aggressive, there are other reasons for overlooking these behaviors in this population. One is related to the idea of sexual latency.

Role of Sexual Latency in Overlooking Sexual Aggression by Children

Very young children explore their sexual parts openly, but by the time they are school age they are discouraged from publicly engaging in sexual behaviors (Martinson, 1981, 1994). Hence, many assume that school-age children live through a period of sexual latency or disinterest in sexual matters. This widely held assumption contributes to a lack of knowledge and understanding of latency-aged sexual behavior. It has also led to a lack of awareness on the part of those who work with this age group that these children could be interested in sexual activity or already have sexual behavior problems or both (Yates, 1982). Furthermore, many parents and professionals do not have much experience observing preadolescents involved either in normal or in abusive sexual behaviors.

Lack of Appropriate Labeling and Reporting of Sexually Abusive Behaviors by Children

Surveys using retrospective reports from college students (Finkelhor, 1980; Greenwald & Leitenberg, 1989; Kendall-Tackett, Williams, & Finkelhor, 1993; Sorrenti-Little et al., 1984) have found peer sexual experiences to be somewhat common in normal populations and abusive child sexual experiences with peers common enough for concern. Abusive experiences, however, are infrequently reported to adults (American Association of University Women, 1993; Yates, 1982) or to the police (Russell, 1983). Gil and Johnson (1993b, pp. 121-125), for example, discussed five case studies from various states. The five children involved in the sexually abusive behaviors were 8 and 9 years of age. Their victims tended to be similar ages or younger and were siblings, neighbors, or schoolmates. In several cases, child protective services initially defined what later turned out to be sexual abuse as "normal sexual play between children" or mutual, consensual "sexual exploration."

Araji, Jache, Tyrrell, and Field (1992) surveyed the 1989 to 1992 case records of 102 children whose families had been referred to a social service agency for child sexual abuse, among other issues. They found 21 cases of children from 11 families in which there was clear evidence of children under the age of 12 sexually abusing other children. Many of the behaviors had not previously been defined as abusive or aggressive because various service providers were reluctant to label these children as sexual abusers or could not envision preadolescents as sexual perpetrators. Fortunately, the study findings led to the agency's awareness of the problem and an increased effort to identify sexually abusive or aggressive children in future cases.

Some professionals, however, express concerns about the identification and intervention process when sexually abusive children are discovered. Kinsey, Pomeroy, Martin, and Gebhard (1953, p. 115) and Johnson (1993c, p. 67) indicate that there can be negative consequences if labels such as sexual aggressor, sexual abuser, perpetrator, or criminal are attached to children. Over 40 years ago, Kinsey et al. (1953) concluded from their research that, when sexual activity between children occurs, there are fewer negative consequences if adults do not intervene. Recent findings regarding sexually abusive or aggressive children, many of which will be reported in this book, challenge this conclusion. The findings also highlight the need to differentiate types of sexual behaviors clearly to ascertain the appropriate labels, theories, interventions, and treatment programs.

Compounding the tendency to overlook sexually abusive or aggressive behaviors by children is that many adults recall participating in exploratory sexual behaviors when they were young (Finkelhor, 1980; Greenwald & Leitenberg, 1989; Haugaard & Tilly, 1988; Kilpatrick, 1992, p. 62). Because they viewed this sexual activity as normal or nonabusive or because of the need to justify having participated in it themselves, or both, there is a reluctance on the part of parents and professionals to talk about any witnessed form of children's sexual behavior whether it is normal or abusive (see Gil, 1993a, for further discussion).

Even today, with the exception of a small, but growing, number of practitioners or researchers or both, there remains a tendency to explain sexually abusive behaviors by young children as something other than abuse. Sexual exploration or sexual curiosity are common terms used, especially with preschoolers (Cantwell, 1988; Gil & Johnson, 1993b, pp. 121-125; Groth & Loredo, 1981; National Adolescent Perpetrator Network, 1988).

Defining sexual behaviors in terms of "reactions" to abuse, including premeditated sexually aggressive acts, is another common explanation. This practice appears more common among those who consider themselves "victim" compared to "offender" therapists. That is, victim therapists are more likely to view sexually abusive children with past abuse histories as only reacting to abuse and label them "sexually reactive." Those who consider themselves offender therapists lean toward the view that these children are offenders who are harming others, and consider this as the first issue that must be addressed. Thus, they are more comfortable with using terms such as "children molesting children," "child perpetrators," or even "criminals" to describe sexually abusive children, whether or not they are also victims of sexual abuse. The use of labels and the labeling consequences are more fully discussed in Chapter 1.

Lack of Literature on Sexually Abusive and Aggressive Children

Another reason that preadolescents' sexually abusive or aggressive behaviors are frequently overlooked is because of the paucity of information that exists in this area. Friedrich (1990, pp. 242-243) offers four reasons for this problem. First, he suggests that clinicians are themselves uneasy about accepting children as sexual beings, and this precipitates an inability to acknowledge or deal with sexual problems in this youthful population. He notes that this point is supported by research indicating that psychiatric staff lack the professional skills and knowledge to manage sexual behaviors in this age of clients and instead respond with avoidance, disgust, restriction, and punishment. Hence, little information about treating sexual behavior problems in children is undertaken, recorded, and shared.

The second reason stems from differences between male and female therapists with respect to recognizing and triggering sexual behavior during therapy. On the basis of discussions with other therapists, Friedrich (1990) believes that male therapists are aware of more sexual behaviors in children because they represent a different stimulus to children—that is, male therapists may cue sexual behaviors in children who have been victimized by males, who make up the largest percentage of known offenders.

A third factor noted by Friedrich (1990) revolves around parents' defense mechanisms. If parents of sexually abused children are guilty, or prone to self-blame, then they also may be likely to deny or be inattentive to sexual behaviors of their children. They may simply "screen out" deviant behaviors, contributing to an underreporting of the problem.

The final reason offered for the poor reporting of treatment for this population comes from a dichotomy that exists in the treatment field. Friedrich (1990) says that the field loosely divides into two largely exclusive groups; victim therapists and offender therapists. The therapists' individual perceptions and understanding of the origins and consequences of sexual behaviors in the child have a pronounced impact on their therapeutic model. The approach of victim therapists is likely to be more supportive and relationship oriented. In contrast, offender therapists tend toward more confrontational interactions. Friedrich (1990, p. 243) and Gil and Johnson (1993b) also note the polarity between service providers: Victim specialists do not want molester referrals; molester specialists reassign their victim referrals.

Dropping Through the Cracks

Sexually aggressive children have also been overlooked because they do not come under the jurisdiction of many agencies or programs due to their young age (National Adolescent Perpetrator Network, 1988, p. 7). Because of age restrictions, law enforcement regulations and the guidelines of treatment facilities often prohibit treating or even investigating cases of preadolescent children who are sexually aggressive. The criminal codes for many states indicate that children under the age of 14 cannot be held "criminally responsible" for their actions.

Social and therapeutic agencies may also refuse to accept cases because children are too young for the type of sex offender programs they offer (J. Burger & J. Heafner, personal communication, May 1996; MacFarlane as cited in Gelman, Gordon, Christian, Talbot, & Snow, 1992; K. Pfeiffer, personal communication, July 1991). On the basis of interviews with child protective service providers and police officers, Gil and Johnson (1993b, p. 129) reported that both providers and police officers expressed frustration at the lack of resources for alleged children who molested others. Similarly, one law enforcement officer who responded to a survey we completed while writing this book indicated that youth corrections typically will not address these children, leaving it up to the Division of Family and Youth Services (DFYS) in his state. He said that "DFYS does not have the staff to deal with the problem, so the kids just drop through the cracks."

Johnson (1993a) reported on a case in New York City that demonstrates that even when children are found guilty in the justice system, there is frequently no program to treat the youthful offender. She notes that it took a jury 2 months to convict a 10-year-old boy of raping a 7-year-old girl, but it took 2 years to find a treatment program for him. Although there are more programs today than when Johnson reported this case study, they are still few and most are still in the early stages of development. Further compounding the problems of these children getting lost in the system is a reluctance by many mental health professionals to assist offenders, partially because they lack expertise on how to treat them. We found this theme voiced many times by those who come into contact with sexually aggressive children who are 12 years of age and younger.

Along similar lines, child protective-type services are primarily concerned with victims of abuse and may not be as vigorous in their pursuit of seeking services to treat children who are abusive. Hence, these children drop out of the system if they do not disclose that they are also a victim (Gil & Johnson, 1993b, p. 128). More evidence related to this problem was identified at a conference I attended in Tacoma, Washington, in February 1994. A clinician in the audience reported that if clients go from victim to offender status in Oregon, they no longer qualify for state funds related to being victims. Hence, to obtain funds to treat these children, there is resistance to identify them as offenders who may be engaged in sexually aggressive acts that cannot be classified as reactions to sexual abuse. This, of course, has labeling and treatment implications. If only victim issues are addressed, then those revolving around offender issues may not be resolved, rendering treatment less effective. John Hunter (personal communication, June 1994) has expressed similar concerns. Lane (1991a, p. 316) argues, in fact, that it is a disservice to preadolescent offenders to minimize and misperceive their offense behaviors or fail to offer offenders specific treatment.

There also exist gender, age, and sexual orientation biases that cause certain populations of children to be ignored. According to Gil and Johnson (1993b, p. 129), both police and child protective workers tend to regard sexually aggressive behaviors by boys, older children (13 years and older), and same-sex behaviors as more serious. These biases, along with those discussed previously, create problems in identifying, reporting, and providing interventions and treatments to preadolescent sexually abusive children who do not fit the stereotypes.

Value and Overview of the Book

Considering Gil and Johnson's (1993a) book on sexually abusive children, one might ask if the problem is great enough, or whether there is enough additional information, to warrant another book. As the primary author of this book, I asked the same question when I first became interested in the subject. A call to F. H. Knopp (personal communication, summer 1992) at the Safer Society Program led to discussions with a small group of professionals who were working with sexually abusive or aggressive children. Following these discussions and attendance at several national and regional conferences and workshops on sexually reactive and sexually aggressive children, it seemed that there was a need for the book proposed herein.

Further indication of the value of a book on sexually aggressive children was uncovered when my colleagues and I began to dig deeper into the literature and talk with professionals around the country who worked in the social work, educational, clinical, justice, and media fields. More awareness that these children existed and information on the topic were found than we anticipated, although much of the information was buried in books and articles on sexual abuse in general or resided in the minds of practitioners who simply did not have time to publish their observations or who had never thought about these children as representing a social problem.

Book Organization

Chapter 1 provides a brief history of how sexually aggressive children have become recognized as an emerging social issue and examines various methods of distinguishing normal from abusive sexual behaviors. The variety of labels used to describe these children are discussed and reasons for the variations are explored.

In Chapter 2, a compilation of social and psychological characteristics associated with sexually aggressive children is presented. This is based on a review of relevant published and unpublished information from a variety of sources.

Chapter 3 provides a more in-depth overview of familial, extrafamilial, and situational factors conducive to various types of sexual abuse. The first section focuses on family environments that have been described by several practitioners and researchers in the field. The second section of the chapter examines the contexts in which intrafamilial sexual abuse occurs. It begins with a general discussion of sibling incest and then moves to the dynamics involved in same-sex sibling incest. The section concludes by illustrating what is known about children who sexually abuse as part of an intergenerational pattern or polyincestuous lifestyle. The third section examines some of the situational dynamics involved in extrafamilial sexual abuse among children. Herein, the locations and circumstances in which children sexually aggress, as well as sexual aggression in foster care and adoptive homes, are described. Also included in this chapter is a discussion of sexual aggression in residential treatment centers, psychiatric hospitals, schools, neighborhoods, and babysitting situations.

Chapter 4 is devoted to a review of theories or frameworks that have been used to explain sexually aggressive children's thinking patterns and behaviors. Most explanations are derived from general psychological and social psychological theories or more specific sexual abuse explanations that borrow from the four-factor model developed by Araji and Finkelhor (1986) or the traumagenic model of Finkelhor and Browne

(1986), or extensions and combinations of these models (e.g., Rasmussen et al., 1992). Most explanations are "trauma-based" models and many represent approaches used with adult or adolescent sex offenders or both, and theory or model modifications are based on developmental levels of preadolescent children. Some examples of how programs and research directly or indirectly apply to various theories or frameworks are provided. Finally, the chapter assesses the current state of theoretical development in this area and offers systems theory as a more comprehensive approach to explanations of children's sexually aggressive behaviors—a theoretical direction in which a number of practitioners and researchers appear to be moving (e.g., Friedrich, Gil, Rasmussen, Burton, Christopherson, and Huke).

Chapter 5 provides an overview of nine programs and practices that have been designed by therapists who are developing individual, family, and group therapies for sexually abusive children and their families. Most of these represent applications of theories or models described in Chapter 4. Descriptions include theories used to conceptualize treatment, goals identified, and the modalities provided to realize goals. A list of 10 factors that can aid in program development and treatment planning are offered in the chapter conclusion. Limitations of the overview are discussed and information is summarized.

The programs and agencies described in Chapter 5 are not an exhaustive list. We are aware of this from a survey we mailed to more than 100 programs and practitioners around the United States who work with youthful sex offenders. Of those who returned the surveys, many reported that they were trying to develop programs that could be used in treating sexually aggressive children but did not have time to describe them in the survey. Because we did not have the time, staff, or financial resources to gather further information via telephone, we have provided only samples of programs specifically designed for sexually abusive children. They appear representative, however, based on information gathered by Freeman-Longo, Bird, Stevenson, and Fiske (1994) at the Safer Society Program.

Chapter 6 is devoted to an assessment of reporting and investigating children's sexually abusive behaviors, offering a critique of gaps in the social and criminal justice systems that impede identifying, processing, and treating sexually abusive children. Recommendations for closing the gaps are offered that include new directions in theory, research, practice, and social and legal services.

1

Identifying, Labeling, and Explaining Children's Sexually Aggressive Behaviors

Sharon K. Araji

As noted in the Introduction, this book is about children 12 or less years of age who act sexually aggressive toward others who are younger or who are viewed as more vulnerable than themselves or both. Many labels are used to describe these children, including "children who abuse" (Cunningham & MacFarlane, 1996), "children who molest" (Cunningham & MacFarlane, 1991; Gil & Johnson, 1993a), "child perpetrators" (Cunningham & MacFarlane, 1991, 1996; Johnson, 1988, 1989), "children with sexual behavior problems" (Pithers, Gray, Cunningham, & Lane, 1993), "sexually aggressive" children (Cantwell, 1995; Friedrich, 1990, Chapter 9; Johnson, 1993b), and "children who sexually act with criminal intent" (Hindman, 1994). As previously noted, in this book I use the term *sexually aggressive children,* although currently there is no agreed-on terminology.

To identify behaviors considered sexually abusive and sexually aggressive for the 12-year-old and younger age group, literature written by professionals who treat sexual behavior problems of this age group or who conduct research on sexual behavior or both is reviewed. Following this review, the commonalities and differences between the descriptions are examined. A synthesis and critical analysis is then offered, with emphasis on how the descriptions influence intervention and treatment.

Distinguishing Normal From
Sexually Abusive and Aggressive Behaviors

During the past decade, information about sexually abusive children has led researchers and practitioners to highlight the need to distinguish children's sexually abusive behaviors from those viewed as normal or normative. Psychologist Paul Okami (1992) published an article critical of researchers' failures to make these distinctions. Labeling clinicians such as MacFarlane "moral crusaders," Okami voiced concern that all sexual explorations by young children (as well as by adolescents) might come to be defined as pathological. Okami contended that behaviors described as normal sex rehearsal play behavior by Kinsey, Pomeroy, and Martin (1948) and Kinsey, Pomeroy, Martin, and Gebhard (1953), and by anthropologists from the mid-1940s to the 1990s, were some of the same behaviors being referred to as preadolescent perpetration behaviors. Okami seems to argue that aggressive, unwanted peer sexual contacts in childhood should be labeled as such but should be clearly distinguished from normal childhood sexual activities that do not produce negative outcomes. Martinson (1994, p. 136) has voiced similar concerns.

While performing research for this book, I found Okami's (1992) and Martinson's (1994) concerns echoed by parents, teachers, clinicians, social workers, and other professionals. Hence, I concluded that any discussion of sexually aggressive behaviors had to include a yardstick that would differentiate these types of behaviors from those considered "normal," "normative," or "appropriate."

Normal, Normative, and
Appropriate Sexual Behaviors

When the term *normal* is used by practitioners and researchers, the term frequently describes sexual behaviors that occur as a result of the natural human biological and physiological developmental process. Those who use the term normal tend to be in areas related to medicine, psychology, or child development. This same group of professionals uses terms such as *pathological* or *abnormal* sexual behaviors to indicate that something has happened to disturb or alter sexual behaviors that would be expected as a part of a natural or normal developmental process.

In contrast to the term normal, the concepts of *normative* or *appropriate* tend to be used when sexual behaviors are defined in a sociocultural way—to indicate what is considered the norm in a given society, culture, or group. Those who use the term normative are likely to be sociologists, professionals in the area of social work, and those associated with the justice system. In contrast to using concepts such as pathological or abnormal, researchers or practitioners in these areas are more likely to use "deviant" or "criminal" to describe sexual behaviors that lay outside the level of social norms or laws.

What is confusing is that the same sexual behaviors that may be referred to as normal, abnormal, or pathological by writers following a developmental perspective are labeled as normative, deviant, or criminal by those following a cultural or sociological perspective. For example, a child psychologist may consider masturbation a normal sexual behavior because it has been observed across societies and history as part of the normal developmental process. Also, from a sex therapist's perspective, masturbation may be considered a behavior that facilitates healthy or satisfactory sexual relationships. Those following a cultural or sociological perspective, however, may define masturbation as a deviant or inappropriate behavior if it goes against group or social norms.

What will become apparent in the following review is that defining and differentiating concepts is a very challenging task because authors sometimes use the previously mentioned concepts, particularly normal and normative, interchangeably and without definitions. Thus, it is left to each reader's judgment to determine how the author is using the term. Although an analysis of the consequences of this practice would be an interesting and valuable undertaking, it is beyond the scope of this book.

Attempts to Distinguish Normal
From Other Types of Sexual Behaviors

There is a developing body of literature (e.g., Beitchman, Zucker, Hood, DaCosta, & Akman, 1991; Gil & Johnson, 1993a; Martinson, 1994; Mian, Wehrspann, Klajner-Diamond, LeBaron, & Winder, 1986) that attempts to distinguish children's normal or normative sexual behaviors from other types. One early method of such distinctions was to compare children who had never been referred to a therapist for sexual abuse and were considered normal with children known to have been sexually abused (e.g., Friedrich, Grambsch, Broughton, Kuiper, & Bielke, 1991).

Friedrich (1990)

Friedrich (1990, pp. 51-56) uses several studies to discuss sexual development in nonsexually abused children compared with those who have been sexually abused. In his discussion, the implication is that nonsexually abused children exemplify normal sexual behaviors, whereas deviations from normal sexual behaviors are linked to children who have been sexually abused—that is, something (sexual abuse) has disrupted the normal course of sexual development. These distinctions are summarized in Table 1.1, which notes the sources Friedrich used in his discussion. The results of being a victim of sexual abuse are viewed as being manifest in sexual behaviors that are advanced beyond those expected in children ages birth through 12 years. Furthermore, the abused children are seen as more compulsive and resistant to treatment and not demonstrating inhibitions associated with normal sexual behaviors during latency.

Friedrich's (1990) method of differentiating normal from nonnormal sexual behaviors is problematic. First, there are ample studies that demonstrate a reluctance by parents to believe or accept the fact that their children have been sexually abused. Friedrich (1990) notes this in some of his later writings about sexually aggressive children. Furthermore, some children are afraid or ashamed to tell parents that they have been victims of sexual abuse. Also, in many cases it is a parent who is the offender and does not want to be discovered. Unless uncovered in some other way, these children would be considered normal using the previously discussed differentiation scheme.

Second, Friedrich and Luecke (1988) note that sexual abuse does not have a singular impact across all children, and that some children appear to be more resistant or immune to the consequences of a traumatic event than others. If this is the case, then it is plausible to assume that some children who are victims of sexual abuse will appear normal. They will slip through the cracks until discovered at a later stage in the life cycle. This may make intervention and treatment more difficult because research has clearly shown that treatment of adult sexual offenders is not particularly effective (Cantwell, 1995, p. 93) and that only about half of adolescent offenders are successfully treated (Ryan, 1987). Finkelhor, Hotaling, Lewis, and Smith (1990) argue that the earlier the intervention of potential sexual offenders, the fewer the number of perpetrators created. These findings are particularly relevant for this book if what Johnson and Feldmeth (1993) have observed about sexually aggressive

TABLE 1.1 Sexual Development of Nonsexually and Sexually
Abused Children

Sexual Development	
Nonsexually Abused Children	*Sexually Abused Children*
Rutter (1971): Erections in young male infants; "orgasmic-like responses" by males as young as 5 months; thigh rubbing by female preschoolers; exhibitionism, voyeurism with other children and adults (also see Gallo, 1979), or sexual exploration games; asking about sex; genital interest, genital play; and masturbation (more pronounced in males) seen in children 2 to 5 years of age.	Friedrich, Urquiza, and Beilke (1986), Friedrich and Luecke (1988), and Yates (1982): Sexual preoccupation and masturbation significantly more evident; behaviors may persist even after therapy.
	Decrease in sexual behavior (at least in public), usually seen in nonsexually abused children, not apparent.
Money and Ehrhardt (1972) and Achenbach and Edelbrook (1983): Children ages 3 to 6 can exhibit flirtations, seductive behaviors, and imitations of parents, older siblings, television, and so on. During latency, they exhibit inhibitions and demand more privacy and so on in response to learning cultural standards.	
Rutter (1971): During prepubescent years, masturbation gradually increases, as does heterosexual play (10% at 7 years of age to 80% at age 13); homosexual play also increases, observed in 25% to 30% of 13-year-old boys.	
Friedrich et al. (1989): The following behaviors would be unusual in nonsexually abused children 2 to 12 years of age: attempting intercourse, inserting objects in vagina or rectum, and touching breasts of adults more than once or on an incidental basis.	

SOURCE: Friedrich (1990). Used with permission.

children is true. They suggest that these children are frequently victims of sexual abuse, but their reactions take longer to manifest than those of victims who they label "sexually reactive" or "extensive mutual sexual behaviors" children.

Third, in general, contemporary writings on deviance, social problems, and crime demonstrate that populations stigmatized by low incomes, minority status, and family dysfunctions are more likely to be identified and labeled deviant. This labeling practice increases the probability that children with these social characteristics will be included in the sexually abused (sexually deviant) group, thereby skewing the public's, researchers', and practitioners' views of which children in a society exhibit normal sexual behaviors compared with deviant sexual behaviors. Hence, we will find children with sexual behavior problems where we look for them. A related consequence of this labeling process is that it has the potential of determining who receives and who is excluded from intervention and treatment.

Gil's (1993a) Descriptions of Appropriate and Inappropriate Sexual Behaviors

Fortunately, there are more refined ways to distinguish normal sexual behaviors from other types than the previously discussed method. In Gil and Johnson's (1993a) book on sexualized children, Gil devotes a chapter to describing age-appropriate (normative) sexual behaviors for children 12 years of age and younger (Table 1.2). At the top of each age category in Table 1.2, Gil identifies several social factors that influence children's sexual behavior developments and the degree of inhibitions expressed at each stage. Children from birth to 4 years of age, for example, have limited peer contact and thus exhibit sexual behaviors that focus on themselves. Children in this age group tend to express no inhibitions about their sexual behaviors, and behaviors tend to be sporadic and random.

The various types of sexual behaviors appropriate for this age include touching and rubbing one's own genitals and watching or poking others' bodies or both. Gil (1993a, p. 22) provides an example of the latter, noting that, when sitting on a woman's lap, young children may poke or squeeze what they call "boobies." Then, they laugh or run away expressing delight.

Children in this age group may also exhibit their genitals and express interest in and ask about bathroom functions. They may repeat slang words used for bathroom body functions or sexual activities or both. This age group may also play "house" or "doctor" as they reach 3 or 4 years of age, imitating sexual behaviors or noises or both that they observe while watching their parents or television. They may also attempt to insert fingers or objects into their anus or vagina or other oral cavities such as their ears and nose. According to Gil (1993a), they stop these actions when it hurts unless there are other factors that intervene and prevent this from happening.

The next age group of children in Gil's (1993a) descriptions includes those 5 to 7 years old. Their sexual behaviors are influenced by increased peer contact, which leads to more varied experimental interactions. As a result of being socialized away from contact with their bodies by age 4 (Lewis, as cited in Gil, 1993a, p. 24), their sexually-related activities are characterized by a desire for privacy and feelings of inhibition. As Table 1.2 demonstrates, some of the same sexual behaviors noted in the 0- to 4-year-old age group continue, although they become more specific with respect to where children touch or rub themselves. The range of behaviors also increases and may include kissing and holding hands.

Further broadening of peer experimental interactions is associated with preadolescent- or latency-age children (8-12 years of age), as can be seen in Table 1.2. The types of appropriate sexual behaviors in which these children engage are also quite expanded, including petting, touching others' genitals, and dry humping. Digital or vaginal intercourse or oral sex may begin in the older children and continue through the three stages of adolescence. According to Gil (1993a), children's reactions vary from disinhibition to inhibition.

Overall, Table 1.2 demonstrates that there is a progressive nature to the sexual behaviors children engage in from birth to 12 years old, a point on which most experts on age-appropriate sexual behaviors agree (e.g., Martinson, 1976, 1991, 1994). The information presented in Table 1.2 is most useful in determining and explaining age-appropriate from age-inappropriate sexual behaviors by considering both the progressive nature of sexual development and the changes in environmental contacts.

Gil (1993a, p. 32) offers examples of age-inappropriate behaviors based on information in Table 1.2. One such example is a 4-year-old child who wants to orally copulate other children. Gil indicates that such a child is demonstrating sexual knowledge beyond what would be expected of this age and stage of sexual development. It is important to note, however, as Gil (1993a) and others such as Finkelhor (1973) and Haugaard and Tilly (1988) have cautioned, that sexual behaviors of children vary across cultures and social groups and may be shaped in either direction by the environment. Furthermore, all children in a given society or culture will not engage in all sexual behaviors listed in Table 1.2. There

TABLE 1.2 Normative Sexual Development in Children

Preschool (Ages = birth-4)	Young School Age (Ages = 5-7)	Latency/Preadolescent (Ages = 8-12)
Limited Peer Contact Self-Exploration Self-Stimulation	Increased Peer Contact Experimental Interactions Inhibition	Increased Peer Contact Experimental Interactions Disinhibition/Inhibition
Touches/rubs own genitals (random) Watches, pokes others' bodies Shows genitals Interested/asks about bathroom functions Uses dirty language Plays house-mom/dad Plays doctor (imitative) May insert/stops with pain	Touches self (specific) Watches, asks Inhibited (privacy) Repulsed by/drawn to opposite sex Tells dirty jokes Plays house Kissing, holding hands May mimic/practice	Touches self/others Mooning Exhibitionistic Kissing/dating Petting Touches others' genitals Dry humping Digital or vaginal intercourse; oral sex in preadolescent or adolescents

SOURCE: Gil (1993a). Reprinted with permission of author.

will be variations from child to child. Because of the range of behaviors that children can participate in, using only sexual behaviors as a measure of appropriateness can be misleading. Gil (1993a, pp. 29-30) indicates that there are other social criteria that must be used when determining the appropriateness or inappropriateness of children's sexual behaviors. The criteria she uses are borrowed from Groth and Loredo (1981) and Sgroi, Bunk, and Wabrek (1988), who developed a set of social factors for determining adolescents' sexually abusive behaviors. Gil proposes that the same criteria in the following list can be used with children 12 years of age and younger:

1. Chronological age difference: Gil proposes that a 3-year age spread warrants concern.
2. Developmental age difference: Children will vary greatly, with some having developmental delays or severe immaturity. These children may become targets of abuse.
3. Size difference: If children are of similar ages, but there exists a substantial difference in height, weight, or physical strength, this should be considered as a variable that may cause problems.

4. Status difference: When one child is given a status, such as babysitter, that sets him or her apart from other children with respect to having authority or power, this status has the potential of being used to coerce cooperation from other children.

5. Type of sexual activity: Gil notes that data about normative sexual behavior among children are minimal, but one way to judge the appropriateness is to view behaviors on a developmental continuum and stay informed as more research and discussion on this topic emerges.

6. Dynamics of sexual play or problematic sexual behaviors: According to Gil, dynamics involved in appropriate age "sex play" compared with "problematic sexual behaviors" are quite different. Sex play is usually spontaneous and includes joy, laughter, embarrassment, and varying levels of inhibition and disinhibition. Problematic sexual behaviors have themes of dominance, coercion, threats, and force. Children involved in these types of behavior appear anxious, fearful, angry, or intense. They demonstrate higher levels of arousal. The sexual behaviors may be habitual and become compulsive in nature. The behaviors are not responsive to parental or caretakers' limits or attempts to distract children from engaging in these behaviors.

Crisci and Brown (as Cited in Kikuchi, 1995)

Crisci and Brown (as cited in Kikuchi, 1995) differentiate between what is considered normal sexual behaviors and those considered abusive by using (a) motivational factors, (b) abuser-victim relationships, (c) types of behavior, and (d) affect expressed. These differentiation factors are very similar to Gil's (1993a) descriptions. That is, Crisci and Brown view the motive for normal sexual behaviors as curiosity, the abuser-victim relationship as involving mutual interest and consent, the affect expressed as "being silly" or "having fun," and the behavior as limited to looking and touching. The example used to demonstrate such an interaction is "I'll show you mine, if you show me yours."

In contrast, abusive sexual behaviors are viewed as involving coercion, bullying, and a power-control imbalance. The sexual behavior is defined as a reenactment of adult sexual acts; the affect expressed is fear, shame, and discomfort; and the example used to depict the behavior is "having sex."

Johnson and Feldmeth's (1993) and Johnson's
(Personal Communication, February 1997)
Continuum of Sexual Behaviors

Table 1.3 shows Johnson and Feldmeth's (1993) and Johnson's (personal communication, February 1997) four-group continuum of sexual behaviors. These groups include normal sexual behaviors (Group I), sexually reactive behaviors (Group II), extensive mutual sexual behaviors (Group III), and sexually aggressive or molesting behaviors (Group IV). These authors view normal sexual behavior as healthy behavior or "sex play" in which children approximately the same age and size explore each other's bodies by touch and sight and do not feel shame or guilt.

Johnson and Feldmeth (1993, pp. 41-42) use several indicators to determine if sexual behaviors are normal or appropriate. First, the sexual behavior is clearly viewed as an information-gathering process or act of curiosity. Second, the children are similar in age, size, and developmental levels. Third, both or all children engage in sex play voluntarily. Fourth, the sex play involves children who have an amicable relationship outside the sexual interaction. Fifth, the sexual behaviors are limited in terms of types and frequency, and children are not preoccupied with sexual behavior. Sixth, if children are caught by others and told to stop, they do so when they are in front of others but the behavior may go underground. When these children are publicly exposed, they may demonstrate feelings of guilt or embarrassment but generally do not express deep feelings of anger, anxiety, fear, or shame. Seventh, the children's sexual activity is usually spontaneous and lighthearted.

Causes

The second category in Johnson and Feldmeth's (1993) continuum of sexual behaviors is sexually reactive behaviors. Children who engage in these behaviors are seen as deviating from age-appropriate sexual behaviors described in Group I, the normal sexual behavior group. Johnson and Feldmeth indicate that children in Group II demonstrate a wider range of behaviors than those in Group I, and their focus on sexuality is out of balance in comparison to their age group. Many of these children have been sexually abused or live in homes that have a high degree of sexual stimulation or both. This stimulation may be associated with watching television shows, viewing pornographic material, or observing sexual activities in their living environment.

Reactions to being discovered while engaging in sexual behavior may be deep shame, intense guilt, and a continuous anxiety about sexuality. Sexual activities frequently involve only themselves, but when other children are involved they are usually similar in age. According to Johnson and Feldmeth (1993), children in Group II do not seek out or use threats or force on their victims. They are more opportunistic, and when told to stop they usually do. Intervention and treatment are generally welcomed.

The third category in Johnson and Feldmeth's (1993) model is extensive mutual sexual behaviors. This group of children participate in "adult-like" sexual activities with other children but, like children in the normal and sexually reactive groups, do not use force or coercion. These children are skilled at keeping their sexual activities secret. Johnson (1991) also describes a lack of affect in this group of children:

> One of the striking differences between these children, and children in the other groups, is their affect—or more precisely, their lack of affect—around sexuality. Group III children do not have the light-hearted spontaneity of sexually healthy children, the shame and anxiety of sexually reactive children or the anger and aggression typical of child perpetrators (Group IV). Instead they display a "blase," matter-of-fact attitude toward sexual behavior with other children. (p. 12)

Most children in Group III have been sexually abused; all have experienced some type of abuse—emotional, physical, sexual, or all three. They come from abusive and dysfunctional environments. Related to such environments, some of these children use sex as a means to an end—for example, as a way of making friends or coping with feelings such as loss, abandonment, fear, loneliness, or all four. For children in Group III, sexual behaviors have become a coping mechanism. These children have organized their previously felt "sexual reactivity" into a way of dealing with their life stresses. They seek out other children with similar conflicts and problems who will mutually engage in sexual behaviors. Not unlike adults who use sex outside the context of a caring and committed relationship to alleviate overwhelming dependency needs, these children also use sex in a maladaptive manner (T. Johnson, personal communication, January 1997).

For children in Group III, sexual arousal and pleasure are rarely the primary drive for engaging in sexual behaviors. Some prepubertal children, however, do experience pleasurable body feelings.

(text continues on p. 16)

TABLE 1.3 Children's Sexual Behaviors: Normal to Disturbed

	Group No.			
	I: *Normal Sexual* *Exploration or "Sex Play"*	*II:* *Sexually* *Reactive Behaviors*	*III:* *Extensive Mutual* *Sexual Behaviors*	*IV:* *Children* *Who Molest*
Sexual behaviors	Sex play, exploration involving touching and initiating gender roles; sample behaviors include autostimulation and self-exploration, kissing, hugging, peeking, touching or exposing genitals or both to other children, sometimes simulated intercourse. (Intercourse is rare and found in only 2% or 3% of children 12 years of age or less)	Range of sexual behaviors is wider than that for Group I; for children in this group, genitals may be focus of their development; frequently, sexual activity includes only their own bodies—masturbation, insertion of objects, and exposing; sexual behaviors often represent repetition compulsion related to previous overstimulating sexuality; may engage in sexual behaviors with others	May participate in full range of adult sexual behaviors, including oral copulation and vaginal and oral intercourse; expresses more pervasive and focused sexual behavior pattern than Group II	Sexual behaviors are similar to those of Group III. These children's thoughts and actions have a pervasively sexual nature
Intensity of sexual behaviors	Balanced, can stop and start at will	Focus on sexuality is out of balance in relation to peer group	Pervasive need for reassurance through sexual contact	Preoccupied by sex; sexualizes most contact with people and things; sexual behaviors are consistent and persistent, not isolated events, and have compulsive and aggressive qualities
Sexual arousal	Arousal/no arousal	Arousal/no arousal	Arousal/no arousal	Arousal/no arousal

Motivation	Curiosity; exploration; needs to be like friends; mimic what is seen in real life or on television; sexual stimulation	Anxiety reduction; posttraumatic stress reaction; reduce confusion or make sense of sexual misuse or victimization; recapitulate previous unassimilated, uncontainable, sexual overstimulation; decrease physiological arousal; sexual stimulation; use sex as a tool for making friends	Coping mechanism to decrease isolation or loneliness or neediness; decrease boredom; decrease depression; make life more bearable; stabilize sense of self; provide an attachment figure; create a connection to otherwise hostile world; decrease physiological arousal; sexual stimulation	Decrease anxiety, fear, loneliness, anger, abandonment fears, or other strong unpleasant internal sensations; reduce confusion; recapitulation of previous physical, sexual, or emotional overstimulation; decrease physiological arousal paired with early or ongoing stress or both; posttraumatic stress reaction; sibling rivalry; compulsive sexual drive; sexual stimulation
Affect regarding sexuality	Silly/giggly/lighthearted; perhaps parental- or religion-induced guilt	Anxiety, shame, guilt, fear, confusion	Needy, confused, sneaky; "What's the big deal" attitude	Anxiety, anger, aggressive, rageful, confusion
Response to discovery	Shyness, embarrassment; "runs and hides"	May be surprised (if dissociated at time of sexual behavior); upset and confused or afraid	Denies or blames other child or does not see problem with the sexual behavior	Acts aggressively and angrily blames other child and/or person who caught them or both; denies behavior
Planning	Spontaneous/planned	Spontaneous/impulsive	Planned	Planned/explosive
Coercion	Mutual involvement	Generally no discussion prior to behavior occurring. If discussion, no coercion, non-coercive	Agreement at conscious or unconscious level; not coercive	Threat/bribes/trickery; manipulation, coercion
Relationship to others involved in sexual behaviors	Siblings (foster, natural, or step); friends	Siblings (foster, natural, or step); accessible children; may approach adults	Mutual sibling incest (foster, natural, or step); willing children; sex may become a stable aspect of relationship	Forced sibling incest (foster, natural, or step); vulnerable children; may be directed at adults
Age difference	Similar age	Similar age; playmates; living companion	Similar age; living companion	Younger, same age, or older; 0 to 12 year difference

TABLE 1.3 Continued

	Group No.			
	I: *Normal Sexual* *Exploration or "Sex Play"*	*II:* *Sexually* *Reactive Behaviors*	*III:* *Extensive Mutual* *Sexual Behaviors*	*IV:* *Children* *Who Molest*
Interpersonal relationship characteristics	All kinds	May be isolated, unsure, wary	Distrusts adults as caregivers— expects to be hurt, unattached; relies on sexual relationships for emotional strength; prone to victimization by adults who take advantage of child's neediness and confusion	Tend to have behavior problems at home and at school; few outside interests; few, if any, friends; lacks problem-solving and coping skills; very limited social skills and relationships with people of any age; no reliable way to get approval
Family/ environment	All types of families	Possibly sexually abusive, other abuses; liberal views; lacks emotional support and cohesion between family members; environment may expose children to pornography or be overly sexualized	Possibly polyabuse in family history; parents/caretakers emotionally distant and unsupportive; extramarital affairs occurring in families; overt and covert sexuality in home; poor boundaries	Psychiatric disorders; criminal justice problems; parental violence; mostly single-parent families; environments tend to lack boundaries, be sexually charged, and have a history of physical abuse between caretakers; parents frequently have history of sexual, physical, emotional, and substance abuse

Possible etiological factors	Natural and healthy childhood that allows curiosity, exploration, and experimentation; TV, videos	Recent or ongoing sexual abuse; emotional abuse; traumatic sexualization; pornography; history of sexual abuse in family; overt sexual lifestyle in home	Sexual, emotional, or physical abandonment, or all three; neglect; extramarital liaisons of parents; inadequate early bonding to caretaker; physiological or hormonal problems; sexually abused in a group; lack of adult attachments; continuous out-of-home placements	Intense rivalry for attention between sibs; lack of positive emotional relationships; physiological/hormonal problems; trauma-induced neurobiological changes; pairing of sex/anger aggression/anxiety; sexual, emotional, or physical abuse, or all three; neglect/abandonment; inherited vulnerabilities; violence in family history; sexualized relationships; sexualized environment in family; poor boundaries; caretakers with many unmet needs
Treatment	Sometimes education of parents or children or both needed regarding sex and sexuality; value clarification	Focus on self-understanding, making sense of previous experiences with overwhelming sexuality; sex education; parental support and education parallel with child's therapy; well-articulated plan to modify sexual behaviors; parallel group therapy for parents and children	Increase attachment to adults to allow children's emotional and dependency needs to be met; teach children to substitute emotional contact for sexual contact (also see Group II treatment)	Intensive treatment, skills, training; intensive treatment for parents; boundary issues; parallel group therapy for parents and children and their siblings; family therapy; intense prevention work in family; violence reduction

SOURCE: Information taken from published material by Johnson and Feldmeth (1993) and from written materials provided by Johnson (personal communication, January 1997). Table reviewed by Johnson (February 1997).

Many children in Group III are in the care of the state or are living in residential, foster, or group settings. They have been chronically hurt or abandoned, frequently lack social or academic successes or both, and have a general distrust of adults. They appear less responsive to treatment then those in Group II.

Johnson and Feldmeth (1993, p. 49) classify the fourth group as "children who molest." According to these authors, there is an impulsive, compulsive, and aggressive quality to these children's sexual behaviors. The children seek out victims who are easy targets. Some form of coercion is always present and, frequently, social and emotional threats are used to keep the victims from telling about the sexual activity. For example, if the victim lacks friends, the sexually aggressive child may threaten never to play with them again. Also, apparent in these children's actions is the lack of empathy for their victims. Children in this group frequently have been sexually abused, similar to some children in Groups II and III, but their reactions appear to take longer to manifest.

Overall, as evident from Table 1.3, Group IV children represent sexual behaviors that are farthest from those considered normal by Johnson and Feldmeth (1993). Their thoughts and actions are pervaded by themes of sexuality; their sexual behaviors continue and increase over time and represent a pattern rather than isolated events. As a group, according to Johnson and Feldmeth (1993, p. 50), they have paired feelings of loneliness, rage, fear, or all three with sex, which has been paired with aggression. Like children in Group III, these children tend to live in dysfunctional environments. They are the most difficult group to treat and require intensive and specialized treatment.

In addition to the specific behaviors and emotional reactions that differentiate children engaged in normal sexual behaviors (Group I) from the three groups with disturbed sexual behaviors, Table 1.3 demonstrates that the motives for sexual behaviors also vary. Children involved in normal sexual behaviors, or sexually reactive behaviors, frequently engage in self-exploration and gratification. Children engaged in sexual play, however, are more motivated by naturally occurring curiosity, whereas sexually reactive children may be driven by anxiety, overstimulation, a desire to understand previously witnessed sexual behaviors, and so on. In some cases, sexually reactive children may be calling attention to their behavior as a signal to adults that they have been abused. Children characterized by extensive mutual sexual behaviors (Group III) are motivated by sexual stimulation as well as coping with dependency needs, whereas children who molest, or Group IV, are motivated by a need to reduce negative feelings of fear, anger, or loneliness that have become associated with sexuality.

In addition to variations in the underlying motives for engaging in sexual behaviors, the nature of the relationship with self and others varies among the groups. Normal and sexually reactive children's sexual behaviors most frequently involve only the "self." When another child is involved, it is usually a child of the same status. According to Johnson and Feldmeth (1993), children in the normal group do not usually choose a sibling for sexual exploration, although sexually reactive children may. Children from the extensive mutual sexual behaviors group, however, choose other children, including siblings, for sexual encounters. There is no consistent status differential between the children involved, however. In contrast to Groups I, II, and III, children who molest (Group IV) choose others who are weaker or more vulnerable to involve in their sexually or physically aggressive behaviors or both; these may be siblings or non-siblings.

As a cautionary note, Johnson and Feldmeth (1993) indicate that when using their model of differentiating the four categories of children's sexual behaviors, there are several considerations to keep in mind. First, the model applies only to children 12 and under who have intact reality testing and who are not mentally retarded. Second, some children may be on the borderline of the various groups or, over time, move between groups or both.

Cunningham and MacFarlane's (1991, 1996) Levels of Sexual Behaviors

In Chapter 1 of their treatment manual *When Children Molest Children* (1991), and in the revised edition, *When Children Abuse* (1996), Cunningham and MacFarlane emphasize that professionals working with children who have been sexually abused must be able to differentiate normal sex play from sexual acts that are abusive. For children 12 and under, they separate the stages of sexual development by age groups: ages 0 to 5, 6 to 10 (latency age), and 10 to 12 (preadolescents). In Table 1.4, I summarize, for each group, what is considered normal and abusive or abnormal. Cunningham and MacFarlane use the words abnormal and abusive interchangeably. The term abnormal is not defined but appears to mean a deviation from sexual behaviors normally expected of a given age group. For example, in the 0- to 5-year-old age group, the authors

TABLE 1.4 Stages of Sexual Development

	Age Group				
Ages 0-5		Ages 6-10		Ages 10-12	
Normal	Abnormal/Abusive[a]	Normal	Abnormal/Abusive[a]	Normal	Abnormal/Abusive[a]
Masturbation as self-soothing behavior	Curiosity about sexual behavior becomes obsessive preoccupation	Continues to fondle and touch own genitals and masturbate	Sexual penetration	Masturbation continues	Highly unusual to be involved in sexual play with younger children
Touching self or others is exploratory or results from curiosity	Exploration becomes reenactment of specific adult sexual activity	Becomes more secretive about self-touching	Genital kissing	Focused on establishing relationships with peers	
Sexual behaviors are done without inhibition	Behavior involves injury to self	Interest in others' bodies becomes more "game playing" than exploratory curiosity—for example, "I'll show you mine, you show me yours" or playing doctor	Oral copulation	Engages in sexual behavior with peers—for example, kissing, fondling, and sexual penetration	
Intense interest in bath-room activities of others	Children's behavior involves coercion, threats, secrecy, aggression, violence, or developmentally inappropriate (precocious) acts	Boys may begin comparing size of penis	Simulated intercourse	Most sexual activity is heterosexual but may be same sex	
May verbalize about toilet functions	Unequal power base and exploitative regarding age, size, power, authority, and lack of consent	Develops extreme interest in sex, sex words, and dirty jokes	Sexual penetration	May be interested in others' bodies, especially the opposite sex that may be in the form of looking at photos or published materials	Highly unusual for this age group to be involved in sex play with younger children

Exhibition of genitalia as means of curiosity	Begins to seek information/pictures that explain body functions	Genital kissing	Sexual experiences are heterosexual, although same-sex sexual experiences are common for this age group
Responds quickly to adult limit setting and redirection concerning sexual behaviors	Swearing begins	Oral copulation	
Sexual behaviors represent only one aspect of general curiosity about their bodies, others' bodies, and world around them	Touching may involve stroking or rubbing	Simulated intercourse	
Touching others is exploratory, not coercive			
Sexual exploration begins during this stage			

SOURCE: Material was taken from Cunningham and MacFarlane (1991).

a. Cunningham and MacFarlane (1991) suggest that for any of the age groups, sexual acts between children that are coercive, involve aggression, bribery, or secrecy, involve a significant age or peer difference, and are developmentally inappropriate should be considered abusive (p. 25).

discuss sex play as being abnormal when curiosity becomes an obsessive preoccupation or when behavior involves coercion or self-injury. Overall, as can be seen in Table 1.4, these authors' descriptions of what sexual behaviors would be considered abnormal or abusive are those that include coercion, threats, aggression, secrecy, or developmentally inappropriate sex acts between younger children or where there is an unequal power base. They indicate that these are the defining characteristics that the literature and their practice experiences suggest.

Similar to Gil (1993a), Cunningham and MacFarlane (1991, 1996) note that informed consent must also be considered when deciding whether the sexual behavior is abusive. The factors they use to measure consent are taken from the 1988 National Adolescent Perpetrator Network's Task Force on Juvenile Sexual Offending definition and include the following:

1. understanding what is proposed based on age, maturity, developmental level, functioning, and experience;
2. knowledge of societal standards for what is being proposed;
3. awareness of potential consequences and alternatives;
4. assumption that agreements or disagreements will be respected equally;
5. voluntary decision; and
6. mental competence.

Compliance and cooperation are also part of the definition, wherein compliance is defined as passive action without overt resistance despite opposing belief or desire. Compliance may occur without consent. Cooperation is defined as participation regardless of belief or desire, and it may also occur without consent.

Ryan and Blum (1994) and Ryan et al.'s (1993) Typology of Problematic Sexual Behaviors

Ryan and Blum (1994) offer simple instructions for parents, using the term *problematic* to describe sexual behaviors that deviate from those defined as normal. They define three ways in which sexual behavior can be a problem. First, the behavior may be a problem for the child if it puts him or her at risk, if it interferes with other developmental tasks or relationships, if it violates rules, if it is self-abusive, or if the child believes the behavior is a problem.

Second, the sexual behavior is considered problematic for others if it causes others to feel uncomfortable, occurs at the wrong time or in the wrong place, conflicts with family or community values, is abusive, or all four.

Third, the sexual behavior may be defined as problematic if it involves other children without their consent, if two children are not equal, or if one child is pressured or coerced by another child.

Ryan et al.'s (1993) training manual for professionals *Understanding and Responding to the Sexual Behavior of Children,* represents a revision of earlier works. Also, as can be seen from Table 1.5, their continuum of normal to sexually abusive behaviors by children 12 years of age and younger is generally consistent with Johnson and Feldmeth's (1993). These authors, however, use the concepts of "yellow flag," "red flag," and "no question" behaviors to describe sexual behaviors that deviate from normal in the developmental sense (or from a societal norm or law in the case of adolescents, in which the term *illegal* is used to describe the most serious category of behavior). To ensure the development of normal sexual behaviors, Ryan et al. (1993) indicate that the socialization process may require an adult to limit, redirect, or educate children about normal or typical behaviors that may occur as children seek an understanding of their bodies, sexuality, and relationships. The authors state that the adult should convey messages regarding the private nature of such behaviors in a way that offers a model of open communication regarding healthy sexual development and learning. Most important, Ryan et al. stress the need to promote empathy by sharing with children the feelings others have when they are the victims of abusive behaviors.

Like the other classification systems discussed, Ryan (1991a) argues that additional factors besides sexual behaviors must be considered when distinguishing normal from problematic sexual behaviors. These include the nature of the relationship and interaction of those involved. Within these two broad categories, the factors that must be considered include consent, equality, and coercion. On the basis of common definitions in the field (from National Adolescent Perpetrator Network, 1988, 1993), Ryan et al. (1993) define *consent* as follows:

1. similar understanding of what is proposed (no trickery, misrepresentation, or confusion);

TABLE 1.5 Range of Sexual Behaviors of Children

Normal	Yellow Flag	Red Flag	"No Question"
Genital or reproduction conversation with peers or similar-age siblings	Preoccupation with sexual themes (especially sexually aggressive)	Sexually explicit conversation with significant age difference	Oral, vaginal, anal penetration of dolls,[a] children, and animals
"Playing doctor"	Attempting to expose other's genitals (e.g., pulling others' skirt up and pants down)	Touching genitals of othe***	Forced exposure of others' genitals[b]
"You show me yours, I'll show you mine" with peers	Sexually explicit or precocious conversation with peers	Degradation/humiliation of self or others with sexual themes	Simulating intercourse with peers with clothing off
Occasional masturbation without penetration	Sexual graffiti (especially chronic or impacting individuals)	Forced exposure of others' genitals	Any genital injury or bleeding not explained by accidental cause
Kissing, flirting	Sexual teasing/embarrassment of others	Inducing fear/threats of force	
Dirty words or jokes within cultural or peer group norm	Single occurrences of peeping/exposing/obscenities/pornographic interest/frottage	Sexually explicit proposals/threats including written notes	
	Preoccupation with masturbation[c]	Repeated or chronic peeping/exposing/obscenities/pornographic interests/frottage	
	Mutual masturbation/group masturbation	Compulsive masturbation/task interruption to masturbate	
	Simulating foreplay with dolls or peers with clothing on (e.g., petting and French kissing)	Masturbation including vaginal or anal penetration	
		Simulating intercourse with dolls, peers, animals, for example, humping	

SOURCE: Reprinted with permission from Ryan et al. (1993). Used with permission.
a. We need to be concerned about behavior with dolls that may be rehearsals for behavior with peers.
b. Although restraining an individual to pull down pants or expose breasts may occur in the context of hazing among peers, it is clearly abusive.
c. Although mutual or group masturbation is not uncommon among children, the interaction must be evaluated.

2. similar awareness of standards for the behavior in the family, the peer group, and the community;
3. similar awareness of possible consequences—that is, pain, punishment, stigma, disease, and so on; and
4. respect for agreement or disagreement without repercussions.[1]

Ryan (1991a) and Ryan et al. (1993) also note that it is important to distinguish between consent, cooperation, and compliance. *Consent* is based on a person's beliefs and desires, whereas *cooperation* implies participation without regard for personal beliefs or desires. *Compliance* means allowing something to happen without resisting, regardless of personal beliefs or desires. Ryan (1991a) stresses that neither compliance nor cooperation equals consent. Hence, a child who cooperates or complies with an abuser's request, using Ryan's definition, has not given his or her consent. Consent must be measured by the four elements previously described.

The second factor in evaluating the relationship and interaction of the sexual experience is equality, which refers to the balance of power and control. Ryan (1991a) notes that some of the indicators are obvious, such as age, weight, height, or intellectual differences. Some are more subtle, such as labels attached during play or other interactions: doctor and patient, king and slave, and boss and worker. Other factors that may be indicators of power differences are reflected in degrees of popularity, self-esteem, assertiveness, and so on.

The third characteristic of the interaction and relationship that must be assessed is the degree of coercion, or pressures used to achieve compliance. This ranges from privacy to secrecy to fear, and the corresponding continuum of pressure includes (a) no pressure; (b) use of authority (manipulation, trickery, and peer pressure); (c) use of coercion, threats, and bribes; and (d) use of physical force, threat of harm, or violence (Ryan, 1991a; Ryan et al., 1993).

Ryan (1991a, p. 399) indicates that there is also a shift in perception that occurs along the pressure continuum. The two ends of this continuum are "privacy" and "secrecy." Within the normal range of sexual behaviors, children may express embarrassment when they are caught engaging in sexual behaviors because these activities are perceived to be private and personal. Privacy, according to Ryan (1991a, p. 399), reflects a "rightful lack of sharing." Secrecy, however, is a "denial of sharing." Ryan (1991a, p. 400) states that a secret is binding and inhibiting. It prohibits external feedback, allowing sexual abuse to occur or continue or both and protects abusers from the consequences of disclosure. The reaction of the victim on discovery when secrets are involved may be fear or shame.

Few of the social factors Ryan et al. (1993) argue must be considered in determining abusive sexual behaviors are found in Table 1.5. In other writings or presentations by these researchers, however, they note that yellow flag behaviors may be accompanied by any combination of manipulation: trickery, peer pressure, and secrecy. Both red flag sexual behaviors and "no question" sexual behaviors may include the use of coercion and threats. Furthermore, Ryan (1990) noted that any sexual behaviors that involve the use of physical force, violence, or threats must be considered abusive. In their training manual, Ryan et al. (1993, p. 21) indicate that sexual behaviors that would be illegal for an older person are clearly deviant and potentially harmful and should always result in a consideration of reporting and referral. They indicate that the motivation and intent for these behaviors in childhood is not always clear, but the question of motivation or intent in no way minimizes or excuses the harmfulness (or unlawfulness) of the behavior.

In comparing Ryan et al.'s (1993) typology of normal and problematic sexual behaviors with Gil's (1993a), Crisci and Brown's (as cited in Kikuchi, 1995), Johnson and Feldmeth's (1993), and Cunningham and MacFarlane's (1991, 1996), it is possible to see patterns developing with respect to sexual behaviors and accompanying social factors that should be used to determine the progression from normal to abusive or aggressive sexual behaviors, regardless of different terminology. For example, Ryan et al.'s (1993) list of normal sexual behaviors is very similar to the ones described by Gil and Johnson and Feldmeth (cf. Tables 1.2, 1.3, and 1.5). Ryan et al.'s last two categories of behavior are similar to Johnson and Feldmeth's children who molest category when involving the use of coercion, threats, violence, or all three. Similar to Gil and Cunningham and MacFarlane, Ryan et al. indicate the need to consider the nature of the relationship and interaction of the victim and abuser, particularly as these relate to the factors of consent, compliance, and cooperation.

Pithers et al.'s (1993) Typology of Normal and Problematic Sexual Behaviors

Pithers et al. (1993) distinguish between normal and problematic sexual behaviors for children 12 years of age and younger. Like Ryan et al. (1993), this group of practitioners use the term problematic to represent behaviors that deviate from those considered developmentally normal for children in this age group.[2] The authors indicate that definitions of problematic sexualized behaviors for children 6 to 12 years of age may include sexual gestures; peeping; drawings; photos; statements; fondling; use of objects; stealing of tampons and underwear; public self-stimulation; touches such as grabbing, pinching, poking, rubbing; exposing; penetration; penetration with animal(s); use of weapon; and oral sexual behavior[3] (A. Gray, personal communication, October 1996).

Pithers et al. (1993) describe three stages of normal sexual development. From 0 to 5 years of age, a children's curiosity about their body leads them to touch both themselves and others. This is considered exploratory looking and touching. From 6 to 10 years of age, curiosity is seen as taking the form of a game, such as playing "doctor." Children also begin to tell dirty jokes and use dirty words. Interest continues in their own and others' bodies, most notably when they see changes (e.g., puberty). At 11 and 12 years of age, self-stimulation (e.g., masturbation) continues. During this period, however, new peer relationships rather than one's self become the primary focus. Some of these relationships, primarily with the opposite gender, involve sexual activity such as kissing and touching. Normal sexual activity may occur with either sex as long as the activity is mutual. Sexual activity with the same gender is not seen as indicating homosexuality.

Using the normal model of sexual development, Pithers et al. (1993) indicate that it is possible to determine problematic sexual behaviors by examining the following five factors: (a) whether the type of sexual activities would normally be expected at this level of development; (b) whether the children involved are of equal size or age; (c) whether sexual activities are mutual or coerced (i.e., intimidation, force, trickery, or bribes); (d) whether the type of secrecy involved falls outside of normal privacy levels; and (e) whether the child has no control over his or her behavior (compulsiveness) or whether the child is preoccupied with sexual behavior (obsessiveness).

Pithers et al. (1993) offer specific examples for each of these five factors. With respect to the first factor, comparing sexual activity to child's developmental level to see if is beyond what would be expected, the authors offer the following as examples of sexual problems:

1. oral or genital intercourse beyond the behaviors expected from children under age 5;

2. sexual behaviors based on threats or suggesting preoccupation with abusive sexuality;

3. children aged 6 to 10 who attempt genital or anal penetration, genital kissing, or oral or genital intercourse; and

4. children aged 10 to 12 who engage in sex play with much younger children or who force someone to engage in sex.

With regard to the second factor, relative power of children, Pithers et al. (1993) view substantial differences between children in the following areas as representative of power imbalances:

1. normal IQ child and a child with severe learning disabilities;

2. size difference such as one child being much taller than other; and

3. leader-follower relationship in which one child is always the leader or the follower.

The third factor Pithers et al. (1993) address is the use of intimidation, force, trickery, or bribery. They note that if any of these are observed in the interactions of children, then it should be considered a risk factor. Examples of these types of behaviors are included in A. Gray and W. Pithers' (personal communication, October 1996) description of coercion. The authors indicate that coercion may exist regardless of age difference and that power differentials stand alone or may be paired with other factors. The factors include (a) aggressive behaviors or statements; (b) intimidating behaviors or statements such as verbal threats, written notes, and displays of aggressive behavior without direct threats; (c) trickery that indicates fake kindness, self-serving caregiving, general threats to "tell on" victim, and using games to access the victim; (d) acting on knowledge of another's weakness for one's own interests; (e) put-downs of another and building self up and putting others down; (f) harassment, such as obtaining compliance or submission by wearing down another's resistance; (g) bribery and enticements through the use of gifts, money, favors, play activities, and offers to exchange chores to gain influence; (h) preplanning to take advantage of the vulnerabilities of another person; and (i) use of the element of surprise to engage in the behavior before the other has the opportunity to resist. In contrast to these types of interactions, they indicate that normal sexual behaviors involve curiosity and game playing.

The fourth factor relates to secrecy. Pithers et al. (1993) indicate that it may be hard to distinguish a child's natural sense of privacy or embarrassment about sexual feelings from the secrecy that allows abusive sexuality to continue. They note that privacy is a rightful protection of one's personal space, whereas secrecy suggests that a child is avoiding the consequences of an action he or she knows or senses is wrong or causes harm.

The fifth and final factor that defines a sexual problem is signs of compulsiveness or obsessiveness or both. Compulsive behavior appears to be beyond the control of the child, whereas sexual obsessions are something the child thinks about continually.

In summary, Pithers et al. (1993) indicate that these are rough guidelines to use when evaluating children's sexual behaviors. Any one factor alone may or may not represent a sexual behavior problem. These authors suggest that if an untrained person has concerns, he or she should consult a mental health professional. For trained individuals, the authors offer the following criteria as guidelines for deciding if referral is necessary: (a) Vermont Department of Social and Rehabilitative Services-substantiated sexual abuse by the child; (b) behavior that, if performed by a juvenile, constitutes a sexual crime; (c) observable, repetitive, problematic sexualized behaviors (as described in the examples from Pithers et al. discussed previously); (d) noncompliance to prohibition of sexual abuse; (e) coercive sexual behaviors; (f) nonsecretive but intrusive sexualized behaviors; (g) diversity of sexualized behaviors; (h) eroticized sexual behaviors—distracted, highly interruptive, and preoccupied; and (i) adult supervision is unsuccessful in extinguishing sexualized behaviors (A. Gray, personal communication, October 1996).

Berliner, Manaois, and Monastersky's (1986) and Berliner and Rawlings's (1991) Classification of Disturbed Sexual Behaviors

Berliner et al. (1986) and Berliner and Rawlings (1991), from the Harborview Sexual Assault Center in Seattle, Washington, propose yet another system for classifying child sexual behaviors. In their continuum, they use the term *disturbance* to reflect sexual behaviors that deviate from those expected as part of normal sexual behavior development, although what is considered normal is not defined. In this classification system, disturbances are categorized into three levels of severity based on objective behavioral criteria.

The first category, "inappropriate sexual behavior," is considered the least disturbed in the model. Typical behaviors include the following: persistent masturbation; public masturbation; masturbation causing pain or irritations; touching breasts and genitals of others; asking others to touch child's genitals; repeatedly or publicly showing genitals; an excessive interest in sexual material and sexualized conversation, art, or conduct with others; and sexualization of nonsexual situations.

Berliner et al. (1986) do not view the previous behaviors as representing psychological disturbances unless the following conditions are present: (a) the behaviors occur in inappropriate situations, (b) the behaviors interfere with the child's development, (c) a persistence of the behavior remains despite intervention, (d) multiple sexual behaviors are reported, and (e) the behaviors are accompanied by other forms of disturbed behavior such as conduct disorders.

Behaviors that indicate a more profound disturbance are labeled "developmentally precocious" and include simulated or completed intercourse in addition to the previously mentioned behaviors. In this category, behaviors are explicit and intentional, but no coercion is present. Berliner et al. (1986) indicate that these behaviors are not always evidence of psychological disturbances but lie outside the range of what would be developmentally normal. As such, the authors suggest the following be included in evaluation: (a) the child's age, (b) family contacts, (c) information about how the behavior was learned, (d) frequency and persistence of the behavior, and (e) the extent to which the child has continued access to sexually explicit materials or opportunities to see sexually explicit activity.

The third category is considered the most serious and is determined by some evidence of aggressive sexual contact or coercion in the child's sexual interaction with others. The first type "aggressive sexual contact" involves the use of physical force, including injury. The second type, "socially coercive" behavior, involves the use of threats or social coercion. Berliner et al. (1986) indicate that these behaviors are serious, unacceptable, and may be associated with other antisocial behaviors. They always warrant assessment and intervention.

Similar to the typologies and classification systems previously discussed, Berliner et al. (1986) place children's sexual behaviors along a continuum and recognize the need to determine the social contexts in which the behaviors occur. For example, the program expresses the need for clinicians to qualify the presence and severity of children's behavior in reference to the developmental, familial, and interpersonal environments in which they are manifest. Similar to several other typologies reviewed previously, Berliner et al. consider behavioral criteria alone to be incomplete evidence of sexual behavior disturbances. Unlike the other typologies, these authors place greater emphasis on the relationship between sexual and psychological disturbances.

Sgroi, Bunk, and Wabrek's (1988) Descriptors

Sgroi et al. (1988, pp. 1-24) describe normal to abusive sexual behaviors for children. Because the methodology is very similar to other classifications previously described, I will only present the factors considered in determining whether sexual behaviors are abusive. These include (a) whether a complaint about the behaviors has been filed, (b) whether the child has exhibited behaviors that indicate he or she has been sexually abused, (c) whether sexual behaviors are consistent with normal behavior for the age of the child, and (d) the relative power of the participants. Sgroi et al. also note the need to take into account whether force or intimidation, ritualistic or sadistic behavior, secrecy, or all of the above are involved.

In addition to similarities with the previous classifications, ritualistic and sadistic behaviors are mentioned as constituting abusive sexual behaviors. Sgroi et al. (1988) also include considering whether a complaint has been filed, a factor that serves as an introduction to programs that use legal terminology and definitions as a means of describing children involved in sexually inappropriate behaviors.

Rasmussen, Burton, and Christopherson's (1992) and Matsuda and Rasmussen's (1990) Types of Sexually Inappropriate Behaviors

To distinguish between various sexual behaviors, Matsuda and Rasmussen, in a 1990 report to the Utah Governor's Council on Juvenile Sex Offenders, used the terms *appropriate* and *inappropriate* sexual behaviors. Although they did not outline what specific sexual behaviors should be included in the appropriate category, they identified the following conditions that warrant the label of inappropriate sexual behaviors in their definition of a juvenile sex offender:

> Any juvenile below the age of 18 who has committed a sexual offense as defined by the Utah Criminal Code Annotated is a juvenile sex offender. Sex offenses by juveniles may include a power differential between perpetrator and victim (perpetrator has greater age, size, or mental capacity); role differential (perpetrator assumes authority over child); predatory patterns (perpetrator sets up the victim); and elements of coercion (perpetrator uses games, tricks, bribes, threats, and/or force). (p. 2)

Under this definition, Matsuda and Rasmussen (1990) identify two types of children 12 years of age and younger who display sexually inappropriate behaviors. The first is labeled the "sexually reactive" child, who is defined as follows:

> A child age eight and under (usually eight or nine), who displays sexually inappropriate behavior towards another which is harmful or unlawful. This behavior is often in reaction to his/her own sexual victimization and/or exposure to explicit sexual stimuli. For court jurisdiction purposes, this child should be considered a dependent. (p. 2)

The second category of children involved in sexually inappropriate behavior is labeled the "preadolescent sex offender," defined as "a child, nine through 12, who displays sexually inappropriate behavior toward another which is harmful or unlawful" (Matsuda & Rasmussen, 1990, p. 2).

Matsuda and Rasmussen (1990, p. 2) offer further clarification of inappropriate sexual behaviors that can be enacted by adolescent sex offenders (children 13-17 years of age), preadolescent sex offenders (children 12 years and younger), or sexually reactive children. These include the following:

> *Victim-perpetrator:* A child who is reacting to his or her own sexual victimization or exposure to explicit sexual stimuli or both.

Delinquent perpetrator: A child who is not a prior victim of sexual abuse but, because of social inadequacy and personality or behavioral disorders or both, responds inappropriately to normal developmental sexual arousal.

Family perpetrator: A juvenile who displays harmful or unlawful sexually inappropriate behavior against a younger sibling or other child living in his or her home or both.

The categories were presented by Matsuda and Rasmussen (1990) to help guide juvenile justice system professionals in their decision making regarding placement and case management of sexually abusive youth.

The previous delineations between sexually appropriate and sexually inappropriate behaviors of preadolescent children are not as clear in a publication by Rasmussen et al. (1992) in the *Journal of Child Sexual Abuse.* The authors indicate that they perceive a difference between behaviors of sexually reactive compared with "sexually aggressive or child perpetrator" types of children. They then continue to use the term sexually reactive to describe all children with sexual behavior problems. Further embedded within their discussion is a statement that suggests that the only factor that differentiates sexually reactive children from sexually aggressive children is "established patterns of predatory sexual behaviors." In a telephone conversation, however, J. Burton (personal communication, September 19, 1994) indicated that the authors were now including the term *children with sexually abusive behavior problems* as a way of differentiating abusive children from those who were only reacting to sexual victimization. L. Rasmussen, J. Burton, and B. Christopherson (personal communication, September and October 1996) indicate that their current work focuses on identifying sexually abusive behavior problems by assessing the sophistication of the behavior and the presence or absence of certain abusive dynamics. These dynamics include (a) differences in power (i.e., age, size, mental capacity, and physical abilities); (b) misuse of authority (e.g., babysitting); and (c) manipulation (e.g., grooming behaviors).

In closing this section, it is worth noting that this typology is the first of those reviewed thus far to use terms associated with the legal or criminal justice system to describe children who have crossed the boundary from normal to reactive to abusive sexual behaviors—that is, delinquent, perpetrator, juvenile sex offenders, and unlawful behaviors.

It's About Childhood, The Hindman Foundation:
Children Who Sexually Act and Culpability

The It's About Childhood program is commonly referred to as Jan Hindman's program and is located in Ontario, Oregon. Whereas Matsuda and Rasmussen (1990) and Rasmussen et al. (1992) used legal and criminal justice terminology to describe children involved in sexually abusive behaviors (e.g., perpetrator and offender) and to discuss sexual behaviors as either harmful or unlawful, the It's About Childhood program extends this idea further than any programs described herein. The program is based on the notion that children who are engaging in what I call sexually aggressive behaviors are committing a crime and should be treated as a criminal. That is, the most extreme sexual behaviors, considering types, knowledge, frequency, number of contacts, and use of coercion, are defined as being criminal in nature; having "criminal intent" (It's About Childhood, The Hindman Foundation, written correspondence and materials, January 1994 and June 1996). Criminal intent is tied to the notion of culpability, which, according to the materials provided, refers to the "knowledge of inappropriateness of the behavior and knowledge that a consequence (e.g., punishment) for the behavior exists." It is assumed that those children who rank high on culpability have criminal intent.

Before further discussing the notion of culpability, the terms that are important to understanding the It's About Childhood program are defined. These include child, sexually act, culpability, sexual curiosity, abuse reactive, criminal intent, and juvenile sex offender.

The term *child* is used to define anyone in the state of Oregon under the age of 18. The authors of the program note that they have purposely chosen this word when describing juveniles in the program because a child may be nearly 18 years of age, but the legal definition in the state determines that anyone under the age of 18 is technically considered a child.

The term *sexually act* has also been designed and used purposely by the staff of It's About Childhood to indicate that children are doing sexual things. They believe that many children engage in sexual activities in a normal or expected manner, and these children may or may not be sexual offenders. Whether the children are acting in a normal manner is determined by the Juvenile Culpability Assessment and by the It's About Childhood evaluation, discussed in a later chapter.

The term *culpability* is extremely important to this program's evaluation of children who "sexually act." Some children are viewed as sexually acting because of curiosity or sexual play. Although these behaviors may seem inappropriate or embarrassing to parents, children may not understand the nature of the sexual activities. Therefore, the behavior may be inappropriate, embarrassing, or even abusive, but if the child does not understand this, he or she would not be "culpable." The term culpability relates to knowledge that children have at the time of the sexual actions. Culpability means knowledge of the inappropriateness of the behavior, and knowledge that a consequence for the behavior exists. When children are culpable, they are viewed as understanding the nature of their sexual actions, that the behavior is inappropriate, and that there may be a consequence or punishment for the behavior. Children who are culpable have criminal intent. This is an important concept and one that is not found in any of the classifications reviewed previously. Using this concept, it is clear that if two children would commit the same sexual act, but only one understands the nature of the behavior and that there is a consequence or punishment attached, only that child is defined as culpable and would be charged with a sexual crime.

The term *sexual curiosity* is used by It's About Childhood to describe sexual activities or sexual intentions of children who do not demonstrate "criminal intent." The authors of the program offer the following differentiation. Children may become curious about their bodies at the same time they are receiving sexual messages from society, such as exposure to pornography or other influences from television or music. With limited knowledge and understanding, children may attempt to act out the behaviors they have heard or observed. Children who have sexual curiosity and act on these feelings, or children who have been improperly influenced by their environment, are not considered to be criminals. They have a low level of culpability. Their behavior occurs because they are curious and basically their actions should be considered as "innocent."

Another term used by It's About Childhood is *abuse reactive*. This term is used to describe children who have been sexually abused in the past. In some situations, children repeat these experiences and may, in some circumstances, reenact those behaviors against other children. If the term abuse reactive is used, it means that the child is repeating a behavior that had happened in the child's past and not acting with criminal intent.

The behaviors described within the sexual curiosity category are generally consistent with the normal, normative, appropriate, and so on categories in the classifications previously described in this chapter. The term abuse reactive is also similar to that of others who use the term, meaning that children are reacting to their own sexual victimization.

Children who commit sexual actions and have criminal intent are viewed as having a high level of culpability. They understand that the behavior is not only inappropriate but also has a consequence or punishment. Children who act with criminal intent will be charged with a sexual crime using the It's About Childhood typology.

In comparing the It's About Childhood continuum to those previously described, sexually aggressive children would probably fall into the criminal intent category, but only if they were knowledgeable that the behavior was inappropriate and had a consequence or punishment attached. In the Juvenile Culpability Assessment Tool, Hindman (1994) warns that levels of culpability cannot be treated as synonymous with risk or dangerousness of the child. She says that some children who have lived in a sexually exploitive environment, or who may be an abuse victim, may not have a culpability level but may be dangerous.

In determining culpability, Hindman (1994) focuses on four areas that have a total of 16 assessment items. The focus areas are (a) intellectual culpability, (b) social culpability, (c) sexual culpability, and (d) criminal culpability. The first category, intellectual culpability, includes measures of the juvenile's age, intelligence, intellectual opportunities (for learning appropriate behaviors and so on), and intellectual inhibitors. The second category, social culpability, includes measures of age differences between offender and victim, time span between the first and last incident (social maturation), social capacity for empathy (antisociopathy), and social skill development. The third category, sexual culpability, includes types of sexual information and sexual abuse information available to the child, the child's sexual victimization history (includes history of abuse, memories of abuse, similarities between current and past sexual activities, and attitudes about previous victimization), and types of sexual behavior. The fourth category, criminal culpability, includes the number of offender's sexual contacts or victims, number of incidents, knowledge of criminal behavior, and level of coercion used. Children who are involved in the TRAC I phase of treatment at the It's About Childhood clinic are labeled "juvenile sexual offenders." These are children who have committed a sexual act, were culpable, and, therefore, had criminal intent. They are juveniles who have been charged with sexual crimes. A scoring matrix of I through IV (high culpability to none) for both those who were sexual abuse victims and those who were not is described in Chapter 5.

Classification Comparisons

The previous discussion of classification systems demonstrates that children engage in a variety of sexual acts alone and with others. These range from sexual behaviors considered normal, normative, or sexually appropriate to those considered problematic, inappropriate, deviant, abusive, aggressive, or even criminal. Although there is not yet a definitive set of symptoms that clearly "marks" children as normal, abused, or likely to abuse (see Beitchman et al., 1991; Conte & Schuerman, 1987; Kendall-Tackett, Williams, & Finkelhor, 1993), the typologies discussed herein are useful because they describe a range of sexual behaviors and associated social and psychological factors that can begin to help assess whether children's sexual behaviors are normal for their age group or whether the children are in need of some type of intervention. Furthermore, although different concepts are used, there is a good deal of consistency of what behaviors and factors can be used to identify normal compared with sexual abusive or sexually aggressive behaviors, and even those that would be labeled as criminal.

In the following section, I identify common factors from the classifications reviewed that can be used to differentiate children involved in sexually aggressive behaviors from those involved in normal or other inappropriate sexual activities. These are presented in Table 1.6 and described in the following section.

Characteristics of
Sexually Aggressive Behaviors

Behavioral Characteristics

Sexually aggressive behaviors represent the extreme end of a sexual behavior continuum. The sexual behaviors are far advanced for children 12 years of age and younger. The behaviors have an aggressive quality, involving use of force, coercion (social or physical), and secrecy. The sexual acts represent patterned rather than isolated events.

TABLE 1.6 Identifying Characteristics of Children 12 Years of Age and Younger Who Exhibit Sexually Aggressive Behavioral Problems

Characteristics of sexually aggressive behaviors

Sexual behaviors are developed far beyond those expected for age of abuser—includes oral copulation, vaginal and oral intercourse, or forcible penetration of anus or vagina with fingers or other objects.

Sexual behaviors have aggressive quality and involve use of force, coercion, secrecy, or all three. The behaviors may be aimed at self, but generally involve others.

Coercion may be two types:

Physical: use of physical force or threat to use physical force, a weapon, or to injure victim(s). Sexual acts may be sadistic or ritualistic in nature.

Social: use of social threats (e.g., "I won't be your friend any more"), bribes, trickery, persuasion, intimidation, peer pressure, and so on.

Secrecy: Types of secrecy used by abuser deny victim(s)—through abuser's use of coercion—the right to disclose their experience and serves to protect sexual aggressor.

Sexual behaviors increase over time, become repetitive or obsessive or both, become compulsive, and represent a pattern rather than isolated events.

When other than self is involved, sexual behaviors are planned, calculated, and predatory—exceed opportunistic sexual activities.

Sexual behaviors may be associated with other antisocial behaviors such as conduct disorders.

Sexual behaviors continue despite intervention.

Under the It's About Childhood program, the sexual behavior may be criminal in nature; that is, if culpability is high—the abuser knows the behavior is inappropriate and is associated with negative consequences.

Motives for sexually aggressive behaviors

Need to reduce negative feelings of fear, anger, and loneliness

Need for power and application of coercion

Self-control

Sexually aggressive children demonstrate little self-control as related to their sexual behavior.

Several additional characteristics of sexually aggressive behaviors in which there is generally consistent agreement among most program areas are that the sexual acts may have a compulsive, obsessive nature; they may be aimed at the self, but by the time behaviors become sexually aggressive they usually involve other victims; behaviors may be opportunistic but many are planned, calculated, and predatory; and the sexual behaviors usually exist in combination with other antisocial behaviors such as conduct disorders. Furthermore, sexually aggressive behaviors

TABLE 1.6 Continued

Sexually aggressive children tend to be impulsive and compulsive in their behaviors.

Emotions demonstrated by sexual aggressors

Abusers demonstrate deep feelings of anger, rage, fear, shame, and loneliness. Practitioners and researchers, such as Johnson and Feldmeth (1993) and Friedrich (1990), argue that these emotions are paired with sex, which has been paired with aggression.

Abusers lack empathy for victims.

Abuse histories

Sexual aggressors may have been sexually abused.

All have been abused in some way—sexually, physically, emotionally, or all three.

Abuser-victim relationship: Equality, power, and control

Abusers choose victims they believe have less power and control, who appear weaker and vulnerable; defining characteristics include differences in age (2-5 years), size, status, intelligence, cognitive development, handicapped, unmet needs, and so on.

Victims may be siblings, other children living in the home, schoolmates, or other acquaintances. Victims may be older than abuser, but abuser has some type of authority or power over victim.

Victims usually do not give informed consent

Environments

Living arrangements lack sexual boundaries; highly sexualized environments that may include frequent exposure to pornography; abusive environments; parents or caretakers are substance abusers or demonstrate other parental dysfunctions.

Outside home environments conducive to socializing children into sexually aggressive activities.

Treatment outcomes

Considering all groups of children with sexual behavior problems and disturbances, sexually aggressive children are most resistant to treatment.

Sexually aggressive children are in need of intensive specialized treatment.

continue even when intervention occurs, and children who exhibit these behaviors are very resistant to treatment.

Several programs, most notably It's About Childhood, add a dimension not included in other programs. If sexual behaviors have the characteristics described previously, and the child knows the behavior is inappropriate and associated with punishment (i.e., the child acts with criminal intent), then the behavior is viewed as a criminal act. This view gives new meaning to sexually aggressive behaviors and has additional implications for intervention and treatment—that is, sexual behaviors defined as criminal would be processed through the criminal justice system, and the child would be labeled criminal. This is not the case in most other programs reviewed in this chapter—that is, in these programs, children with sexually aggressive behaviors are very frequently viewed as sexually reactive or exhibiting inappropriate sexually abusive problems. As a consequence, they are assigned to foster care or to social or psychological services or both. The child is not viewed as a criminal. As demonstrated in the following several quotations from leading practitioners in the area of sexually abusive children, whether to label these children as criminal will probably be a hotly debated issue as this field develops.

Lucy Berliner
(Personal Communication, June 1996)

I am opposed to conceptualizing sexual misbehavior in children primarily as crimes. When children are old enough or possess the *mens rea* necessary for their acts to be prosecuted, then the sexual misconduct becomes criminal in nature. As you know, states set the age below which children are presumed incapable of forming the intent to commit a crime and the age above which it is a rebuttable assumption. The ages may vary. But the more important point is that when children twelve and under are the focus, in general, misconduct should be primarily considered a behavior problem not a crime. Just as this is true for nonsexual aggressive behavior, it should be true for sexually aggressive behavior. I can see no advantage in labeling and treating prepubescent children with behavior problems as criminals for treatment or intervention purposes. Even in those rare cases where the criminal justice system becomes involved with younger children, the treatment should be the same. The point is to accurately assess the nature and cause of the behavior and construct an intervention that eliminates it.

Dave Fowers
(Personal Communication, August 1996)

We have regularly discussed labels, responsibility, treatment, and accountability with our Utah Network on Juveniles Offending Sexually (NOJOS). Our consensus is somewhat inconsistent because of the extremes of feelings and the various viewpoints represented by the cross section of NOJOS members (law enforcement, attorneys, child advocates, secure facility staff, mental health, etc.).

My feeling is somewhere in the middle. Offenses in Utah are "delinquent" up to age 18 and then can be called "criminal." Offenders prior to age 12 are not brought into the Youth Corrections system. Often times the only legal court record before the age of 8 is one of "dependency." I think sexual or aggressive behaviors committed before the age of 12 need to have a special sanction. We have been trying to develop a term or "label" that would recognize specific mitigating factors, but would nevertheless hold youth and agencies responsible to participate in intervention processes or programs that would reduce the possibility of re-offense. As described in our manual, entitled *Juvenile Sex Offender Specific Protocols and Standards Manual* (third edition), a continuum of services need to be in place to facilitate the most effective placement in terms of cost, supervision, treatment, security, and safety.

We have a long way to go. Presently there is not a very good match between the legal and clinical definitions of older offenders. The situation with the younger population is even worse or non-existent.

William (Bill) Friedrich
(Personal Communication, May 1996)

It's important to use accurate terms that reflect the nature of the behavior. Sexual reactivity may not be sexual aggression, and sexual offending may not be sexual aggression. The use of the word *offending* adds ambiguity.

Eliana Gil
(Personal Communication, July 1996)

Regarding your question about advantages/disadvantages of applying criminal justice labels, this is a complex issue. While research on adult and adolescent offenders indicates that the adjudication process and legal interventions, when coordinated with rigorous treatment efforts, tend to produce the best results, we must assume that the legal system acts as a strong external limiter because adolescents and adults understand and fear legal repercussions.

With respect to children who molest, I believe that their sexually abusive behaviors must be stopped early, before the behaviors become a deeply established pattern of relating to others. Children must also be assessed to see if they have a history of abuse that may influence their behavior.

I also am aware that some children's offenses are very serious and don't look much different than those of their adolescent and adult counterparts. Certainly, if a child under age commits a serious violent sexual crime, he or she must be given immediate help to control dangerous behaviors. In my thinking, this might mean a hospital or a residential treatment program. But of what possible use or consequence would it be to send a child to juvenile detention, or to have the child adjudicated and placed on probation or confined, without treatment, to criminal facilities? These are places where children are likely to come under the influence of some powerful role modeling from older, aggressive youth with patterns of criminal behavior.

In addition, when children get labeled criminals so early, the labels may prejudice others' responses toward them. Children don't need skepticism: They need serious, focused, and unwavering help. I'm afraid most children will not find labeling and legal intervention as helpful.

Having said the above, the "abuse excuse" should be approached with caution. I believe prior abuse is a treatment concern, but should never be used to justify a child's behavior. After all, there are many children who are abused, and never abuse others. So additional variables must be considered.

Jan Hindman
(Personal Communication, September 1996)

When I read your question, I see you are concerned with the important issue of describing children as "criminals." I have very strong feelings about this issue, and I will hope to answer your questions.

There are basically two factors that are used nationwide to determine if a child has committed a criminal sexual offense. These are (1) age differential (vary from state to state varying two years to six years) and (2) the sexual activity. I do not believe that these two items alone are adequate to determine whether a child has criminal intent, which of course must occur for criminal charges or labels to be appropriate.

As an example, John Hinkley shot President Reagan in front of two million people on television. He was "not guilty" because he was "not culpable." In other words, he did not have criminal intent due to mental illness. Whether we agree or disagree with the decision, adults have a protection in most states, concerning culpability.

My definition of culpability has two parts. First, the person must know the behavior is inappropriate, but secondly, the person must know there is a consequence for the behavior. Each state decides when a person can give sexual consent. In most states the age of majority is 18. It is assumed that unless there are several circumstances all citizens over the age of 18 have a duty to know the law.

We have naturally assumed that children know that sexual activity is wrong even though we rarely teach children about sexual rules. If we take the two criteria, children could engage in sexual activity with the same type of behavior and the same age differential when in one situation it could be normal sexual curiosity and in another situation it could be highly criminal. The difference is what children know when they commit these activities.

Therefore, and finally, I have developed a "Juvenile Culpability Assessment." This sixteen-item test is used to attempt an assessment of the child's culpability. It adds fourteen items to the two items commonly used. The culpability assessment is less than perfect at this time, but it is still a valuable tool to determine whether children should be charged with crimes, whether they are at risk of becoming a sex offender, or whether they are simply engaging in normal sexual curiosity.

Lucinda Rasmussen
(Personal Communication, October 1996)

Ordinarily children are not considered legally culpable for behavior that would be criminal if committed by an adult. Sexual abuse is viewed as taking place when a person who has greater power of authority uses some type of manipulation or coercion to initiate sexual contact against a child. It is possible for children under 11 years old to use sexual behavior to intentionally exercise power, authority, manipulation, and coercion against other children who are younger, smaller, less intelligent, or more vulnerable. Clinicians and juvenile justice professionals are then faced with the difficult decision of what to do to help these children recognize that their behavior is unacceptable and to prevent them from continuing to hurt others. Effective intervention holds individuals accountable for harmful behavior while providing adequate opportunity for rehabilitation.

It is sometimes difficult to achieve and maintain a rehabilitative focus on juvenile justice. However, intervention in a juvenile justice system should include two components: clinical intervention to provide treatment and ensure rehabilitation of the offending child/adolescent, and juvenile justice supervision to provide consequences for illegal behavior and ensure community protection (Matsuda & Rasmussen, 1990). Both components of intervention must be applied in tandem.

An effective juvenile justice response to these young children includes referring them to appropriate treatment resources in the community. Involving the families in the treatment process is crucial to the success to treatment. Adjudicating the children in juvenile court and using court orders to ensure compliance to treatment may be advisable, particularly when parents are resistant to seeking treatment for their children. However, juvenile justice intervention with preadolescent children is only advisable when the philosophy of the local juvenile justice system supports treatment and rehabilitation. If the focus of court intervention is directed more toward imposing punitive consequences than treatment, adjudicating a preadolescent child in juvenile court is not helpful and may in fact be detrimental.

Gail Ryan
(Personal Communication, September 1996)

When a seven year old steals a candy bar from the store, we do not label the child "criminal" but we do make sure s(he) knows the behavior is illegal. Children need to learn that there are values, rules, and laws about sexual behavior but, even with older youngsters, we need to label the behavior without labeling the child.

Motives for Acting Sexually Aggressive

Not all programs reviewed herein address the issue of motives. Of those that do—for example, Johnson and Feldmeth (1993) and Crisci and Brown (as cited in Kikuchi, 1995)—the motives behind children acting sexually aggressive are the need to reduce feelings of fear, anger, or loneliness or to achieve power over victims through acts of coercion. Some professionals believe that a significant number of sexually aggressive children are also addicted to the behaviors.

Self-Control

Some professionals indicate that sexually aggressive children appear to have little self-control in relation to their sexual behaviors. Their acts are impulsive or compulsive or both.

Emotions Expressed

Sexually aggressive children demonstrate deep feelings of anger, rage, shame, and loneliness. Several professionals (e.g., Friedrich, Johnson, and Feldmeth) have observed that these emotions are paired with sex, which has been paired with aggression. This latter observation would explain the aggressive quality of the group of sexually aggressive children's sexual behaviors compared with other groups such as sexually reactive children. With respect to their victims, sexually aggressive children express no empathy.

Abuse Histories

Sexually aggressive children may have been sexually abused but not necessarily. All have experienced some type of abuse—physical, sexual, or emotional—usually multiple types. Some professionals who work with sexually aggressive children believe that histories of physical abuse are equally or more closely related to sexually aggressive children's behaviors than are histories of sexual abuse (D. Kennedy, personal communication, August 1993).

Abuse-Victim Relationships

This is an important defining characteristic of sexually aggressive children because these children seek out others who are perceived as less powerful, unequal in status, and who can be controlled. As noted previously, sexually aggressive children use coercion on their victims, hence victims do not fully agree to participate in the sexual acts; they do not consent to participation. Because sexually aggressive children view their victims as "prey," their behaviors demonstrate a predatory nature.

Environments

The majority of sexually aggressive children live in dysfunctional-type homes or environments that include families that lack boundaries, especially in the area of sexual activities. Families or living arrangements may be characterized as abusive. Environments outside the home may also be conducive to learning sexually aggressive behaviors. These risk factors are discussed further in Chapters 2 and 3.

Treatment Outcomes

Of all children demonstrating problematic sexual behaviors, children who act sexually aggressive are the most resistant to treatment. This may be related to Johnson and Feldmeth's (1993) observation that this type of behavior takes longer to manifest than other types such as sexually reactive behavior. Cantwell (1995) also reports that sexually aggressive children are addicted to the behavior. Hence, by the time sexually aggressive children are recognized, their behaviors and related cognitive and affective patterns may be well ingrained.

Conclusions and Analysis

Although data collection and research on sexually aggressive children is in its infancy, the material presented in this chapter and summarized in Table 1.6 can be of some help in attempting to identify these children compared with children who exhibit normal sexual behaviors or who have other sexual behavior problems. As was apparent in this chapter, most practitioners and researchers use a continuum of sexual behaviors to demonstrate the progression of normal to sexually aggressive behaviors. In all continuums, sexually aggressive behaviors fall at the extreme end and are viewed as most resistant to intervention and treatment.

Although there is some agreement among researchers and practitioners concerning specific sexual behaviors that can be characterized as sexually aggressive, this chapter demonstrated that there is a wide variety of labels that are used when describing these sexually abusive behaviors. The labels tend to vary by discipline or perspective of the practitioners or researchers. As evident in this chapter, the labels or conceptualizations of these children's behaviors or both can have far-reaching intervention and treatment outcomes. For example, the It's About Childhood approach, compared with other more clinical programs described in this chapter, would probably increase the chances of children ending up in the criminal justice system.

Notes

1. Ryan et al. (1993) did not initially refer to the final category as illegal but made a distinction in their most recent revisions to note that these behaviors are illegal for adolescents. The use of the term illegal behaviors seems to represent an extension in thinking about extreme sexually abusive behaviors as being not only developmentally inappropriate but also violating societal norms that have been encoded into laws. The second change in thinking is found in a revision of the fourth criteria used to define consent. Previously, Ryan (1991a, pp. 398-399) conceptualized the four criteria as follows: (a) The victim fully understands what the abuser is proposing: The use of trickery or misrepresentation (trying to fool the victim) by the abuser is absent; (b) the victim is knowledgeable about the family's, peer group, and culture's standards for sexual behaviors; (c) the victim is aware of the possible consequences of the sexual behavior, such as pain, punishment, disease, and so on; and (d) the victim has the option to agree or disagree with the abuser's proposal without repercussions. The reason Ryan

gave for changing the wording in the fourth criterion was conveyed in a letter. She said, "it is very important to change the use of 'victim' and 'perpetrator' labels in the definition of consent, since neither is a victim if the four conditions are met" (G. Ryan, personal communication, July 2, 1996, and September 23, 1996). This does not equate with dismissing the behavior as nonproblematic but may indicate that it is a different kind of problem.

2. In addition to using the term problematic, Lane (1991a) also uses sexually abusive when describing a range of sexually problematic behaviors. To establish a benchmark for what behaviors should be considered problematic or abusive, Lane utilizes Martinson's (1991) work on normal sexual development in infancy and young children.

3. Gray and Pithers (A. Gray, personal communication, October 1996) exclude from the definition of problematic sexualized behaviors (a) children with major psychiatric disorders who are nonresponsive to psychotropic medications, (b) private self-stimulation behaviors exclusively, and (c) sexualized verbalizations exclusively.

2

Sexually Aggressive Children
Social Demographics and Psychological Characteristics

Sharon K. Araji

Once it is recognized that new groups such as sexually aggressive children present social problems, then it is common for practitioners and researchers to become interested in not only the behaviors that constitute the problems, as discussed in Chapter 1, but also the defining social and psychological characteristics of the population. Hence, this chapter is a natural extension of Chapter 1 and focuses on social and psychological factors associated with sexually aggressive children. Both types of information are important for the development of appropriate and effective prevention, intervention, and treatment strategies.

To accomplish the chapter objective, published studies, unpublished data from survey research, and personal correspondence with clinicians and service providers who have contact with sexually aggressive children are reviewed.

Identifying Social Demographics and Psychological Characteristics Associated With Sexually Aggressive Children: Published Studies

Following a review of several empirical studies that focused on sexually aggressive children, six broad social and psychological categories that should be examined when describing this group of children were identified. These include abuser and victim characteristics, family characteristics and environments, victimization experiences, sexual and aggressive preoccupation, school performance, and social relationships and skills.

Abuser and Victim Demographics: Johnson's (1993c) Report From Three Research Studies

Information presented in Studies 1, 2, and 3 that is shown in Table 2.1 is adapted from Johnson (1993c) in Gil and Johnson's (1993a) book. The table shows that in Johnson's 1988 and 1989 studies and Friedrich and Luecke's 1988 study, the average age at first perpetration by boys was 8.7 (range, 4 to 12 years) and for girls 6.7 (range, 4 to 9 years).

In Johnson's (1988, 1989) studies (Table 2.1, Studies 1 and 2), the average age of the boys' victims was 6.7, and for girls it was 5. The average age difference between the girls who molested siblings and their sibling victims was 4.2 years (Table 2.1, Study 2), whereas the average age difference between the brother-molester and the sister-victim was 4.5 years (Table 2.1, Study 2). When the sexual behavior was between two brothers, the average age difference was 3 years (Table 2.1, Study 2).

Johnson's (1993c) report indicates that girls begin their sexually aggressive behaviors earlier than boys (6.7 and 8.7 years, respectively), and their victims are also younger (5 and 6.7 years of age, respectively). As Table 2.1 demonstrates, however, the average age differences between male and female perpetrators and their victims are very similar: 3 or 4½ years.

Although Studies 1 and 2 in Table 2.1 show that, on the average, victims were younger than perpetrators, this age difference pattern does not hold across all situations.

For example, in both the Johnson (1988, 1989) and Friedrich and Luecke (1988) studies, many of the child molesters were the same age or younger than their victims, in some cases as many as 4 years. This suggests that equally or more important than the biological age differences between perpetrators and victims is the perpetrator's psychological assessment as to whether he or she can control the victim. Interestingly, relative to the sample size, Johnson found that girls used more force and physical coercion than boys in gaining victim compliance.

The average number of victims for boys in Studies 1 and 3 in Table 2.1 was approximately 2, with a range of 1 to 7. For girls, in Friedrich and Luecke's (1988) study (Table 2.1, Study 3), the average was 2 victims, whereas in Johnson's (1989) study (Table 2.1, Study 2) the average was 3.3 with a range of 1 to 15. All the children knew their victims, who were frequently siblings. Johnson found that of the 47 boys in her 1988 study (Table 2.1, Study 1), 46% molested siblings. Johnson and Feldmeth (1993, pp. 48-50) also reported that in cases in which victims are siblings, the young sexual perpetrators may be family scapegoats and their chosen victims a favored child of the parent(s).

Johnson (1993c) reports that, unlike many adult pedophiles, sexually aggressive children did not slowly develop a caring, warm relationship with their victims and then take advantage of them—what some refer to as "grooming behaviors." Most children who molested simply chose victims who were available or vulnerable, who could be easily forced, bribed, or threatened into silence, or all of these. In this sense, victimizations tended to be opportunistic. As will be shown later in this chapter, there is not total agreement on this observation.

Abusers' Victimization Experiences

In the Johnson (1988, 1989) and Friedrich and Luecke (1988) studies shown in Table 2.1, between 50 and 75% of the male abusers had been victims of sexual abuse, whereas 100% of the females had been sexually victimized. Many of the children were also victims of severe physical and emotional abuse as well as neglect.

Sexual Preoccupation and Fantasies

Children in all three studies demonstrated a high degree of sexual preoccupation. Johnson (1993c), drawing from Friedrich and Luecke's study (1988), reported that on Draw-a-Person, Kinetic Family Drawings Test, the Rorschach, the Thematic Apperception Test (TAT), and the Robert's Apperception Test, Friedrich and Luecke reported that there was more reference by sexually aggressive children to sexual themes or sexual content than would normally be expected. Johnson (1988) and Friedrich and Luecke also found that sexual themes were coupled with aggression. Also, although the children did not report elaborate sexual fantasies about sex, where fantasies were reported children were more aware of the aggressive compared with the sexual content.

(text continues on p. 55)

TABLE 2.1 Demographics of Sexually Aggressive Children: Nine Studies

Study No.

	1 (Johnson, 1988)	2 (Johnson, 1989)	3 (Friedrich & Luecke, 1988)	4 (Cantwell, 1988)	5 (English & Ray, 1991)	6 (Araji, Jache, Tyrrell, & Field, 1992)	7 (Araji, Jache, Pfeiffer, & Smith, 1993)	8 (Bonner et al., 1996)	9 (Pithers & Gray, 1996)
Subjects Number	47 Boys	13 Girls	14 Boys, 4 girls	3 Case studies, with multiple children each	89 Cases; 72 males, 17 females	10 Males, 11 females (11 families)	222 Preadolescent sex offenders; identified by 26 survey respondents	70 Females, 100 males, (control group, 50 cases)	72 Children; 47 males, 25 females
Age	4-12	4-12	4-11	10 and younger	5-12	3-11	12 years and under	6-11	6-12
Race	44% Caucasian, 28% Black, and 28% Hispanic	62% Caucasian, 31% Black, 7% Hispanic	NIA[a]	NIA	67% Caucasian, 33% non-White	80% Caucasian; 5% each: Black, Alaska Native; 10% each: Black/White, Alaska Native/White	Asian = 0-10%, Black = 0-50%, Caucasian = 25-100%	76% Caucasian; 12% African American; 12% Hispanic, Asian, or Native American	NIA
Average age at intake	9.7 Years old	7.5 Years old	7.3 Years old	NIA	NIA	6.2 Years old	NIA	NIA	NIA
IQ	Average to low-average (no NR)	Average to low-average (no NR)	Range = 70-139, Mean IQ = 98	NIA	Normal range	NIA	NIA	NIA	NIA

Victimization history	50% Sexually abused; pervasive severe and erratic physical punishment	100% Sexually abused; pervasive severe and erratic physical punishment	75% of boys and 100% of girls were sexually abused	NIA	6% Sexually abused, 3% physically abused, 6% neglected, 8% emotionally abused, 6% multiple abuses, 1% no abuse	86% Sexually abused (did not break down by gender)	165 (74%) of 222 victims of sexual abuse	18 Females and 1 male neglected; 94.6% females abused, 5.4% males abused; 92% females physically abused; 8% males physically abused; 77 females emotionally abused; 6 males emotionally abused	(Based on 66 cases) 95% Sexually abused; 100% females, 93% males; 52% males, 42% females physically abused; 38% females, 31% males emotionally abused; 8% females, 12% males neglected; for 6- to 9-year-old group, 63% females, 52% males, multiple abuses; for 10- to 12-year-old group, 65% females, 63% males, multiple abuses
Average age at first molestation	8.7 Years old, range 4–12	6 Years old, range 4–9	NIA	Hard to assess, but seems to be 4 or 5 years	3 or 4 years old, range 0–3	6.6 Years old, range 3–11	NIA	NIA	3.4 Years old, range 2.8–6.5
Average number of victims	2.1, range 1–7	3.3, range 4–9	2 for boys, 2 for girls	Hard to assess, but seems to be more than 1 year	3.4, range 0–3	1.9, range 1–6	1.9, range 1–6	NIA	Almost 2

(continued)

51

TABLE 2.1 Continued

	Study No.								
	1 (Johnson, 1988)	*2* (Johnson, 1989)	*3* (Friedrich & Luecke, 1988)	*4* (Cantwell, 1988)	*5* (English and Ray, 1991)	*6* (Araji, Jache, Tyrrell, & Field, 1992)	*7* (Araji, Jache, Pfeiffer, & Smith, 1993)	*8* (Bonner et al., 1991-1996)	*9* (Pithers & Gray, 1996)
Average age of victims or other age-related characteristics	6.7 Years old	5 Years old	NIA	Hard to assess, but seems to be around 4 or 5 years	Younger female child in home, relative, 33%; younger female child, nonrelative, 38%; younger male child in home, relative, 26%; younger male child, nonrelative, 34%; peer-age male, nonrelative, 38%	5.1 Years old	5.1 Years old	NIA	Younger siblings, 44%; other relatives, 5.6%; friends, 37.6%; houseguests, 10.4%; animals, 1.6%; babysitters, 0.8%; most victims, females, 54.5%
Average age difference between child who molests and victim	Boys and female siblings, 4.5 years; boys and male siblings, 3 years	Girls and siblings, 4.2 years	NIA	Hard to assess, but appears to be at least 2 years	NIA	NIA	NIA	NIA	NIA

Family/ environment									
Family type	60% Single mother/sole provider; 23% other (study does not specify); 17% with biological parents	46% Single mother/sole provider; 23% relatives (removal from home due to unfit parents); 8% mother/stepfather; 8% stepmother/father; 8% adoptive parents; 8% biological parents (perpetrator being molested by father)	93% Single parent of families for sexually aggressive group; 67% for comparison group	NIA	NIA	27% Single mother; 36% blended; 9% foster; 27% biological parents	Similar to Araji, Jache, Tyrrell, & Field (1992) study	27% Parents divorced/separated, 25% parents married to a 2nd spouse, 15% married to 1st spouse, 9% not married, 8% live with partner, 3% widowed (13%, no information)	71% Biological parents (at time of abusive behavior); at time of testing: 65% biological parents, 35% nonbiological parents (14 foster parents, 6% adoptive parents, 1 nonrelative guardian, 4 residential care placements)
Average number of children in family	2.5	2.5	NIA	2.4	NIA	NIA	NIA	NIA	NIA
Social class	47% Lower, 53% middle	85% Lower, 15% middle	NIA	16% White-collar, 32% blue-collar, 18% unemployed, 27% unknown	NIA	16% White collar, 32% blue collar, 18% unemployed, 27% unknown	NIA	Primarily lower class to poverty level	NIA

(continued)

TABLE 2.1 Continued

Study No.

	1 (Johnson, 1988)	2 (Johnson, 1989)	3 (Friedrich & Luecke, 1988)	4 (Cantwell, 1988)	5 (English & Ray, 1991)	6 (Araji, Jache, Tyrrell, & Field, 1992)	7 (Araji, Jache, Pfeiffer, & Smith, 1993)	8 (Bonner et al., 1991-1996)	9 (Pithers & Gray, 1996)
Family/environment/parent/caretaker characteristics	Drug/alcohol abuse in 73% of parents and/or grandparents of children	Majority were characterized by dysfunctional family relationships; parents/caretakers poor role models with personality problems	Maternal chemical dependency in 57% of cases of SA groups, 80% in NSA comparison group; good emotional support of child in 6% of cases in SA group, 83% in comparison group	NIA	NIA	Majority characterized by dysfunctional family environments	(12 of 26 survey respondents answered questions) Responses ranged from 25% to 100% of parents having been sexually abused themselves; 8 of 12 responses were above 70%	Based on 160 caretakers, almost 50% reported being physically, sexually, and/or emotionally abused and/or neglected. Respondents were overwhelmingly female	Families indicative of parental and familial distress including high marital violence, sexual victimization/perpetration in extended families, parental arrest, other psychological/behavioral disturbances, and poverty

NOTE: SA = sexually aggressive; NSA = nonsexually aggressive; NIA = no information available.

54

I believe the previous information demonstrates the need for an awareness of the relative importance of the aggressive compared with the sexual content of the fantasies when evaluating the fantasies of sexually abused children, particularly if the previous findings continue to hold across research. That is, the aggressive themes can be helpful in defining children who have a combination of "sexual" and "aggressive" behavior and thus identifying appropriate intervention and treatment programs.

Family and School Relationships

Family

For the majority of sexually aggressive children, a history of parent-child problems existed prior to the young abusers' sexually aggressive acts. In fact, most homes were characterized by a host of problems, such as broken families, domestic abuse, substance abuse, overly sexualized atmospheres with no boundaries, parents with histories of abuse, or multigenerational abuse. When the sexually aggressive children were victims of sexual abuse in the home, most were sexually molested by family members, fathers being the most prevalent offenders. Few fathers, however, were living in the homes when sexually aggressive children began their molesting behaviors.

School

As can be seen in Table 2.1, most of the children in the Johnson (1988, 1989) and Friedrich and Luecke (1988) studies (Table 2.1, Studies 1-3) had average to lower IQs. Many experienced learning problems and other academic problems and demonstrated conduct disorders, deficit disorders, and hyperactivity. Few children had "a best friend" and most had very poor peer relationships. Most relationships were characterized by aggression, antagonism, fear, uncertainty, and impulsiveness apart from sexual problems. Social skills, problem solving, tolerance, and positive coping skills were also found to be very poor among sexually aggressive children. In general, sexually aggressive children's relationships tended to be strained and conflictual, and positive relationships with anyone were minimal or nonexistent. School and peer interactions appeared to reflect problematic home environments.

Friedrich and Luecke (1988)

Although Johnson (1993c) included the 1988 study by Friedrich and Luecke in her conceptualization of sexually aggressive children as discussed previously, I examined this study more closely because Friedrich and Luecke distinguished between sexually aggressive (SA) children (n = 16), nonsexually aggressive (NSA) children (n = 6), and those who had only behavioral problems (BP) related to histories of sexual abuse (n = 22). Criteria used by Friedrich and Luecke to determine whether children's behavior was sexually aggressive included evidence from multiple sources (the victim, caregiver, abusing child, or all three). Additional evidence included documentation that the behavior was persistent (had occurred two or more times), that there had been coercion and genital contact, that the referred child was at least 2 years older than the victim(s), and that the sexual behavior was significantly more aggressive than mutual exploratory behavior developmentally common in children 12 years of age or less. The following sections provide a summary of the similarities and differences between the SA, NSA, and BP groups (see Table 2.1, Study 3).

Demographic Differences

Almost all perpetrators in the three groups were male. In fact, the only group that had any females was the SA group, in which 25% (4) were girls. Children from all three groups tended to be from lower- to lower-middle-class families, and the predominant family form for all groups was a single parent, usually a female. In the case of SA children, all but 1 of the 16 were from single-parent families.

The mean ages of the three groups varied. For the NSA group, it was 6.6 years; for the BP group, it was 8.9 years; and the SA group fell in the middle, at 7.6 years.

The SA group had a mean IQ of 97.8, whereas the NSA group's mean IQ was 107.5. Friedrich and Luecke (1988) interpreted the IQ results as suggestive that the two groups differed with regard to cognitive abilities, although both groups fell within the average range. Approximately half of the SA children, however, were in the low-average range or borderline range, which is more than twice what would be expected in a normally distributed sample.

The group differences described in the following sections pertain to (a) the type of the sexually aggressive child's own sexual victimization experiences; (b) the primary perpetrator(s) of the sexually aggressive child's sexual abuse; and (c) the psychological, behavioral, and social consequences of the sexually aggressive child's history of own abuse.

Type and Frequency of Sexual
Victimization History

In comparison with the NSA and BP groups, SA children had experienced more severe types of abuse that usually involved genital contact and intercourse. Friedrich and Luecke (1988) reported that 100% of the SA group who had been sexually abused (13 of 16) had experienced oral, anal, or vaginal intercourse. The authors also noted that the frequency and severity of the sexual abuse was greater than would be expected in a random sample of sexually abused children and appeared to contribute to a predilection for sexually aggressive behavior. For example, 12 of the 16 SA group exhibited clear signs of sexual preoccupation as measured by spontaneous drawings (Draw-a-Person or Kinetic Family Drawings Test) of genitalia or sexual acts, sexual content on the Rorschach, the TAT, or the Roberts test, an elevated sexual problems score on the Child Behavior Checklist, or all three. The sum of raw scores of six items from the Achenbach Child Behavior Checklist revealed much more sexualized behavior for both males and females in the SA group (5.9 and 6.8, respectively) compared with the NSA group (1.1) and the BP (1.3).

Data from the Child Sexual Behavior Checklist also demonstrated that, overall, abused compared with nonabused children showed far higher numbers who could be defined as sexually aggressive and who were involved in the full range of adult sexual behaviors. Friedrich and Luecke (1988) also noted that the sexually aggressive behaviors of the children they studied were more extreme than those seen in Fehrenbach, Smith, Monastersky, and Deisher's (1986) study of a large sample of adolescent sexual offenders. Twenty-three percent of the adolescents in the Fehrenbach et al. (1986) study were involved in rape, whereas the majority of the behaviors of the young children in the Friedrich and Luecke sample (Table 2.1, Study 3) could be classified as rape.

Perpetrators of Sexually
Aggressive Children's Abuse

Friedrich and Luecke (1988) found that the primary perpetrator in the SA group tended to be older than those of the other two groups (NSA and BP). In the case of the SA group, the primary abusers were more likely to be 17 years of age and older, whereas for the other groups they were between the ages of 12 and 16.

Consequences of the Sexually Aggressive Child's Own Abuse History

Children in the SA group appeared to be more psychologically impaired than children in the other two groups, especially in the areas of aggressiveness and conduct or oppositional disorders. Friedrich and Luecke (1988) indicated that all 16 SA children satisfied criteria for DSM-III diagnosis (American Psychiatric Association, 1980), which was usually characterized by aggressiveness. There were eight diagnoses of conduct disorder and four of oppositional disorder. Two of the children were exhibiting adjustment disorders. One child was dysthymic and 1 was schizophrenic. In comparison, four of the six NSA children had a DSM-III diagnosis, but none of these were conduct disordered. With respect to DSM-III. diagnoses of the 22 boys in the BP group, Friedrich and Luecke found the majority would be described as adjustment disorders with mixed features.

More SA children than children in the other two groups had problems with age-appropriate social skills. They also had problems with "taking the role of the other" or feeling empathy.

Sexually aggressive children, more than children in the other two groups, were found to have home- and school-related problems. Friedrich and Luecke (1988) assessed parent-child relationships for the three groups through interviews in the SA and NSA groups and through therapist reports and family assessment questionnaire data in the BP group. The authors usually had a conjoint interview with the parent and child and interviewed each, individually, about their relationship.

Eight (50%) of the SA parent-child relationships were rated as poor when measured by (a) lack of support of the child, which included blaming; (b) a history of scapegoating and projection; and (c) a history of neglect, even periods of abandonment. In some cases, a fourth feature, that of an eroticized mother-son relationship, was also noted. Only 1 of the 15 SA cases was described as having a good parent-child relationship. Marked pathology in the parent was also frequently evident, and anger was a predominant feature in family discord, as was impulsivity, impaired interpersonal relationships, and alienation.

In comparison to the SA children, five of the six NSA children were described as having good parent-child relationships. With respect to the quality of parent-child relationships and parental pathology in the BP group, one half of the families gave some evidence that parent-child relations were very problematic. With respect to therapist ratings on family quality, however, the treatment group was found to have overall positive family qualities, especially as measured by "unconditional support of the child" and "overall conflict in the family."

Regarding the school environment, all 11 of the school-aged SA children had school problems. Eight were in learning disabled or other special education programs and were also frequently reported as having behavioral problems. Although some boys in the NSA and BP groups had school problems, or were receiving below-average or failing grades in one or more subjects, school difficulties were found to be much more prominent in the SA group. According to Friedrich and Luecke (1988), these problems reflected the degree to which the children's lives were disrupted.

In discussing findings from their study, Friedrich and Luecke (1988) set forth several conclusions that are important to our attempt to identify particular social and psychological characteristics that distinguish sexually aggressive children. These authors noted that, without exception, the SA group was exposed to (a) physical violence, (b) sexualized adult behavior, (c) sexual abuse that involved various types of intercourse at a percentage that far exceeds that reported in large samples of sexually abused children, or all three. They further noted that there was a pairing of physical violence or threats with these children's sexual abuse victimizations. Friedrich and Luecke indicated that when this pairing is present, denial takes place because the situation represents a "not me" nature. The authors also noted that the sexually abusive experiences served to add a sexualized channel to aggressiveness that was already emerging in these children because of conditions existing in the home. These authors add that because the child's behavior becomes influenced by the trauma event, there is a need to master it, which takes the form of repetition compulsion or repeating (modeling) the abusive act perpetrated against them. Friedrich and Luecke reported that the SA children tended to parallel in their victims their own victimization experiences.

Because Friedrich and Luecke (1988) used Finkelhor and Browne's (1986) conceptualization of the sources of trauma inherent in sexual abuse as a guide in their study, they indicated that three of the four components in the conceptualization were present in SA children: The children frequently felt powerless, betrayed, and were traumatically sexualized. Importantly, Friedrich and Luecke noted that the relationship between the traumatic event and the outcome behavior could be moderated by buffering variables. These included individual factors, such as cognitive abilities and absence of significant psychopathology, and interpersonal variables, such as social skills, school adaptation, and parent-child relations.

Cantwell (1988)

The same year that the Friedrich and Luecke (1988) study was published in *Professional Psychology: Research and Practice* and Johnson's (1988) study was published in *Child Abuse and Neglect*, Cantwell's (1988) article on young sexual abuse perpetrators also appeared in *Child Abuse and Neglect*. Cantwell's study involved three case studies, some of which reported multiple perpetrators or victims or both. As shown in Table 2.1 (Study 4), many of the characteristics reported by Cantwell were similar to the Friedrich and Luecke (1988) and Johnson (1988, 1989) studies. The child perpetrators Cantwell described were 10 years of age or younger; there was a mixture of males and females, although overly represented by males; and much of the abuse was incestuous. Also, although it was hard to assess from the study, the average ages at the time of the first molestation acts appeared to be 4 or 5; the perpetrators seemed to have more than one victim; and the victims were 4 or 5 years of age and usually approximately 2 years younger than the perpetrators. Cantwell offered no definition as to what characteristics defined a "child perpetrator."

English and Ray (1991) and
Ray and English (1991)

In 1991, English and Ray completed several state reports that focused on children with sexual behavior problems in the state of Washington. These reports compared sexually aggressive children by age, breaking them into two groups: those who were 12 years and younger and those who were 13 to 18 years of age. The relevant results of these reports are shown in Table 2.1 (Study 5).

The subjects in the English and Ray (1991) study included 200 children identified by public agencies in the state of Washington as being sexually aggressive. The 200 cases were randomly drawn from 691 case files. In addition, all children who had been selected to receive specialized sexually aggressive treatment in a new state program were included in the sample.

The final sample size was 271 with 89 in the specialized sexually aggressive treatment group and 182 in the service-as-usual group. By age group, 89 (32.8%) of the children were 12 and under, and 182 (67.2%) were between 13 and 18 years of age. Sexually aggressive behavior was defined as having both a sexual component and an aggressive component that included physical force, verbal threats, deception, or inequality in size, age, or development. The sample was also categorized by sexual offense. These included (a) rape (forced sexual intercourse), (b) molest (defined as sexual touching of intimate parts for the purpose of gratifying sexual desire), and (c) sexually inappropriate behavior that does not include contact (e.g., peeping, exposing, or sexually aggressive language).

Children's Demographics

Only group demographics in the English and Ray (1991) reports that can be compared with other studies are shown in Table 2.1 (Study 5). Prior to this comparison, however, I believe it is important to discuss how the 12 and under age group is similar and different from the 13 to 18 age group.

The majority of the sample was more than 12 years of age (67.2% and 32.8%, respectively). For both age groups, males were overrepresented: 90.7% males to 9.3% females for the more than 12 years of age group, and 80.9% to 19.1%, respectively, for the 12 and under age group. As can be seen, substantially more female offenders were found in the younger age group.

The majority of both groups were Caucasian (79.7% for the older age group and 67.4% for the younger age group), although there was a higher percentage of African American children in the 12 and under age group (32.6% compared to 20.3%). Although I am unsure of the percentage breakdown by race in the geographic areas in Washington, where the sample respondents lived, I believe it is safe to assume that the percentage of African American children is probably overrepresented in the study and that of Caucasians, underrepresented. This would appear particularly true for children 12 years and younger.

The modal family type for both groups was single parent (48.6% for the older group and 55.9% for the younger group), although children under 12 years of age were more likely to live with both their natural parents (19%) than were those more than 12 years of age (14.5%). A substantially larger percentage of older children (27.2% compared with

17.9%), however, were living with stepparents. The least number of children of both age groups were living with adoptive parents: 9.8% for children 13 to 18 years of age and 7.1% for those 12 and under. For purposes of this book, the previous findings indicate that more than one half (55%) of sexually aggressive children (12 years of age and younger) were living in single-parent families, whereas the remainder (45%) were living with natural parents, stepparents, or adoptive parents.

The English and Ray studies (1991) found that both the 12 and under and the 13 and over age groups ranked high as recipients of various types of abuse. In every category of abuse, children 12 and under were more likely to be victimized. The comparisons included the following: sexual abuse, 96.1% to 81%; physical abuse, 92.6% to 75.5%; neglect, 86.1% to 62.9%; emotional abuse, 67.7% to 41.7%; and multiple abuses, 95.5% to 70.6%, respectively. There was also a significant difference in the number in each group who had experienced "no abuse." For the older group, 11.8% fell into this category, whereas only 1.1% of the 12 and under group had not experienced any abuse. Using the chi-square measure, all the differences noted previously were significant at the $p < 0.01$ level.

Sexual Offenses and Associated Deviant Behaviors

Comparing the three divisions of sexually aggressive behaviors described by English and Ray (1991) (raping, molesting, and sexually inappropriate behaviors), it was found that the older compared to the younger group of children was significantly more likely to have committed rape (t test, $p = .001$). The older children were also more likely to have engaged in molestation-type behaviors, although the difference in group means was not statistically significant (t tests). The younger children engaged in more sexually inappropriate behaviors than the older children, although no statistically significant differences were found.

English and Ray (1991) also examined the behavioral history of both age groups of children as well as behaviors that were observed while the children were being supervised by agencies. With respect to a behavioral history, the researchers found some children in each age group engaged in fire-setting, bed-wetting, animal mutilation, and what the authors referred to as scatological behaviors (i.e., disturbed behaviors related to bodily functions such as urination and elimination). The only two categories in which the two groups varied significantly were bed-wetting and scatological behaviors, with the 12 and under age group having a greater percentage of involvement (41% to 20.2% and 20.5% to 7.9%, respectively). They also found that nearly one in three of all the children had documented histories of animal cruelty, which was not included in an animal mutilation category.

English and Ray (1991) listed 12 categories of behavioral problems the children in their study exhibited while being supervised by state agencies involved in the study. These included sexual aggression, disobedience, verbal aggression, physical aggression, nonviolent criminal behavior, depression and suicide ideation, property damage, running away, school problems, hyperactivity, alcohol and drug problems, and scatological problems. Using the t test of differences, they found statistically significant differences between the groups on 6 of the 12 behaviors. The 12 and under age group was more likely to exhibit sexual aggression ($p < 0.05$), hyperactivity ($p < 0.05$), and scatological behaviors ($p < 0.05$). The older group was more likely to run away ($p < 0.00$), be involved with alcohol and drugs ($p < 0.00$), and to have school problems ($p < 0.05$). With respect to disobedience, verbal aggression, and nonviolent criminal behavior, the two groups were highly similar in terms of the percentage involved in such acts. The younger group had higher percentages involved in physical aggression and property damage, whereas the older group had greater percentages who were experiencing depression and suicide ideation.

Together, this group of findings suggests several conclusions. First, the behaviors reported for the two age groups seem to parallel deviant behaviors associated with preadolescent and adolescent stages of development in the normal population. For example, experimenting with alcohol or drugs or both and running away are more commonly associated with adolescents who are seeking a self-identity, conforming to peer pressure, or seeking independence from parents—that is, rebellion. Bedwetting and hyperactivity, however, are less developmentally mature ways of breaking norms or releasing anger and aggression.

Second, the findings suggest that the younger age group of perpetrators externalize their aggressions, whereas the 13-year-old and older age group may begin to turn their anger and aggression inward through depression and suicide ideation.

Third, these findings are valuable because they seem to indicate that just as sexual behaviors and sexual abuse have developmental histories, so do other deviant behaviors that accompany these—for example, progressing from bed-wetting to fire-setting to animal cruelty to substance abuse, and so on.

Victims of Sexual Aggression

Most of the children in the two age groups had engaged in sexually aggressive acts with others. Only three (1.6%) in the older age group and three (3.4%) in the younger age group had no known victims. English and Ray's (1991) statistics indicated that the modal number of victims for the 13- to 18-year-old group was 1 (36.8%), whereas for the 12 and under age group it was 2 (31.5%). The two groups were comparable on the 3 to 5 victim category (27.5% for the older group and 23.6% for the younger group) and the 6 to 10 victim category (7.7% for older children and 6.7% for the younger children). The younger children were more likely to have more than 10 victims (10.1% to 4.4%), whereas the older age group had more in the "over 100 victims" category (3.8% to 0%), although only a few 13- to 18-year-olds (seven) fell in this category. No statistical levels of significance were reported for these comparisons. This group of findings indicates that the majority of both age groups have multiple victims.

Types of Victims Targeted

Overall, the English and Ray (1991) reports indicated that females were more likely to be the chosen victims for both age groups, particularly the older (13-18) group. The "younger female relative in the home" was the victim of 53.3% of the 13- to 18-year-old group and 32.6% of the 12 and under age group. Approximately 38% in each age group chose a "younger female non-relative." A "female peer-age group non-relative" was the targeted victim of 38.2% of the 12 and under age group and 22.5% of the 13- to 18-year-old age group.

With respect to male victims, the largest targeted group for children 12 years and younger was a peer age nonrelative (41.6% compared to 25.3% for the older group). The 12-year-old and younger group was also more likely than the older group to target younger male children in the home (25.8% and 21%, respectively). There was more similarity between the groups with respect to choosing young male nonrelatives, although the younger children were still more likely to victimize these targets (39.3% and 32.4%, respectively). Regardless of the percentage differences between the groups, there were no statistically significant differences reported. As a whole, these findings suggest that for the 12 and under age group that is the focus of this study, both female and male children are at risk of becoming victims, both in and out of the home setting.

Risk Factors Associated With
Sexually Aggressive Children

English and Ray (1991) and Ray and English (1991) used a model that English developed in 1987 to assess the likelihood of sexually aggressive children reoffending. The model included 32 factors divided into three categories: (a) family and environment characteristics, (b) sexually aggressive youth characteristics, and (c) victim characteristics. The values attached to each characteristic ranged from low (1) to high (5). The overall risk estimate using this model was 3.4 for the 12 and under age group and 3.7 for the 13- to 18-year-old group. These numbers indicate moderate to moderately high risk levels of reoffending for both age groups. Each of the three categories is more specifically described in the following sections.

Family and environment risk characteristics. English and Ray (1991) reported that both age groups showed moderate to moderately high risk levels on family factors, although the younger group presented an even more dysfunctional family portrait than the older group. Using the Mann-Whitney *U* test, the 12-year-old and younger group depicted significantly higher family histories of violence, lack of positive anger management, blurred boundaries regarding privacy, a history of family abuse, and parents who were unable to cope with the child's alleged abuse. Although no statistical significance was reported, other disturbed family characteristics found in both groups were poor parental attitudes toward sex, confused parental roles, absence of parent, and one or more parents who were physically or emotionally withdrawn from the child.

The younger group was found to be significantly higher on levels of social isolation (3.8% compared with 3.3%) and have more current stressors in their lives (4.4% compared with 4.1%). Both groups had moderate levels of geographic isolation (3.2%).

Sexually aggressive youth risk characteristics. English and Ray (1991) listed 14 factors that they classified as "child risk factors." These included a prior history of sexually aggressive behavior, level of aggression, level of coercion, level of sophistication in committing sexual acts, lack of empathy, escalation of sexual violence, resistance to intervention issues, denial of responsibility for behaviors, history of psychiatric problems, history of substance use or abuse, history of abuse and neglect, level of social skills, age-appropriate knowledge of sex, and intellectual functioning. Again, using the Mann-Whitney U test, these two groups differed significantly on 9 of the 14 factors. The only factor that the younger group scored significantly higher on was a history of abuse and neglect (3.8% compared to 3.4% risk levels).

The older age group was found to have significantly higher levels of aggression, levels of coercion, and levels of sophistication in committing sexually aggressive acts. They were less empathic, showed higher levels of escalating sexual violence, and exhibited greater resistance to acknowledging the seriousness of their behaviors and responding to the distress of their victims. Although both groups were low on substance-related histories, the older group had significantly higher risk scores than the younger group (1.7% compared with 1.1%, respectively).

The two groups did not differ significantly on the remaining five factors. These included prior history of aggressive behavior, history of psychiatric problems, level of social skills, age-appropriate knowledge of sex, and intellectual functioning. With respect to the preadolescent group of sexually aggressive youth, this set of findings is supportive of Friedrich and Luecke (1988), who suggested, based on their findings, that the lives of sexually aggressive children are severely disruptive to normal human development.

Victim risk characteristics. English and Ray (1991) reported moderate to low-moderate risk on factors identified in the offenders' victim risk category. The factors included in this list were degree of trauma, verbal ability to report, level of assertiveness, victim's awareness, victim's functioning, and victim's abuse history. The only factor that significantly differentiated the two age groups was the victims' verbal ability to report. This factor placed victims at greater risk with the 12-year-old and younger offenders (2.2% to 1.9% levels, respectively). Obviously, this is a function of the younger age of the preadolescent offenders and thus the younger ages of their victims whose communication and cognitive skills would be less developed.

Overall, findings from the English and Ray (1991) and Ray and English (1991) reports generally agree with those of other studies reviewed. Because these authors divided and compared groups by age (12 years and under and 13 years and over), however, the findings allow us to pinpoint risk factors that may be most salient for the age group that is the topic of this book—sexually aggressive children 12 years of age and under. First, English and Ray's (1991) findings indicate that preadolescents and adolescents have many factors in common that place them at risk of becoming sexually aggressive. Of the 14 "youth risk" factors considered, however, the only one that is significantly different for preadolescents is the history of abuse and neglect. The younger group tended to have significantly more abusive and neglectful histories than the adolescent group.

Second, preadolescent perpetrators tend to be younger and, thus, so do their victims. As such, they are less likely to have the cognitive and verbal skills to explain or report the sexual abuse being perpetrated on them. This makes sexually aggressive children's victims even harder to detect than those of sexually aggressive adolescents.

Third, the data also suggest that in comparison with adolescents, the targets of preadolescent perpetrators' aggression are less likely to be themselves. This seems to suggest that preadolescents have not yet reached the developmental level of turning their aggressions inward.

Fourth, if intervention does not occur with sexually aggressive preadolescents, the behaviors become more sexually sophisticated and show an escalation of aggression, coercion, and violence, greater resistance to intervention and treatment, and decreased levels of empathy for victims. This is of great concern because if no intervention occurs, and the cycle of abuse continues, not only may the number of victims increase but also so could the number of sexual abusers.

Unpublished Research

The previous discussions were based on published studies and reports that directly focused on sexually aggressive children. In the next several sections, unpublished data that I have collected from surveys or conversations or both with program providers across the United States are reviewed.

Araji, Jache, Tyrrell, and Field (1992)

In the summer of 1992, I arranged to have two students conduct a content analysis of all sexual abuse case files between 1987 and 1992 in a social service agency in Alaska. The objective was to see if any preadolescent sexually aggressive children were embedded within the cases. The definition used to identify sexually aggressive children was that the perpetrator had to be 12 years of age or younger and had used some form of coercion—verbal, physical, or trickery—to involve victims in sexual activities beyond the normal limits expected of the age group.

The agency made available 102 case files. The case files included intake social histories and demographics, therapist notes, psychological evaluations, court documents, and correspondence between the agency and other "outside agencies" when involved. From these files, 21 pre-adolescent sexually aggressive children from 11 different families were identified. Given the voluminous nature of the case files and project time constraints, only information related to the first occurring perpetration was selected. This information is presented in Table 2.1, Study 6.

As can be seen in Table 2.1, the 21 children were approximately equally divided between male and female: 10 males and 11 females. The ages ranged from 3 to 11 years, with 6.6 being the average age of first disclosed perpetration activity.

The average age of the perpetrators' victims was 5.1 years. The average number of victims was 1.9, with a range of 1 to 6. Most of the children were Caucasian (80%). Alaska Natives made up 5% of the sample, as did African Americans (5%). The remaining 20% were racial mixtures of African American/White (10%) and Alaska Native/White (10%).

All but one (96.2%) of the sample members were victims of sexual abuse. Most of the primary perpetrators were adult males or females.

The majority of the 21 children were referred to the treatment agency by the State Division of Family and Youth Services (DFYS), although only 11 were referred as a direct result of their sexual behaviors. Two were referred by family members and one by a private treatment facility.

Nineteen of the 21 children were living at home at the time they were referred to the agency, and two were living in foster homes. The other two children were in treatment for sexual victimization issues when their perpetration activities were discovered.

Eight of the 21 children in this study were found in one family. Because the family and agency interactions in this case file demonstrate a number of issues being discussed in this book, I decided to report the case in more detail.

In this family (with eight children), only the eldest daughter was a victim of adult sexual abuse. She was molested at the age of 2 by a male and a female babysitter. She admitted to therapists that around the age of 8, she began "sexually abusing" her 5-year-old brother for a period of 2 years. She stated that it involved "fondling," but she did not elaborate. When she "found out that it wasn't right," she stopped the behavior. She told therapists that she knew her younger brother continued to have "sexual interaction" with his younger brothers and sisters and that she felt guilty about her past history of sexual abuse and felt responsible for her brother's behavior. Also, a year after she began molesting her brother, his primary teacher discovered him and a 6-year-old female classmate with their hands in each other's pants. He admitted to having engaged in similar behavior on three or four occasions. The incident was reported by the school to the DFYS and the police department. Charges were brought against the boy but were eventually dropped.

Five years later, this family came to the attention of the police, DFYS, and the family treatment agency when the second eldest son reported to the school nurse that his brothers and sisters were "doing bad things together."

This child, 9 years old at the time, denied that he was ever a victim of his older brother or sister and, of the total family members involved, was the only one that reported no sexual abuse experiences. He did admit that he "touched his 8-year-old sister on her private parts a long time ago," perhaps when he was 6 and she was 4, but stated that "it happened only once." He denied any current sexual involvement.

Upon his disclosure of the sexual activity occurring between his siblings, DFYS removed the six eldest children from the home and placed them in foster care. The police charged the eldest son, 11 years old, with delinquency of a minor with three counts of sexual abuse of a minor. He was accused of intercourse with vaginal penetration with his 8-year-old sister. The charges were eventually dropped in lieu of treatment. The therapists' notes for this case involving six siblings indicated that all of them, except for the 9-year-old boy, were first victims and then perpetrators.

There was much discussion in this case about what was normal and nonnormative sex play. A private physician conducted psychiatric evaluations and was adamant about not labeling the 11-year-old a perpetrator as the police had done. The doctor wrote, "Labeling a child as a sexual perpetrator is clearly absurd," and explained that the sexual activity was normal childhood exploratory behavior due to the nearness in age of the two children. The agency therapists labeled the child abusers' sexual activities as "sexually acting out" and worked with the children on the differences between "good touch and bad touch" in both victimization and perpetration situations. The label "perpetrator" was not given to any of the children by the agency where the files were reviewed, indicating a hesitancy to view these children as sexual perpetrators.

All 21 children uncovered in the case files were seen as being victims in a cycle of abuse. In the seven cases in which the children were already in treatment for sexual victimization, six of them began their perpetrating activity on an average of 3 months into treatment.

In summary, this case study demonstrates the "contagious" nature of sexual abuse, even when it begins at an early age. That is, the initial family perpetrator was victimized at the age of 2 by two babysitters—a male and female. She says she later (at about 8 years of age) began perpetrating against a 5-year-old brother, who then began molesting his other siblings. Only one sibling escaped the incestuous sexual activities, at least by self-report. Eventually, the sexual activities moved into the school setting and then came to the attention of social services and the police. At each of the levels (school, social service agency, and psychiatrists), we can see problems previously discussed that relate to accepting these children as sexual abusers. There was a reluctance to label them as sexual perpetrators, and even when charges were brought against one of the children, they were dropped. The implication of these events is that these children may have received inappropriate interventions or treatments or both. This may have allowed both the number of new victims and, if the cycle continued, the number of new sexually abusive children to increase over a substantial period of time.

Araji, Jache, Pfeiffer, and Smith (1993)

In the summer of 1993, approximately 75 surveys were mailed to various practitioners or programs around the United States that treat sex offenders. The names were obtained from the Safer Society Program (Fay Honey Knopp) and from therapists the survey developers knew. Thirty-six surveys (approximately 50%) were returned, and 26 contained enough useful information to be included in this chapter.[1] Because we were interested in only preadolescent abusers, if the individual or program focused on only preadolescent victims, the respondent was asked to note that and return the uncompleted survey.

Description of Sexually Aggressive Children

Survey information that could be compared with the other studies described herein is reported in Table 2.1, Study 7. Together, the 26 survey respondents had seen a total of 222 preadolescent sex abusers. The mean number each had treated was approximately 11, with a range of 1-50 offenders. Of the 222 offenders, 164, or 74%, were also victims of sexual assault. Of the 164, approximately 50% were victimized by children 12 years of age and under. Of this group, 81% were victimized by male preadolescents, 22% by female preadolescents, and 16% by both. Approximately 50% of the 164 victimized children were victims of adolescent offenders, 13 to 20 years of age.

The types of behaviors that the 222 preadolescents were involved in by gender were as follows: voyeurism (22 males and 2 females); exhibitionism (51 males and 4 females); French kissing children under 11 years of age (19 males and 12 females); forced French kissing (3 males and 1 female); use of threats (10 males and 2 females); coercive touching of breasts, buttocks, vagina, or genitals (77 males and 63 females); simulated intercourse (58 males and 17 females); digital penetration with objects or fingers (51 males and 36 females); penile intercourse (55 males and 9 females); anal intercourse (33 males and 1 female); bestiality (28 males and 2 females); and ritualistic or sadistic sexual abuse (5 males and 4 females). Adding all acts that involved some form of coercion gave us a sum of 320, or 78%, of the total 412 reported acts for males. For females, the number of acts that involved coercion totaled 135, or approximately 88%, of the total ($n = 153$) sexual acts committed.

As can be seen in Table 2.1, Study 7, the sexually abusing children generally had more than one victim. For males, the number ranged from 1 to 13. For females, the range was 1 to 15. For both male and female offenders, the modal age category of victims was 6 to 9 years.

Several other questions in the survey provided additional information about these young offenders. One of the questions related to whether the children usually acted alone or in groups. Another question focused on the pattern of abuse, whether it was a one-time occurrence or not. Eighteen of the 26 respondents (approximately 70%) answered both questions. Of these, 11 (61%) indicated that the sexually aggressive children acted alone, whereas 7 (39%) responded that they acted alone and in groups. With respect to the second question, only 1 respondent (10%) indicated the abuse was a one-time occurrence, 11 (61%) responded that it was multiple occurrences over an extended time period, and 6 (33.3%) said they found a combination of single and multiple occurrences in the children they treated.

Description of Families

As can be seen in Table 2.1, Study 7, the parents of these children depict similarities with and differences from those of the other studies shown in the table. The parents are probably most like those in the English and Ray (1991) studies and the Araji et al. (1992) study because the children represented in the sample come from a variety of family types. Single-parent, female-headed, and blended families were the modal categories. The children's parents also appeared to cut across social classes, although our question was based on respondents' perceptions of parents income, occupation, and education. Only 9 (32%) of the 26 respondents were able to answer the question.

Lastly, the only information we have analyzed to date that is compared with studies that describe the functional and dysfunctional characteristics of the family relates to parents' sexual victimization history. As can be seen in Table 2.1, 12 of the 26 respondents indicated that between 25% and 100% of the parents of the children they treated were themselves victims of sexual abuse; 8 of the 12 respondents indicated that this was true for more than 70% of the parents.

Bonner, Walker, and Berliner (1991-1996)

Bonner et al. (1991-1996) were involved in a 5-year assessment and treatment program funded by a federal grant from the National Center on Child Abuse and Neglect. The goals of their project were to (a) assess the continuum of sexual behavior problems in children ages 6 to 11 via referral information and intake measures, (b) develop a useful typology of children with sexual behavior problems, (c) compare the efficacy of two treatment approaches (dynamic play and cognitive and behavioral) for children with sexual behavior problems, (d) develop treatment manuals for replication of the treatment programs, and (e) conduct follow-up assessments of the children over a 2-year period to compare current levels of behavior with referral behaviors.

Children were assessed at two sites: the Department of Pediatrics at the University of Oklahoma Health Sciences Center, Oklahoma City, Oklahoma, and the Sexual Assault Center at the University of Washington, Seattle, Washington. Children and caretakers, assessed at the Oklahoma site only, received 12 weeks of group treatment: 1 hour for children per week and 1 hour for parents or caretakers per week. The assessment and treatment were offered at no cost to the participants.

The study population involved 205 children with sexual behavior problems. Fifty children without sexual behavior problems served as a control group. Of the study population, 50 were assessed at the University of Washington and 155 were assessed at the University of Oklahoma. For the 50 controls, 25 were assessed from each of the two sites. The definition of behavioral problems followed the one used by Berliner, Manaois, and Monastersky (1986) which was described in Chapter 1.

The only statistics currently available regarding participants in the study relate to demographics of the 205 children with sexual behavior problems—that is, the study group. The largest percentage of the 205 children in the study group were referred through mental health centers and clinics (49%). The distant second referral agency was the Department of Human Services (25%). Ten percent were referred by schools, 7% through foster care, 4% from police and attorneys (the legal system), 3% through newspaper advertisement, and 2% were referred by physicians.

The age, race, and victimization histories are included in Table 2.1 (Study 8) for comparisons with other studies. The age range was 6 to 11 years of age. In this age range, 28.3% of the children were 6 years old (13.2% boys and 15.1% girls), 23.4% were 7 years of age (17.6% boys and 5.8% girls), 15.1% were 8 years of age (9.8% boys and 5.4% girls), 9.8% were 9 years of age (4.9% boys and 4.9% girls), 5.9% were 10 years of age (3.9% boys and 2.0% girls), and 11.7% were 11 years old (9.7% boys and 2.0% girls). It is noteworthy that boys and girls are quite evenly distributed in the 6-year-old and 9-year-old categories, but in the 7, 8, 10, and 11 years of age categories there are significantly more boys than girls.

With respect to race, 76% of the 205 children were Caucasian, 12% were African American, and 12% were Hispanic, Asian, or Native American.

Information from 170 children (70 girls and 100 boys) indicated that a substantial number experienced physical abuse (40.6%), sexual abuse (67%), emotional abuse (45.9%), and neglect (23.5%). The male and female children were about equally distributed across each type of abuse and the neglect category.

With respect to the marital and familial characteristics, slightly more than one fourth (27%) of the 205 children's parents or caretakers were separated or divorced. Only slightly less (25%) were married, but to a second spouse. A distant third group (15%) were married to a first spouse. Less than 10% (9%) had never been married, 8% lived with a partner, and 3% were widowed. For 13% of the parents or caretakers, information was not available.

With respect to educational levels, information was available for 69% of the caretakers. Of these, 38% had completed high school and 16% had received the general equivalency diploma. Fifteen percent had some college education.

Information about abuse histories was available for 160 caretakers (130 females and 30 males). The data indicated that the children's caretakers also had histories of abuse. Of the 160 caretakers (130 females and 30 males), 75 (46%) indicated they had been victims of child physical abuse. The breakdown included 69 females and 6 males (92 and 8%, respectively). Almost a similar number, 74 (46.3%), had experienced sexual abuse as children. Of the 74, female children were significantly more likely to fall into this category compared with males (94.6% compared with 5.4%, respectively). Not surprisingly, childhood emotional abuse was reported by the largest number of caretakers (83). Of this number, 77 (92.7%) were females and 6 (7.3%) males. For caretakers, 19 reported being neglected. This consisted of 18 (94.7%) females and 1 (5.3%) male.[2]

Although only demographic data were available from this study, it is useful because it does support some findings from previously discussed studies. For example, this study shows that both male and female children are involved in sexually abusive acts and that many of the children are victims of multiple types of abuse and may represent the latest generation in a cycle of abuse. Like other studies discussed in this chapter, most of the study population was from clinical or social service agencies. The study does have a control group, however, that will allow, when analyses are complete, determination of how and perhaps why children who engage in sexually abusive acts differ from children who do not.

W. Pithers and A. Gray (Personal Communication, February 1997)

Similar to Bonner et al. (1991-1996), W. Pithers and A. Gray (personal communication, February 1997) are involved in an evaluation study of two different treatment modalities. The first, sex abuse specific treatment, is a modified relapse prevention approach including an external supervision dimension called the prevention team. The second modality, abuse prevention treatment, offers an array of interventions including assertiveness, self-esteem, decision making, positive sexuality, and relationship skills. In this study, children were separated by ages, 6- to 9-year-olds and 10- to 12-year-olds, and randomly assigned to one of the two treatment conditions. Instruments used to assess the sexually abusive children included an Intake Interview, the Child Behavior Checklist, the Youth Self Report for ages 11 to 18, the Child Sexual Behavior Inventory, the Eyberg Child Behavior Inventory, the Children's Actions Tendency Scale, the State-Trait Anxiety Inventory for Children, the Harter Perceived Self-Competence Scale, and Goal Attainment Scaling.

Because interactions with caregivers affect children, caregivers complete an assessment battery that includes an Intake Interview, Family Environment Scale, the Brief Symptom Inventory, the Parenting Stress Index, the Social Support Scale, and the State-Trait Anger Expression Inventory.

Although Gray and Pithers began their National Center on Child Abuse Neglect study at about the same time as the Bonner et al. (1991-1996) group, they were able to provide information beyond demographics. I begin with a discussion of demographic variables, however, so the findings can be compared with other studies in Table 2.1, Study 9.

Referral Sources

The referral sources in the Gray and Pithers study are similar to those of Bonner et al.'s (1991-1996) in that the majority (60%) of the 72 children were referred by mental health practitioners, with a distant second being social services (28%). In comparison to the Bonner et al. study, approximately twice the number of children (21%) were referred by schools. Ten percent of the children were from parents who self-referred their families, and a similar percentage (3%) of referrals came from legal-related sources. Some children were referred by several sources.

Age and Gender

The 72 children in the study ranged from 6 to 12 years of age, with a mean age of 8.4 and a median age of 8 years. For boys, the mean age was 8.5 and the median age was 8.9. The mean and median age for girls was 8.4. There were significantly more boys (65%, $n = 47$) in the sample than girls (35%, $n = 25$).

Of the 72 children, the 6- to 9-year-old group made up 64% of the study sample, whereas 36% were 10 to 12 years of age. Six-year-old children were overrepresented in the sample relative to all other ages ($\chi^2 = 13.94$, $n = 72$, $p < 0.03$), with other ages being equally represented. This finding differs somewhat from those of the Bonner et al. (1991-1996) study, although their 6-year-old category had the largest number of girls

($n = 31$) and the second largest number of boys ($n = 27$). In the Bonner et al. study, the 7 years of age category had the largest number of boys ($n = 36$).

Male and female children were found in both age groups in the Gray and Pithers's study. Of the 6- to 9-year-old children, 64% ($n = 28$) were male and 36% ($n = 16$) were female. For the 10- to 12-year-olds, 68% ($n = 19$) were male and 32% ($n = 9$) were female. The majority of all age and gender groups had been victims of sexual abuse as well as other forms of abuse.

Victimization Histories

At the time of intake, Gray and Pithers indicated that six parents were reluctant to provide information about their children's victimization history. Thus, victimization data are based on 66 cases. The children in the sample had experienced a wide variety of childhood abuse, but sexual abuse predominated. Of the 66 children, 95% were victims of sexual abuse. All the females had been sexually abused and this was also found for 93% of the males.

Physical abuse was the second most common type of victimization because it was experienced by 48% of the entire sample; 52% of the males and 42% of the females were affected. One third (33%) of the children had been emotionally abused with some percentage difference between females (38%) and males (31%). With respect to neglect, this was found in only 11% of the sample (12% of the males and 8% of the females).

Overall, for the 6- to 9-year-old group, 52% of males were victims of multiple forms of abuse as were 63% of the females. For the 10- to 12-year-old group, this was found for 65% of the males and 63% of the females. Compared with those in the Bonner et al. study, these statistics demonstrate both commonalities (e.g., the proportions that endured emotional abuse) and divergences (e.g., the proportion that were sexually abused).

With respect to children's victimization histories, the average number of victimizers per child was 2.5 (standard deviation [SD] = 2.0). The vast majority of the children's abusers were male (73.2%). In 25% of the cases, abusers were female, and in 1.8% of the cases the abuser's sex was unknown. With respect to reporting, 40% of the cases were reported to Child Protective Services, and the abuse was substantiated in 19% of the cases. For 18% of the children, at least one of the child's abusers admitted responsibility. Criminal charges were filed against 11% ($n = 21$) of the abusers and convictions resulted in 9% ($n = 17$) of the cases.

Gray and Pithers caution that because a substantial percentage of abuse to children was perpetrated by other children (40% of the abuse to the children was performed by other children and adolescents), the reported abuse data about criminal charges and conviction may not be representative. In these cases, 16.7% of the abusers were 5 to 10 years of age and 22.7% were between ages 11 and 18. Young adults, aged 19 to 25, represented about 6% of the children's abusers, whereas adults between ages 26 and 35 comprised 13.6%, those ages 36 to 50 made up 15.2%, and 4.5% were adults ages 50 to 60. The abuser's age was not known in 21.2% of the cases.

The average age of children at the time of their victimization was 3.4 years (SD = 2.9). The mean ages of abusers for 6 to 9-year-olds were 2.8 years for males and 3.3 years for females. For the 10- to 12-year-old group, it was 5.0 years of age for males and 6.5 years for females.

Psychiatric Diagnosis

The follow-up data were based on 59 of the 72 children for whom information about psychiatric diagnosis was available. Of the 59 children, 55 (93%) met the *DSM-IV* criteria for at least one psychiatric diagnosis. The most common diagnosis was conduct disorder, which was found in 73% of the sample (52% of the females and 84% of the males). This was followed by attention deficit/hyperactivity disorder (ADHD), identified in 37% of the sample (42% of the males and 25% of the females). Oppositional and defiant disorder was found in 27% of the sample (29% of the females and 26% of the males). Posttraumatic stress disorder was identified in 18% of the cases (19% of the females and 17% of the males), and adjustment disorder with mixed emotional features was diagnosed in 8% of the sample (11% of the females and 5% of the males). In comparing all the disorders, only the conduct disorder diagnosis differed significantly across the sex of subjects (χ^2 = 3.87, n = 72, p < 0.05), with a greater proportion of males (84%) than females (52%) receiving this diagnosis.

Considering the 55 children who had received a psychiatric diagnosis, 23 (42%) had been dually diagnosed and 14 (25%) had received more than two diagnoses. The most common dual diagnoses (n = 5) involved a pairing of conduct disorder with either oppositional and defiant disorder (ODD) (n = 6) or ADHD. The most common multiple diagnosis was conduct disorder, ADHD, and ODD (n = 7). Of the sample,

8.4% had participated in psychotherapy within 6 months of entry into the research project.

Childhood Perpetration Behavior

Perpetration data were available for 67 of the 72 children in the study. Together, the 67 children had 125 victims ($M = 1.87$). Although each child in the study was responsible for almost two victims, only approximately 21% of the children admitted having engaged in any sexual misbehavior during their intake interview.

Siblings were the most common victims (44.0%), followed by friends (37.6%). "Others" (e.g., houseguest) accounted for 10.4% of the victims; other relatives, 5.6%; animals, 1.6%; and babysitters, 0.8%. Thus, children with sexual behavior problems tended to abuse the people with whom they had trusting relationships, proximity, and frequent contact. Overall, most of the children's victims were female (54.5%), although female perpetrators had a higher percentage of female victims (65.7%) than male perpetrators (50.0%).

Only 10 of the 67 children displayed hands-on or hands-off behavior exclusively, whereas 57 children displayed both hands-on and hands-off behaviors. Most children engaged in several types of sexually abusive behavior. Across the entire sample of children, the most common behaviors were fondling (63%), sexual statements (49%), and exposing (35%). None of these behaviors would be considered sexually aggressive.

As suggested by the preponderance of siblings abused by children, most of the sexual misconduct occurred in the natural parents' home (66.7%), a foster parent's home (18.1%), or an adoptive parent's home (8.3%). The remainder of the sexual misconduct took place either in residential care (5.6%) or in the home of a guardian (1.4%).

Place of Residence at Time of Sexualized Behavior Testing

At the time of the child's sexualized behavior, 71% ($n = 51$) of the children lived with their biological parents. At the time of testing, 65% ($n = 47$) of children resided with their biological parents, whereas 35% ($n = 25$) resided with nonbiological parents. Nonbiological caregivers consisted of 14 foster parents, 6 adoptive parents, 1 nonrelative guardian, and 4 residential care placements. Thus, between the time of the problematic sexual behavior and entry into this study there was a small decrease in the percentage of children living with their natural parents. This decrease may be associated with the finding that 56.7% of the children had abused a sibling.

Gray and Pithers's Assessment of Study Findings

Although in-depth parental and familial data were not available at this time, Gray and Pithers indicated that their data are clearly demonstrating that families of children with sexual behavior problems have an array of characteristics indicative of parental and familial distress, including high rates of (a) poverty; (b) violence between parents, and children who have witnessed violence; (c) sexual victimization and perpetration within the extended family; (d) physical abuse of the children who have exhibited sexual behavior problems; (e) parental arrest; (f) denial of responsibility for perpetration of sexual abuse by members of the extended family; (g) special educational services; (h) prior therapy for children; and (i) clinical scores on behavioral rating instruments.

Gray and Pithers note that several significant differences emerged between the younger age group (6- to 9-year-olds) and older group (10- to 12-year-olds). Younger children, relative to older children, had (a) been sexually and physically abused at an earlier age, (b) witnessed physical violence between parents, (c) performed problematic sexual behaviors at an earlier age, (d) demonstrated a higher annual rate of problematic sexual behaviors, (e) engaged in a higher percentage of "hands-on" sexual behaviors, and (f) scored higher on measures indicative of sexual behavior problems (i.e., Child Behavior Survey and Child Behavior Checklist Sexual Problems Subscale).

Kylie Gardner (Personal Communication, July 1993)

In the summer of 1993, I had several lengthy telephone and personal interviews with Kylie Gardner, who was working in a state social service agency in Idaho but who had previously worked with preadolescent sexual offenders in another Pacific Northwest state agency. Gardner completed, in-depth, the Araji et al. (1993) survey described previously. The information described herein is based on Gardner's oral and written recollection of 50 preadolescent offenders seen during a 2-year period at a private for-profit outpatient center in a state other than Idaho. As will become apparent, her recollections reveal both similarities and departures from information discussed in this chapter.

Of the 50 preadolescents Gardner had observed in treatment, 80% were victims of sexual abuse. Of these, 50% had been victimized by children age 12 and younger. Only 30% were victimized by adults age 21 and older; 80% of those were male.

The largest number of preadolescent sexually aggressive children Gardner had treated were male (90%), and most, both male and female, were victimized by males. The most common type of sexual behavior by male and female preadolescent offenders was "coercive touching" of the breasts, buttocks, vagina, and genitals. Only males were involved in simulated intercourse (40%) and bestiality (30%). Females were more likely than males to engage in digital penetration with objects or fingers (50% compared with 30%). If various types of sexual intercourse were combined, however, the penetration percentages by gender become closer because males were the only ones involved in penile (10%) and anal (2%) intercourse.

The young perpetrators' typical victims were biological siblings. This was more the case for females (100%) than for males (60%). Both sexes had abused a variety of other victims, including stepsiblings, relatives, and friends.

Both sexes molested male and female victims. For male perpetrators, the majority of both male and female victims tended to be 6 to 9 years of age (90%), and the remainder (10%) were 3 to 5 years old. For the most part, the same was true for female offenders. A few offenders of both genders chose children with mental disabilities because they were easy targets.

The least number of victims that either male or female perpetrators had was one; the most for females was eight and for males six. The average number for males was two or three and for females it was three.

Both male and female offenders acted either alone or in groups. Gardner reported that often the sexual abuse was a "free for all against one or more victims." For both genders, the perpetrating behavior was multiple offenses over a period of time rather than one-time occurrences.

Approximately 25% of the perpetrators of both genders used verbal coercion on their victims such as threats to "beat them up" or bribes. Approximately 5% of the males used physical coercion that included such things as tying up the victim and then multiple offenders abusing him or her. Females were seen as less likely to use physical coercion, which is in contrast to what Johnson (1993c) reported. Gardner also observed that offenders generally lacked empathy for their victims.

With respect to family demographics, approximately 80% of the 50 children were Caucasian and 20% Hispanic. Gardner's assessment of this is that the distribution reflects the ethnic and racial groups in the area where she had worked. She noted, however, that a large oriental population resided in the area, but no offenders or victims were referred or reported to her agency in the time period covered (2 years) in her observations. This probably does not indicate that sexually aggressive children are not present in these racial and ethnic groups, but the absence is more reflective of the closed and private nature of the Asian culture and communities.

Similar to the previous clinical and agency studies reviewed, Gardner reported that most of the families were in the lower-income bracket and were generally in blue-collar occupations, and the parents tended to have high school or some college education. She also reported that a high percentage of the parents had been sexually abused themselves, that the family environments lacked sexual boundaries, and that children witnessed their parents engaging in extensive sexual activities.

Third, in contrast to other studies, most of the children Gardner treated came from two-parent families. I believe that this may be reflective of the fact that Gardner's clients were from a private nonprofit organization and may represent higher-income groups in which more families may be intact. Data from the other studies reported herein were from public social service agencies or therapists who received referrals from public agencies. Clients who come in contact with these agencies frequently have many family-related problems, are from lower-economic groups and have higher percentages of single-parent or broken families.

Although the findings from Gardner's observations are generally consistent with the research findings reported in other studies reviewed in this chapter, I did observe some differences. First, Gardner views sexually aggressive children's primary motivation for engaging in sexual abusive behaviors as fulfillment of their own gratification. This somewhat contrasts to other practitioners and researchers, who are more inclined to view the behaviors as sexually reactive or involving issues of power and control to express dominance over victims.

Second, Gardner strongly believed that the young male and female offenders were not involved in sexual abuse of other children as a way of compensating for something missing or something that they (the perpetrator) wanted in their lives.

Third, she also did not view these youthful sexual abusers, particularly males, as seeking revenge or acting out their own sexual victimizations. In fact, based on her observations of the 50 preadolescent offenders, she concluded that these children are less abuse reactive than the current literature leads us to believe.

Finally, Gardner strongly believed, for both sexes, that the sexually aggressive behaviors represented more than opportunistic abuse. She viewed the sexual abuse as planned and predatory, with some children engaging in grooming activities.

Basically, Gardner's observations seem to be that these children's actions reflect learned patterns of sexually aggressive behaviors that have become rewarding for a variety of reasons. Furthermore, the pre-adolescents she observed are more characteristic of "youthful predators" than "opportunistic abusers."

Case Study

The following case study serves as an example of many of the behavioral, social, and psychological characteristics of sexually aggressive children that were identified in this chapter and in Chapter 1. The victimization scenarios described, which are not complete descriptions, were all reported by a 9-year-old male abuser. He had multiple victims, both male and female, related and unrelated. The scenarios generally reflect language used by the child.[3]

About Victim 1: My name is (male) and I am responsible for putting my penis in an adoptive sister's vagina. One time I put it one-half way in her. I stopped because she was crying and I didn't want to get caught. She was 4 years old.

About Victim 2: My name is (male) and I am responsible for molesting my 4 or 5 year old cousin. This all happened in my bedroom. He was the fourth child I molested. I threatened him to pull his pants down. What I said was, "if you don't pull your draws I will tell your mother and she will yell at you." (Victim) pulled his pants and underwear down. My hands were on his back. I was thinking about what I did to my sister and what sister looked like when she was naked. Then I forced his mouth on my penis with my hand on his head. I told him not to bite me or I would kill him. It felt good so I didn't want to stop. I heard his mother, so I told him to get dressed. I was scared someone would catch us.

About Victim 3: My name is (male) and I am responsible for molesting (victim) who was six years old. I asked (victim) to go to the frog pond with me. I knew he'd say yes. We went into a very secluded spot near the frog pond. I said, "if you want to go to the frog pond, pull down your pants." Part of my plan was knowing that victim had molested his sister, so I figured he would do things that I asked him to do. Then he said, "what are you going to do?" When I told him he said "no," so I threatened to beat him up and said I wouldn't bring him candy and treats from the store. I threatened to destroy things he likes, like his bike, if he told.

About Victim 4: My name is (male) and (victim) was 6 1/2 years old. I picked (victim) because he had a problem, like stuttering. I used to stutter so I know it is hard to understand kids who stutter. I know that adults sometimes don't even bother listening to him because it takes him so long to talk. He probably wouldn't talk much and people would not understand him. I molested him one time. This happened at the frog pond. I told him to pull down his pants. I threatened to put a snake in his bed if he didn't do this.

About Victim 5: My name is (male) and I am responsible for molesting a male victim. He was 7 years old. We lived at group home together. We were at a beach. I picked him because he wasn't swimming. He trusted me so he went with me. I threatened to beat him up if he told on me. I was afraid he'd tell the director who was strict. I pulled down his pants. He asked me why I was doing this. I said, "I'm doing something you wouldn't want to know." He did what I asked because I threatened him. I felt like I didn't care if he cried because we were in the woods and far from others so they couldn't hear him crying, so I couldn't get caught. I continued to threaten him all of the time I was molesting him by either saying I would beat him up or sexually assault him again. I felt a tiny bit sad, but I didn't stop because it felt good. Finally, it ended because he ran from me. I was scared he would tell. A month later I molested him again.

Analysis

What does this chapter, in combination with Chapter 1, tell us about children who act sexually abusive? First, the material reviewed in this chapter leaves little doubt that young children are involved in sexually abusive behaviors, and that these behaviors must be appropriately labeled when observed by parents, teachers, practitioners, and researchers. This chapter demonstrates some social and psychological factors that can be used to identify sexually abusive children, noting similarities and differences among abusive groups. The chapter also highlights some similarities and differences between preadolescent and adolescent sexual aggressors. This is helpful to practitioners who are primarily using information about adolescents in their attempts to intervene and treat sexually abusive children.

Second, there must be increased acceptance by parents and professionals that children can begin sexually abusive behaviors at early ages; the modal ages seem to be 6 to 9. In contrast to most of the literature on adolescent and adult sexual abusers wherein males make up the majority of reported or known perpetrators, female children compose a substantial proportion of the known sexually abusive children and appear to be engaging in equally aggressive acts. This finding raises some interesting questions when sexually aggressive perpetrators in the preadolescent, adolescent, and adult populations are compared. Because relatively few female perpetrators are reported in the adolescent, and especially adult sex offender populations, what happens to the preadolescent female sexual offenders? Are they simply hidden because gender role stereotypes blind us from looking for them? Do females stop, on their own, their sexually aggressive behaviors? As they reach adolescence, does gender role socialization cause them to drop the perpetrator role and continue to engage in abusive behaviors in which they are only victims—for example, victims of rape, domestic violence, pornography, or prostitution? As a function of gender role socialization, do they, more than males, turn their aggression inward and become victims of depression, eating disorders, substance abuse, and suicide? Because of gender role stereotypes, do males simply not report their victimizations by females?

Third, most sexually aggressive children have multiple victims—those they view as vulnerable and whom they can control. The victims may be male or female. Siblings appear to be targets of much abuse, especially for the female perpetrators. Nonsibling targets tend to be friends or acquaintances—few, if any, appear to select complete strangers. Evidence suggests that many sexually aggressive children are "opportunistic" in the selection of their victims, although some groom their victims just like adolescents and adults.

Fourth, for many adults and adolescent sex offenders and other criminals who come to the attention of school authorities, social service agencies, and the police, dysfunctional and abusive family life appear as a part of their backgrounds. This is also true for sexually abusive children. The particular red flags in the backgrounds of these children are that they suffer multiple types of abuses and the abuses appear to be very severe and of longer duration than comparative groups (e.g., see the Friedrich & Luecke [1988] study and the English & Ray [1991] reports). Where sexual abuse occurred, it tended to be more intrusive, involving genital contact or penetration or both. Some studies (Friedrich & Luecke, 1988) suggested that in comparison to other groups of sexually abused children, the perpetrators who victimized sexually aggressive children tended to be older. Physical abuse, as well as neglect, also seems to be included in the abuse histories of sexually aggressive children. In fact, Johnson and Aoki (1993) report that data from a study they conducted on 158 children between 6 and 11 years of age who were in residential treatment indicate that physical abuse may be a significant contributor to the development of sexual behavior problems in sexually abused children.

The interactions in the homes of sexually abusive children involved aggression, conflict, and nonnormative sexual environments—for example, no sexual boundaries, exposure to adult sexual activity or pornographic material, or all three. This type of environment no doubt leads to the generally consistent findings across studies that the prominent psychological disorders that set this group apart from other sexual abuse groups are conduct and oppositional disorders. Specific behavior manifestations that serve as clues to those disorders for this age group are found in the English and Ray (1991) reports.

The aggressive, conflictual, and sexualized homes also serve as the basis for Friedrich's (1990) hypothesis of how aggression and sex get linked together, hence creating sexually aggressive children. Although this idea is explained more fully in Chapter 4, Friedrich basically argues that a child living in the previously described home begins to develop aggressive characteristics and disorders that, at some point, get linked with sexual activity. It is the linking of aggression and sex that produces sexually aggressive behavior. As was apparent in this chapter, the aggressive behaviors, with or without the sexual component, manifest themselves in the school environment and in the interactions with peers and adults—that is, conduct or oppositional disorders or both.

With respect to social demographics that characterize this group, it appears that in publicly supported social service agencies, or clinics, the predominant family form may be a single parent, mostly likely headed by a female. This family structure, however, may not characterize the clientele of private clinics, therapists, or organizations. Taken together, the chapter findings suggest that sexually aggressive children are found in single- and dual-parent families and other types of family structures such as stepfamilies.

All studies reviewed herein suggest that sexually abusive children are predominantly found in lower- to lower-middle-income families, in which parents have a high school or college education or both. As more empirical research on these children becomes available, however, the social class variations will no doubt expand.

With respect to the racial and ethnic statuses of sexually aggressive children, the findings as a whole suggest that groups or samples may reflect racial and ethnic variations in the geographic areas where the children are being observed or studied.

What I concluded from the information about families of sexually aggressive children is that social demographics, such as family structure, social class, and racial or ethnic background, play a lesser role in creating sexually aggressive children than do the dynamics or interactions that take place within families. Although I identified a number of family problems or dysfunctions that act as contributors, the ones that appear particularly salient to producing sexually aggressive behaviors in children are homes in which children (a) are recipients of multiple types of abuse that include physical violence and in some cases sexual abuse; (b) experience abuse that is extreme and of longer duration in percentages that exceed those reported in large samples of sexually abused children; (c) are victims of sexual abuse experiences that involve genital contact and various types of intercourse; (d) are exposed to sexualized adult behaviors in some format; and (e) exist in families characterized by aggression, anger, conflict, and little parent support, and in which the child may be a family scapegoat.

Conclusions

Chapter 1 focused on behavioral characteristics of sexually aggressive children. This chapter extended that information by identifying social and psychological factors that are associated with or contribute to children's sexually aggressive behaviors. The evidence reviewed in the chapter points to family interactions as a primary source of the problem. The family interaction patterns are characterized by (a) multiple and extreme types of abuse, including neglect and abandonment, over long periods of time, and (b) aggressive, angry, conflictual, sexualized, repressive, or all five sexual climates that are conducive to children linking together aggression and sexual acts. Information in this chapter suggests that once identified, appropriate interventions and treatments must begin immediately to prevent further victimizations from occurring and to break the cycle of abuse and prevent a potential increase in the number of new perpetrators. That is, a high percentage of sexually aggressive children were first victims of sexual abuse.

Furthermore, appropriate intervention at the preadolescent level may prevent escalation of sexually aggressive behaviors in terms of sophistication and violence. It may also be more effective in terminating sexually aggressive and related behaviors than if identification and intervention or treatment occur later in the life cycle. For example, the English and Ray (1991) reports indicated that adolescents (ages 13-18) had significantly higher levels of aggression, levels of coercion, and levels of sophistication in committing sexually aggressive acts than did the younger group. They were also less empathic, showed higher levels of escalating sexual violence, and exhibited greater resistance to acknowledging the seriousness of their behaviors and responding to the distress of their victims. Also, although both groups were low on substance-related histories, adolescents had significantly higher risk scores than the younger group. They were also more likely to internalize as well as externalize their aggressive behaviors, as demonstrated by depression and suicide ideation.

In conclusion, I cannot overstate the need to apply caution when using information provided in this chapter. It represents only the social and psychological characteristics of sexually aggressive children that were derived from a few studies, some of which are practitioners' observations, that are only recently available in this newly emerging field of practice and research. There are, undoubtedly, other social and psychological factors yet to be determined and written about or shared.

Notes

1. Some of the reasons respondents gave for not completing the surveys include the following: (a) survey was long (70 questions if only male offenders had been treated; 100 questions if both male and female offenders had been

treated) and no one in the agency had time to complete it; (b) program descriptions were returned in lieu of completing surveys; and (c) programs or practitioners did not treat preadolescent offenders.

2. Information about the ongoing Bonner et al. (1991-1996) study was obtained from personal communication with the Oklahoma site (fall 1996).

3. To maintain confidentiality and anonymity, the name of the perpetrator, the respondent to the survey, and the program are omitted.

3

Sexually Abusive Children

Family, Extrafamilial Environments, and Situational Risk Factors

Sharon K. Araji/Rebecca L. Bosek

The material reviewed in Chapter 2 demonstrated that the interactions and climate within a child's family are important determinants of sexually aggressive behaviors, perhaps more salient than demographics such as social class, race, and family structure—for example, single-parent and two-parent families. Recognition of the role families play in creating sexually aggressive children has been noted by many practitioners and is reflected in the following statement by Gil (1993b):

> When we assess whose sexualized or molesting behaviors have brought them [children] to the attention of concerned professionals, we must immediately address the family environments in which these children live. Extreme and persistent sexualized and molesting behaviors do not emerge in a vacuum. (p. 101)

In this chapter, we take an in-depth look at the familial environments that contribute to young children acting sexually abusively or aggressively. Because some preadolescent children's environments extend beyond the home, we also review information about extrafamilial environments and situations that may precipitate or facilitate sexually abusive behaviors.

The chapter objectives are accomplished by reviewing observations, writings, and research of many different professionals and researchers. The chapter is divided into three primary sections. The first section describes family dynamics, environments, and climates that can contribute to sexual abuse. In this section, there is a focus on overt and covert abuse in families as well as family systems that contribute to the development of a range of sexual behaviors, particularly sexually aggressive behaviors.

The second section focuses on variations of intrafamilial sexual abuse. Because much of preadolescents' sexual abuse is aimed at siblings, the section includes a discussion of sibling incest and also what is known about children who sexually abuse as part of an intergenerational pattern or a polyincestuous lifestyle.

The third section of the chapter focuses on some of the situations and dynamics involved in extrafamilial sexual abuse among children. In this section, locations and circumstances outside the home where children sexually aggress are described. These include foster care, adoptive homes, residential treatment centers, psychiatric hospitals, schools, neighborhoods, and babysitting situations. The final section offers a synthesis and critical analysis of the chapter material.

Family Environments: Current Descriptions

This section describes and briefly discusses the practice and research value of four prominent practitioners' or researchers' typologies of family environments that are conducive to creating normal to sexually aggressive behaviors. The typologies are presented in Table 3.1.

Gil (1993b)

As shown in Table 3.1, Gil's (1993b) typology is divided into two categories: "family dynamics" and "family systems." In discussing dynamics of sexually abusive families, Gil says years of practice have led her to conclude that there are two primary types of abusive families: overt and covert. *Overtly abusive* families are those that literally engage in abusive behaviors. In contrast, *covertly abusive* families create a sexualized atmosphere in which inappropriate abusive attitudes are communicated, but these families do not engage in corresponding abusive behaviors. That is, the families only create a climate or atmosphere that sends a message that the abuse "could" happen at any time. In summary,

TABLE 3.1 A Continuum of Family Environments That Contribute to a Range of Sexual Behaviors: Normal to Aggressive

Reference		Types of Family Environments
Gil (1993b)	Family systems	
	Family dynamics	
	Overtly abusive	Sexualized families
	Covertly abusive	Sociopathic families
		Repressed families
		Emotionally barren families
Johnson (1993b)		Natural and healthy; sexually neutral homes; open or communal living homes; sexually repressed homes; "sex is dirty" homes; homes with overt values and covert norms; sexually overwhelming homes; sexually and emotionally needy homes; homes where sex is an exchange commodity; sexually abusive homes; multigenerational sexually abusive homes
Ryan (1991b)		Exploitive families; rigid or enmeshed families; chaotic or disengaged families; perfect families; previously adequate families; multigenerational sexually abusive families
Larson & Maddock (1986)		Affective-exchange process families; erotic-exchange process families; aggressive-exchange process families; rage-expressive exchange process families

the focus of attention in overtly abusive families is on behaviors; in covertly abusive families, it is on cognitions.

Overt Abuse Described

Recall from the previous chapter that sexually aggressive children were likely to come from families in which they were victims of multiple types of abuse. In describing families involved in physical and sexual abuse, Gil (1993b) suggests that families who perpetrate either of these abusive behaviors are more similar than different. Both sexually and physically abusive families exhibit low self-esteem, impulsivity, and low frustration levels. They reflect an inability to identify or meet needs and lack problem-solving skills. They demonstrate affective and expressive problems as well as communication deficits. They exhibit feelings of helplessness and hopelessness and experience frequent and unresolved losses. Social isolation among family members and the community is common. Gil notes that the pain, agony, stress, isolation, feelings of despair, and substance abuse found in overtly abusive families may manifest themselves in sexually or physically abusive behaviors or both. Similar findings have been reported by other researchers such as Friedrich (1990).

Gil (1993b) draws on the concept of "power" to explain how children in overt sexually or physically abusive families can be singled out for victimization. She cites Gelinas' (1988) descriptions of incestuous families in which relational imbalances exist, resulting in unfair treatment of specific family members. Over time, Gelinas suggests that the unfair treatment converges on one child, who becomes the primary victim of incest.

Gil (1993b, p. 103) extends Gelinas's (1988) idea about incestuous families and says that relational power imbalances also operate in physically abusive families so the person with the least power is singled out as a victim of physical violence.

Several ideas emerge from the previously noted observations that are important to understanding sexually aggressive children as they have been described in previous chapters of this book. The first important idea relates to the notion that the relational dynamics represent a pattern of "unfairness" and that, over time, one child may be progressively singled out for unfair treatment—that is, the child may become the object of multiple abusive behaviors over a long duration of time. This may explain why one of the social characteristics somewhat consistently found associated with sexually aggressive children is that they are the family scapegoat.

The second idea relates to power dynamics that set up the abuser-victim relationship in both sexually and physically abusive families. Specifically, the dynamics being learned by the child are that whoever has the power and control in a relationship is the one who administers the physical or sexual abuse or both, whereas the least powerful person becomes the victim.

Third, the observations of Gelinas (1988) and Gil (1993b) provide insight into why sexually aggressive children become progressively angry and frustrated. If the child comes to perceive the abuse he or she is receiving as unfair but unescapable, the emotions that develop may be anger and frustration. Behaviorally, these emotions can be manifest in conduct or oppositional disorders or both, both of which are reportedly associated with sexually aggressive children. Because many sexually aggressive children are victims of both physical and sexual abuse, this abuse combination provides insight into how aggressive and sexual acts may get linked together.

Parent-Child Role Reversals

Gil (1993b, pp. 103-104) also discusses a common factor found in many overt physically and sexually abusive, as well as neglectful, families: parent-child role reversals. In these types of families, a child at various times assumes the parent role.

When the parent-child role reversal factor is combined with the previous discussion of family power dynamics and scapegoating, the picture becomes more focused as to how children may become sexually abusive, why siblings are frequently sexually abusive children's victims, and why a favored child in a family may become the first or the most frequently victimized available target or both. That is, the "child-victim now parent" assumes a position of power and control over other children, giving him or her the opportunity to imitate, model, or practice what he or she has learned about "power equals aggressor" and "powerlessness equals victim." It follows that the child-victim now parent will assume the aggressor role looking for an appropriate victim. The situation also helps explain why the chosen victim(s) may be several types. For example, if the child-victim now parent is placed in charge of only one sibling or even a nonsibling, then this child is the only target. If the aggressor can persuade, trick, coerce, or force the child to comply with

his or her demands, then this child becomes a "victim of opportunity"—
that is, the child is the only person available at the time. If, however, there
is more than one child to choose from, the child-victim now parent may
choose the child perceived as least powerful—just as the parent(s) chose
the child for victimization. This type of victimization reflects a reenactment of the parent's own victimization experiences.

A third type of victim might be the object of revenge or anger. In this
scenario, the victim could be the parents' favored child. The child-victim
now parent may see the favored child as partially or solely responsible
for the abuse he or she receives at the hands of his or her parents or
caretakers—abuse the child-victim now parent characterizes as unfair.

Covert Abuse Described

Because covert abuse operates at the cognitive rather than the behavioral level, the family's specific underlying problems are more difficult for an observer to detect than problems that are overtly manifested.
To demonstrate the dynamics of covert abuse, we use two examples
presented by Gil (1993b, pp. 106-107)—one relating to physical abuse
and the other to sexual abuse (incest).

In the case of physical abuse, Gil (1993b) described environments
that continuously send threatening messages to a child that violence can
erupt at any time. She offered a case study of a young woman who was
extremely fearful of her father because almost daily he threatened to "kill
her in her sleep." Then he would make her sit for hours and watch him
clean his guns. Gil writes that the father never did physically harm his
daughter, but the situation created a threatening perception that violence
was possible at any time. For us, it appears reasonable to assume that
living in this type of environment could lead children to become highly
anxious, another characteristic found associated with sexually aggressive children.

When sexual abuse, rather than physical abuse, is the topic of
concern, Gil (1993b) indicates that the family climate conveys an incestuous or sexual compared to physically violent message. The example
Gil provides of the dynamics involved in covert incest comes from an
adult survivor who described the following interactions with her father:

> My father never laid a finger on me. He would just watch and
> watch and watch, with his ugly stare. I knew what he was

thinking. I knew where he was looking. He just always looked and made a gargly sound with saliva. (pp. 106-107)

Gil (1993b) says that this young girl was spared behavioral incest, but the incest dynamics were still present. She also indicates that in most cases of nonbehavioral incest, one parent remains aloof or absent, whereas the other is intrusive. The intrusiveness can be emotional or verbal or both.

Motivations for
Covert Abuse

Covert abuse appears to be a complex process whereby parents transmit to a child, consciously or unconsciously, their own unresolved problems, frustrations, or desires. According to Gil (1993, p. 108), however, for some yet unexplained reason, when the message is relayed to the child, the child does not let the feelings remain at the cognitive level. Instead, the child overtly performs the acts the parent wants to engage in but restrains himself or herself from doing. In cases such as this, triangulation occurs as the child becomes the vehicle through which the parent meets a need or is able to vicariously experience, through the child's behavior, an act that the parent wants to engage in but cannot bring himself or herself to perform.

A specific example of the triangulation process from parent to child is seen in the case of a 13-year-old boy who raped his 11-year-old sister. In a family therapy session, Gil (1993b, p. 109) reported asking who in the family was most and least upset about the rape incident. The mother reported being distraught and suicidal, but the father minimized the incident and called it "understandable" for an adolescent to be curious about sex. Gil later discovered that the father had been "setting up" the adolescent boy for more than a year by making statements such as "Your sister is hot!" "Look at the way she moves those buns!," "Check out this chick," and "First guy to get into her pants is gonna be one lucky guy." The father constantly called the boy's attention to his sister as she walked by, and whenever the boy had a girlfriend the father would compare her with the boy's sister and discourage the relationship. Finally, the boy attacked his sister and raped her.

Gil (1993b) indicates that the father had successfully transmitted his incestuous desires toward his daughter, and although he could feel self-righteous for not committing the crime, he was responsible for eliciting his son's interest and ultimate act in the form of rape.

In summary, it is apparent that covert abuse can manifest itself in several ways. It can remain at the covert level, such as the case of the young child whose father threatened physical violence but never did engage in overt abuse, or it can be transmitted through a child who ultimately engages in the overt behavior that the parent desires but restrains himself or herself from enacting. In either case, it appears that covert abuse can be as damaging to children as overt abuse.

Family Systems

In addition to discussing the dynamics of abusive families, which included overt and covert abuse, Gil (1993b) describes four family environments or systems associated with children who display sexualized or molesting behaviors. As indicated in Table 3.1, the first of these is sexualized families. In this type of family, members have an intense preoccupation with sex, and sexually laden themes permeate all aspects of everyday life. There is a continual erotic quality to interactions. Children are repeatedly exposed to adult sexuality and engage in sexual behavior beyond what is generally considered age appropriate. The children are used to meet the sexual needs of the parents. Overall, the sex education children receive in these families is not appropriate to their developmental levels.

In the second family type, sociopathic families, the sexual behaviors of children are part of a larger pattern of criminal activities and other problematic behaviors. Frequently, there is much illegal activity, and there is little structure and discipline. Children are allowed to do as they wish. Neglect is common, and children may be emotionally, physically, or sexually abused.

In repressed families, the third type mentioned by Gil (1993b), children do not have a chance to learn about healthy sex and sexuality. Sex is considered sinful, and sexual feelings, thoughts, and behaviors are discouraged. Parents in repressed families use authoritarian commands and religion to teach their children to avoid all feelings, thoughts, and behaviors related to sex and sexuality. Verbal or physical punishment or both may be used to control the behavior of the children.

The fourth type of family considered by Gil (1993b) is emotionally barren. In these families, parents are unable to meet the emotional and physical needs of their children. They lack the understanding and the skills necessary for successful parenting, and they may get their needs met through their children. Hence, it is common for role reversals to take place.

Johnson (1993b)

On the basis of clinical observations, Johnson (1993b) describes 11 family environments or systems that form a continuum from those that promote healthy sexuality to those that pose risks to normal sexual development. We have included all 11 family sexual environments for descriptive, information, and comparison purposes. These are listed in Table 3.1 and include natural and healthy homes, sexually neutral homes, open or communal living homes, sexually repressed homes, "sex is dirty" homes, homes with overt values and covert norms, sexually overwhelming homes, sexually and emotionally needy homes, homes where sex is an exchange commodity, sexually abusive homes, and multigenerational sexually abusive homes.

In natural and healthy homes, parents feel secure in their sexuality and children are free to ask questions about sex and explore their sexuality. Sexual issues are dealt with according to the developmental level of the children. Emotional, physical, and sexual boundaries between family members and others are respected.

In sexually neutral homes, sex and sexuality are not denigrated but neither are they discussed. In these homes, there is ambivalence regarding issues related to sex and sexuality. Although conversations regarding sexual issues are not held, sexuality is not considered disgusting, repulsive, or repugnant. In this environment, physical affection is limited, and needs for nuturance are primarily met through food.

Open or communal living homes, the third family type mentioned by Johnson (1993b), have an atmosphere in which children are taught that sex is an extension of love and they are free to explore their sexuality. Children have access to information about sex and sexuality, and there is early teaching of the subject. With the exception of intercourse, children may witness sexual behavior between parents, and children may engage in sexual experimentation.

In sexually repressed homes, sex is considered private and sexuality is not displayed. Hence, children are not educated about issues related to sex and sexuality and they do not witness parents displaying sexual behavior. Children learn early that anything having to do with sex is a taboo topic.

Johnson's (1993b) fifth family environment is called "sex is dirty" homes. Here, sex is considered disgusting and only for the purpose of procreation. Sex and sexuality are not considered positive, healthy, or natural. Children's attempts to learn about sex or engage in sex play are severely repressed. Parents may use anger, intimidation, or physical force to curtail interest in the topic.

In the environment Johnson (1993b) calls homes with overt values and covert norms, overt messages tie sex to religious teachings and social values. At the same time, family members engage in behavior contrary to these teachings and values. Male dominance, extramarital affairs, and abuse are common. Women and children have little control over their lives or bodies.

Sexually overwhelming homes are characterized by Johnson (1993b) as displaying overt sexual behavior and pornography. Alcohol and drug use and abuse may be common. Males are dominant over females. Family emotions are changeable and explosive.

Although sexually aggressive children may come from a broad range of family environments, Johnson (1993b) reports that children who act sexually aggressive generally come from the last 4 of the 11 types of family environments. The first is labeled sexually and emotionally needy homes. Children in these families are used to meet the emotional, physical, and sexual needs of parents. The parents may use their children as replacements for adult partners until adults can be found to fill this role. Boundaries among family members are not respected. Anger and aggression are common.

The next family is described as homes where sex is an exchange commodity and is characterized by adults using sex as a way to gain material possessions. Sometimes, children are engaged in the exchange process. Alcohol, drug abuse, and illegal activities are common, as are violence and physical aggression.

The third type of family mentioned by Johnson (1993b) as conducive to sexually aggressive behaviors is called sexually abusive homes. Here, children are molested by one or both parents. In some cases, the perpetrator is an extended family member. The nonoffending parent may not know about the sexual abuse or may do nothing to stop it. Alcohol and drug abuse may take place. Bribes and threats of physical aggression or death may be used to ensure silence.

Finally, in multigenerational sexually abusive homes, sexual abuse may occur simultaneously in several generations across the nuclear and extended family, representing a "cycle of abuse." Powerful family members sexually abuse those who are less powerful, and emotional and physical force are commonly used to gain compliance.[1]

Ryan (1991b)

Ryan (1991b) reports that families of juvenile sex offenders have several characteristics in common. These characteristics are a lack of positive emotional development, an inability to deal with feelings in a healthy way, keeping secrets, disruptions in attachment, and lack of care. She developed a typology of five family types to describe these families. As shown in Table 3.1, these include the exploitive family, the rigid or enmeshed family, the chaotic or disengaged family, the perfect family, and the previously adequate family.

In the exploitive family, Ryan (1991b) notes that family members may be viewed as property. In these families, parents expect children to meet their needs, and children believe the degree to which they are successful in meeting their parents' needs determines how much their parents care for them. Children learn that needs are not met freely but must be gained through successful manipulation of others.

Interactions in the rigid or enmeshed family are dysfunctional. Family members pull together and become isolated from others. There is little contact with people outside the family, and family members hold the belief that this is the preferable way to live. Secrets are common, and boundaries among family members are poor.

In the chaotic or disengaged family, problems and crises predominate. Parents serve as role models for a variety of unacceptable behaviors. There is no "limit setting" on the behavior of the children. Children are frequently unsupervised, and in these families they experience emotional impoverishment. Boundaries in these families are poor and parent-child role reversals may occur.

The perfect family presents a facade of healthy and acceptable behavior. These families appear as the model of traditional life with males and females assuming traditional roles. Family members expend much energy in maintaining the image of perfection because there is a great fear the family will fall apart. Often, the parents in these families have a childhood history of abuse or neglect. Their attempts to create a perfect family may represent a means to change their own family of orientation. If deviant sexual behaviors occur in these families, there is an attempt to demonstrate that the juvenile sexual offender's behavior is the single family abnormality.

The previously adequate family consists of a functioning family system that experiences change. Ryan (1991b) provides two examples of change: marriage and adoption. She says either change results in new patterns of interaction within the existing system that may set the stage for dysfunction. In these families, there may be intense anger among family members, and sexual boundaries may be poor.

Larson and Maddock (1986)

Larson and Maddock (1986), who focus on incestuous families, report poor boundaries are common in families in which incest is committed by adults against children. In these families, incest is thought to serve one of four functions in interpersonal exchanges. These include the affective-exchange process, erotic-exchange process, aggression-exchange process, and rage-exchange process. The four functions are shown in Table 3.1.

In the affection-exchange process, a family member of one generation uses sexual abuse as a means to express affection for a family member of another generation. Family members do not feel emotionally close to others and have not experienced healthy forms of physical contact. Violence and physical force are typically not used to gain compliance, but there is great effort expended to keep incestuous relationships a secret.

Families that engage in erotic-exchange processes sexualize many aspects of their daily lives. Sexuality and sexual behavior may be either covert or overt, and group sex may be a part of the process. People outside the nuclear family may also be involved in the sexual abuse. Children may engage in sexual acting out in school or the community. Similar to the affection-exchange process, violence is usually not necessary for adults to gain children's compliance.

In the aggression-exchange process, anger and sexuality merge. A powerful family member sexually abuses a weaker family member in an attempt to harm another family member, and violence may be a part of the process. The victim serves as a scapegoat. In these families, family members use sexualized anger to deal with failed hopes and expectations.

Finally, some families use the rage-exchange process, which is characterized by extreme anger and rage. Sexual abuse may involve severe physical violence, and the perpetrator chooses a very weak family member to victimize. Often, the perpetrator has a history of childhood neglect or abuse and may even be psychotic.

Value of Family Typologies and Environments to Understanding Sexually Abusive and Aggressive Children

The terminology used to describe the various categories of family environments varies among the four typologies discussed previously in terms of what specific family environments are more or less likely to promote or maintain or both sexually abusive and aggressive behaviors in children. Our assessment is that common threads run through many of the family types, but they also vary enough to offer different insights into how sexually aggressive behaviors develop. Viewed in combination, the typologies offer a greater understanding of how family environments contribute to children becoming sexually aggressive when viewed separately. An overall assessment of the value of the typologies for practice and research is discussed in the final section of this chapter.

Sibling Incest

The previous section primarily focused on parents as perpetrators and children as victims. This section focuses on child to child abuse. As discussed in previous chapters, many victims of sexually abusive children tend to be siblings. This is understandable because children are generally introduced to sexual abuse within the family and, given the young ages of many preadolescents who became abusers, siblings are the most or only accessible targets. In the next several sections, we describe various types of sibling incest, why it may be ignored, and what implications ignoring or minimizing sibling incest has for concealing children's sexually abusive behaviors.

Sibling Incest Defined

Sibling incest, as discussed in this chapter, is a sexual relationship between two individuals who share one or both parents. The relationship may include a brother and sister, brother and brother, or sister and sister. Full, half, and stepsiblings are also included. Incestuous behavior can be arrayed on a continuum from physical contact that is sexually stimulating to actual intercourse (Justice & Justice, 1979). Of course, the concern in this book is when the sexual behavior involves unequal power relationships, force, or coercion—that is, when it becomes sexually aggressive.

Sibling Incest: How Common?

Sibling incest is quite widespread (Finkelhor, 1980; Greenwald & Leitenberg, 1989; Sorrenti-Little, Bagley, & Robertson, 1984) but for several reasons tends to be ignored or underreported or both (De Jong, 1989). Pierce and Pierce (1990) note that one reason this type of incest remains hidden is a tendency to label it as experimentation or exploration. In this sense, it is not seen as serious or cause for alarm. A second reason, offered by Sgroi (1978), is that family members are generally tolerant of incestuous relationships between siblings when they are young, close in age, and violence is not a factor. Third, Cole (1982) suggests that parents who discover brother-sister incest are unlikely to "turn in" a sexually abusive son to authorities. Fourth, Canavan, Meyer, and Higgs (1992) indicate that an assumption is made that victim trauma is minimal because generational boundaries have not been violated, and the age of the child who is sexually aggressive and the status of current laws render it difficult to assign legal responsibility.

Brother-Sister Incest

Brother-sister incest is thought to be the most commonly reported type of sibling incest (Loredo, 1982). This form of incest is well documented in the adolescent population (e.g., O'Brien, 1991) and also reported as occurring both before and at puberty (e.g., Pittman, 1987). From discussions in previous chapters of this book, it is clear that it is also fairly common among sexually aggressive preadolescent children. Brother-sister incest usually involves a range of sexual behaviors between an older brother and a younger sister, and the age difference between the two siblings varies.

Bank and Kahn (1982) define two general types of brother-sister incest. The first, "power-oriented incest," involves exploitation and co-ercion and deliberate attempts to do mental or physical harm. We consider this type of incest as sexually aggressive. The second type of brother-sister incest is described as "nurturance-oriented," mutually consensual behavior characterized by feelings of loyalty, love, and compassion.

Russell (1986) criticizes the examples provided by Bank and Kahn (1982). She argues that the authors fail to recognize the presence of coercion and lack of mutuality involved in any incestuous relationship.

Recognizing that children from emotionally impoverished families may turn to each other to meet emotional needs, Everstine and Everstine (1989) suggest that incestuous relationships, even when consensual with a small age difference, may be harmful. They also note that incest may cause difficulties in the formation of later romantic relationships. Due to the different ways males and females are socialized, Cole (1982) also questions whether incest between an older brother and a sister is really consensual or harmless. It seems to us that this gender-related rationale applies to brother-sister incest, even if the brother is the same age as the sister or younger.

In contrast to the objections noted previously, the following ideas tend to support Bank and Kahn's (1982) two-category notion of incest. Forward and Buck (1978) suggest that sibling incest may be harmless when, for example, siblings are young, close in age, do not have trust between them betrayed, the behavior is a result of curiosity and exploration, and the adults who discover the behavior do not traumatize the children. Additional factors that have been suggested for considering whether incest is harmless include children being of similar size, equal status, and engaging in sexual behavior considered typical for children of a particular age group (Gil, 1993a). Finally, the subjective interpretation of both siblings must be that the event was not exploitive or coercive.

Same-Sex Sibling Incest

To the public, same-sex sibling incest is considered particularly abhorrent due to societal taboos against incest as well as misconceptions that the behaviors represent homosexuality. Additionally, professionals

often consider same-sex sibling incest to be extremely rare, and this belief
has led to cases being unrecognized, mislabeled, or underreported (Kaslow, Haupt, Arce, & Werblowsky, 1981). Consequently, little is known
about the specific dynamics. In the case of sexually aggressive preadolescent offenders, more research in this area is definitely needed because
many of these children's victims are "victims of opportunity," in which
there is less emphasis on the sex of victims than in the cases of adolescent
or adult sex offenders.

In the majority of cases of same-sex sibling incest, the sexual behavior is initiated by an older sibling (Kaslow et al., 1981), although younger
children have been known to engage in sexually aggressive behavior
toward older siblings (e.g., Pomeroy, Behar, & Stewart, 1981). As is the
case with other forms of sexual aggression, children involved in same-
sex sibling incest may use some form of coercion to gain compliance
(Johnson, 1993c).

Among very young children, choosing a victim of the same sex is
not thought to imply homosexuality (Courtois, 1988) nor is it thought to
lead to children developing a preference for individuals of the same sex
(Forward & Buck, 1978). According to Johnson (1993c), sexual preference
may play less of a role in victim selection than the availability of a
particular child or jealousy based on perceptions a sibling has received
some kind of special treatment. Nevertheless, during treatment the issue
of the same-sex molestation deserves thorough discussion. Gil (1987)
cautions that children who choose same-sex victims often have general
concerns about sexuality and possibly questions regarding sexual identity. We do not believe, however, that this applies to very young children
who act sexually aggressive.

The majority of children involved in sibling incest do not tell anyone
about the abuse for various reasons. Examples include the perpetrator
using threats and coercion (Finkelhor, 1980), the perpetrator telling the
victim that he or she would not be believed even if he or she told (Daie,
Witztum, & Eleff, 1989), the victim not feeling parents would care enough
to stop the abuse (Laviola, 1989), and fears of being blamed or punished
(Laviola, 1992). Additional reasons given in cases of brother-sister incest
are victims feeling responsible for the abuse (Cole, 1982) and the sister-
victim having protective feelings toward a sexually aggressive brother
(Russell, 1986).

Furthermore, when children who are victimized do disclose, many
report detrimental consequences. The responses of parents may range
from telling the child not to tell lies to beatings and ostracism (Kaslow

et al., 1981). After studying emotional, physical, and sexual abuse among siblings, Wiehe (1990, 1991) found parents who do not want to deal with the abuse resort to "lashing out at the messenger." It is oftentimes easier for parents to ignore, deny, or blame the victim than to take the necessary steps to stop the abuse. When parents do not take measures to intervene, however, the messages given to both children (the aggressor and the victim) are unfortunate. The child who has been victimized learns parents will not provide necessary support and protection. The child who is sexually aggressive may begin to feel the parents either do not care about the abuse or somehow condone it. Consequently, sexually aggressive behavior may be reinforced, thereby increasing the likelihood of recurrence.

Intergenerational Incest

Intergenerational incest takes place when sexual abuse occurs in sequential generations within the nuclear and extended family. Additionally, these families may contain siblings and cousins who sexually aggress against each other, and family members may be sexually abused either concurrently or serially. In all cases, children who have been sexually or physically abused by family members are at risk for molesting younger or more vulnerable siblings (Green, 1988). Mathews, Mathews, and Speltz (1990) suggest some preadolescent females who are sexually aggressive may be intergenerationally predisposed. According to the authors, young females often choose victims who are relatives and who are close in age to their initial sexual abuse.

Two studies conducted by Johnson (1988, 1989) provide preliminary information on intergenerational incest in the lives of sexually aggressive children. The author reports many of the parents or grandparents of the children had themselves been sexually abused. Moreover, many of the sexually aggressive children reported a personal history of sexual abuse. The children named immediate or extended family members as the perpetrators, particularly in the case of females. In describing their first victim, sexually aggressive children often chose siblings or cousins.

The aforementioned studies indicate that sexually abused children continue the intergenerational cycle of incest by becoming offenders themselves. Children with no histories of overt sexual abuse, however, may begin to molest siblings. Often, children obtain knowledge of the original adult-child incest through either observing the event or hearing about it. Correspondingly, the youth sexually aggresses against the same child. This phenomena has been documented in preadolescent boys who sexually aggress against younger female siblings (e.g., Laviola, 1992; Smith & Israel, 1987). Boys who sexually aggress against younger sisters as a result of being aware of adult-child incest may view the sister as damaged and may be imitating the father (de Young, 1982). Kirschner, Kirschner, and Rappaport (1993) concur with this observation and suggest that this type of incest takes place in families in which females are devalued and powerless.

An additional characteristic of some incestuous families is what Sanford (1980) describes as a "women as property" mind-set. Evidence of this form of familial denigration of females is provided by case examples that describe preadolescent brothers "selling" or "trading" their sisters for money or favors (e.g., Canavan et al., 1992). In other cases, youths may begin "sharing" their sister(s) with friends (e.g., Cole, 1982).

In some families, more than one sibling may be involved in the sexual aggression. Documented case examples have provided evidence that two siblings may sexually aggress against a third (e.g., Forward & Buck, 1978), or a group of related children may victimize a younger relative (e.g., Johnson, 1993b).

Polyincestuous Families

According to Faller (1991), polyincest takes place when sexual abuse is found intergenerationally as well as across the extended family. The author notes that these families frequently contain multiple perpetrators, multiple victims, and instances of group sex. Oftentimes, those who are sexually abused, in turn, sexually exploit others.

The question arises as to whether polyincestuous families view sexual abuse as a lifestyle choice or normal occurrence. After studying a large number of polyincestuous families, Faller (1991) concludes that some families contain a member, typically an adult offender, who holds some type of belief system that justifies sexually abusing children. Of course, most are aware of large-scale organizations such as North American Man/Boy Love Association that promote sex between adults and children. Faller adds that many child victims of polyincestuous abuse reported distress over the abuse, and he further notes that the child victims may have expected to be sexually abused but did not want it to happen.

In Faller's (1991) study, the frequency of very young children sexually aggressing against other children was quite high. Although Faller does not break down the children into age groups, the mean age was 6.7 years, suggesting a young population. The author notes that in almost half of the families, at least one victimized child was sexually aggressive. In many instances, the polyincest was discovered after the children had exhibited sexualized talk or behavior in foster care (Faller, 1991).

Little is known about polyincestuous families and much less is known about children who sexually aggress in this context. Further research is required to examine the pathways by which children sexually aggress when incest is pervasive in extended family systems.

In summary, this section discussed the family contexts or situations in which intrafamilial sexual abuse occurs. As was readily apparent, family members generally have little respect for the emotional, physical, or sexual boundaries of others; a climate of intrusiveness exists. These families are characterized by numerous dysfunctions, coercion, and exploitation. Power is abused by older or high-status family members, and being younger or weaker exposes a person to sexual and physical victimization. Once a child is victimized, he or she may turn to victimizing others. The sexual abuse may take place indefinitely, and once an established pattern of sexual abuse is developed, the pattern often repeats itself over successive generations—that is, a cycle of abuse is perpetuated.

Abused and Sexually Aggressive Children in Extrafamilial Locations and Situations

Foster Care

Due to a history of abuse or neglect or both, some children are in need of a placement outside the home, such as in foster care. Children placed in foster care may have emotional, cognitive, and behavioral deficits related to their own abuse, their abuse of others, or a combination of both factors. Frequently, they also have medical, psychosocial, developmental, and school problems requiring intervention (Hochstadt, Jaudes, Zimo, & Schachter, 1987).

Sexual abuse victims in foster care may be at high risk for either revictimization or sexual acting out (McFadden, 1989). In some cases, sexual aggression may occur (Klee & Halfon, 1987), and the sexually aggressive child may be either a biological child or a foster child (Faller, 1990). In some foster families, more than one sexually aggressive child may molest (e.g., Brant & Tisza, 1977).

In addition to sexual aggression, abuse-reactive sexual behavior may occur in foster care and has been observed in children as young as 3 years old (A. Skversky, personal communication, December 1993). Foster care may offer a potentially sexually aggressive child the first opportunity to react to his or her own abusive victimization, and it is not uncommon to hear foster caregivers relate that child victims exhibited, to the best of their knowledge, their initial perpetrating activities after being removed from the home and placed in foster care. Hence, the question of the conditions under which to place sexually abused, sexually aggressive, or both children in foster care deserves attention.

In some instances, having one or more sexually abused children residing in the same foster family may inadvertently set up a situation in which children sexually abuse others (Faller, 1990). Similarly, placing physically or sexually aggressive children in the same foster home with younger children may result in abuse (McFadden & Ryan, 1991). Finally, foster care may not be appropriate to meet the needs of sexually aggressive children who continue to abuse and have chronic histories of multiple failed placements (Henderson, English, & MacKenzie, 1989).

Often, foster parents are uncertain whether their foster children have been sexually abused (Treacy & Fisher, 1993). Furthermore, some children may not disclose a history of sexual abuse until after they have been placed in foster care (Henry, Cossett, Auletta, & Egan, 1991), and many foster parents lack training in how to deal with such disclosures (Rushton, 1989). They also do not know how to handle the behavioral manifestations of sexual abuse or sexual aggression (Kehoe, 1988). Sexually abused children entering foster care may use sexual behavior as a way to test limits or receive comfort from foster caregivers (Roberts, 1986), and the intrusiveness of the sexual behavior taxes the knowledge, skills, and resources of even the most well-meaning foster parents (Treacy & Fisher, 1993). Many foster parents find sexually aggressive children too difficult to handle, or are unprepared to meet the numerous demands of working with these children or both.

Severity of behavior problems is one factor associated with continuous disrupted foster placements (Cooper, Peterson, & Meier, 1987), and any display of explicit sexual behavior in foster care may result in foster children getting shuffled from placement to placement (James, 1989;

Yates, 1982). The result of repeated moves through the foster care system is an escalating cycle of failed placements with limited options for the future. For these children, the choice of a new foster home placement may rest more with the availability of bed space than the placement being the most suitable one for a particular child. This sets up a circumstance whereby foster children may be revictimized or victimize others or both.

Adoptive Homes

Children over the age of 3 become available for adoption when parental rights are terminated for neglect or abuse (Berry & Barth, 1989). Individuals adopting these children should be aware that they (children) may have difficulties making attachments and bonding (Barth, Berry, Carson, Goodfield, & Feinberg, 1986) and may display psychological and behavioral difficulties resulting from trauma during early development (Kadushin & Seidl, 1971). Some adoptive parents report not being told about the severity of the child's emotional and behavioral problems prior to the placement (e.g., Barth & Berry, 1988). In some cases, adoption workers may be reluctant to disclose full details because doing so may hinder a child's chances for placement (Berry, 1990). Johnson (1990) stresses preadoptive evaluations should include information about the child's history as well as resulting emotional and behavioral problems. Furthermore, the author notes this information should be shared with potential adoptive parents.

Abused children may abuse others, place themselves in positions that increase the likelihood of reabuse, or misinterpret nonabusive situations (McNamara, 1988). Adoptive parents have reported difficulties dealing with children who are sexually active or display inappropriate sexual behavior or both (Valentine, Conway, & Randolph, 1988). In some cases, the sexually acting out of the child may arouse negative feelings among other family members, leading to disruption of the entire family system (Katz, 1977).

Adoptive parents have expressed the need to receive training to deal with sexual acting out and other problematic behaviors (Berry, 1990). McNamara (1990) suggests that parents adopting abused children be taught about the behaviors of traumatized children, how these behaviors relate to past abuse, and what interventions can be used to deal with them. In some cases, therapeutic interventions may be required to help the parents adjust their expectations of the child so there is consistency between parental expectations and the child's strengths and limitations (Winkler, Brown, Van Keppel, & Blanchard, 1988).

The need for adoptive parents to have training on how to deal with problematic sexual behavior as well as a variety of other issues is critical. Children who display sexual behavior problems in adoptive homes face disrupted placements (Ryan, 1990, 1991a). Having gone through a previous adoption disruption places the child at risk for subsequent disruptions (Barth, Berry, Yoshikami, Goodfield, & Carson, 1988). For some children, this could mean repeated moves through the system with limited opportunities for continuous exposure to healthy family life. Training for the parents coupled with therapy for the child and family can assist in maintaining the newly formed family unit.

Residential Treatment Centers

Typically, children enter group care after other options have been exhausted (Maluccio & Fein, 1983). Children may enter residential treatment from a variety of different living situations: Some may have been living with biological or extended family members; others are referred for residential treatment after repeated problems in foster care (Steinhauer, 1991) or adoptive placements (Cole & Donley, 1990); or children may enter residential treatment from group homes (Bagley & Shewchuk-Dann, 1991).

Children are referred to residential treatment centers for a variety of emotional and behavioral problems. Despite this, referral information for children who sexually aggress is sometimes inadequate. Although some children are referred for their sexually aggressive behavior (Nielson, Young, & Latham, 1982), in other instances sexual aggression is not listed as a primary reason for referral (Bagley & Shewchuk-Dann, 1991). This lack of accurate and complete referral information may have serious consequences for the sexually aggressive child as well as for other children in the residential treatment center.

For example, based on results from a study of 158 children between the ages of 6 and 11 who were in residential treatment for sexual and other problem behaviors, Johnson and Aoki (1993) offer the following cautions about children who molest in residential care:

1. There are children in residential care who caregivers consider to have very serious sexual behavior problems. These children

may force and coerce other children into sexual behaviors despite the best efforts of the staff.

2. When a child is identified as a perpetrator of sexual abuse, the agency must assess its ability to keep the other children safe.

3. Clinical information indicates that being molested by another child has serious consequences, and Johnson and Aoki (1993) indicate that this may be more true in residential care, where children are away from families and may feel especially vulnerable.

4. It is advisable for children who molest other children to be housed together, separate from other children.

5. Children who molest have many problems in addition to being sexually abusive. For example, they may be physically aggressive and attempt to dominate and manipulate others to meet their needs. When children who molest are housed together, a structured, instructive, supportive, and constructive environment and close supervision should be provided both day and night.

Similar observations to those of Johnson and Aoki (1993) have been reported by Araji, Jache, Pfeiffer, & Smith (1993) and Plach (1993). Attention to the previous information is important to prevent sexually aggressive children from continuing their molestations in residential treatment centers. Allowing the abusive behaviors to continue serves to reinforce patterns of sexual aggression in the sexually aggressive child and leaves other children open to victimization or revictimization.

Because child care workers in residential treatment centers spend the majority of their time working with the children, they are critical to the success of any treatment program (LeCroy, 1984). They are expected to deal with children's issues regarding sex and sexuality in a calm and unemotional manner (Lambert, 1976, 1977). As part of their duties, they may be called on to talk about and question children regarding incidents of sexual acting out (McNeil & Morse, 1964). They may regularly make decisions about whether children's sexual behavior is normal experimentation, an indicator of childhood disturbance, or whether the behavior is intended to provoke staff (Crenshaw, 1988). According to Johnson and Aoki (1993), the major reparative work staff need to be specially selected, trained, and supported to work with these children, and therapy should be focused on the sexually aggressive behaviors. Additionally, we believe it is important that child care workers in residential treatment centers receive ongoing training and supervision on the topics of childhood sex, sexuality, and sexually aggressive behaviors.

Parental involvement is important for all children in residential treatment. According to Krona (1980), parents should be actively involved in assessment, treatment, and discharge planning. Also, Carlo (1985) stresses the importance of parental involvement and support as a means of lessening the gap between the residential treatment center and the child's home environment.

Magnus (1974) has provided a list of ways that staff at residential treatment centers can involve parents in the child's treatment. First, parents must learn their own parenting roles and what has happened in the family that resulted in their child being placed in residential treatment. Second, parents should be treated as fully functioning and valuable members of the treatment team. Third, they should be given written information about the treatment program and their role in treatment. Fourth, parents will benefit from a tour of the center. Fifth, one staff member should be assigned the responsibility of coordinating information and treatment for the family.

Other suggestions by Magnus (1974) relate to duties that treatment center staff could perform to facilitate the treatment process. These include determining whether parents require transportation or information about social services they can access to meet basic living needs and whether some parents may require assistance with employers to attend meetings. Additionally, attempts should be made to arrange meetings when parents are available.

Another set of suggestions by Magnus (1974) relates to supports parents may require. First, parents of children already in care can serve as supports to parents whose children are just entering the treatment center. Second, weekly discussion groups for parents may provide a format for talking about relevant issues. Third, an open meeting time in which parents can discuss concerns may be beneficial.

A fourth set of suggestions relates to the treatment process itself. These include making parents feel welcome at the residential treatment center, encouraging visits when deemed as therapeutic. After visits, informal meetings with parents should be scheduled to discuss issues. Parents should participate in some unit activities to put their child's behavior in perspective and learn new ways to handle it. They should also do shopping and other tasks related to meeting their child's needs. They should attend some residential school sessions with their child to gain insight into how their child behaves, and family issues that are troublesome should be dealt with prior to the child's leaving the residential treatment center.

The involvement of parents (or primary caretakers) is critical to the process of working with sexually abusive children. For treatment gains to be maintained, these people must have a clear understanding of their child's sexual aggression and what can be done to help the child prevent relapse. Once this is accomplished, these individuals can assist their child to transfer learned skills from the residential treatment center to the home environment.

Not all children in residential treatment will return to live with their biological families (Maluccio, Fein, Hamilton, Ward, & Sutton, 1982). Some children leave residential treatment to live with relatives, in foster homes, adoptive homes, or another form of group care. As soon as the primary caretakers who will be taking care of the child have been identified, they should be involved in the treatment process.

Psychiatric Hospitals

Little is known about children who sexually aggress in psychiatric hospitals, and we were able to find only one related article. Kohan, Pothier, and Norbeck (1987) conducted a study of 110 inpatient child psychiatric units and found staff expressed several needs. According to the authors, these needs included (a) providing supervision so children do not sexually act out, (b) using intensive one-to-one staffing with some children, (c) avoiding placement of children in pairs that are nontherapeutic, and (d) designing environments that decrease opportunities for children to sexually act out.

Schools

Another extrafamilial environment from which sexually aggressive children choose victims is the school. Case examples indicate sexual aggression can take place in a variety of areas either within or near schools. Examples include school bathrooms (Gil & Johnson, 1993b), school buses (Cantwell, 1988), or while walking to and from school (Rogers & Tremain, 1984). Additionally, some children may sexually aggress on school playgrounds (Araji et al., 1993).

Children who sexually aggress in school settings are exhibiting behavior that requires intervention. In some instances, the behavior may be an indicator of their own sexual victimization (e.g., Fortenberry & Hill, 1986); in other cases, it may be an indication of some form of trauma or exposure to inappropriate stimuli.

Neighborhoods

As children get older, there is increasing independence from parental and caretaker supervision. Although parents usually set limits on the distances children may travel, most children are allowed to play near their own homes. Hence, when young children sexually aggress, they are usually not a long distance from their homes. Given this situation, it should not be surprising that some children molest others in their own neighborhoods if an opportunity arises (Araji et al., 1993). In these situations, a child may have no definite plan to engage in sexual aggression but may capitalize on an opportunity if he or she comes upon a circumstance in which it is unlikely adults will detect the child's behavior. In other cases, children may set out in a predatory manner searching for a victim. The same types of phenomena described previously may occur among a group of children who are wandering aimlessly in a neighborhood with no specific purpose or activity. For these children, teasing may lead to physical altercations that, in turn, culminate in sexual aggression. Groups of children, however, may set out in search of a victim or victims.

In Other People's Homes While Babysitting

Children may behave in a sexually aggressive manner when they babysit in the homes of others (e.g., Araji et al., 1993), particularly if they come from environments in which they have been victimized or witnessed sexually aggressive behaviors toward children. Babysitting allows a child to acquire a position of greater authority or status through which he or she can gain compliance of a chosen victim (Gil, 1993a).

Fehrenback, Smith, Monastersky, and Deisher (1986) studied 305 children and adolescents who engaged in sexual aggression. The authors found nearly half of the incidents took place during babysitting jobs in either the child abuser's own home or other people's homes. The authors identified three factors as characteristic of many sexually aggressive youth: (a) a willingness to babysit, (b) an availability to babysit, and (c) an ability to get along well with children. Not surprisingly, these are some of the very factors parents look for when choosing an ideal babysitter.

In summary, this section described some common extrafamilial locations and situations in which children have been known to sexually exploit others. There are other nonfamilial environments in which children act sexually aggressive but about which we have little information. The following list is included because we are aware of at least one example in which sexual aggression by children has occurred: churches, camps, and homes in which a sexually aggressive child's mother was a child care provider (Araji et al., 1993). Additionally, we are aware of situations in which victims reported being molested by other children in day care settings.

Summary

In summary, this chapter demonstrates the important roles that particularly familial environments play in the development of children's sexually aggressive behaviors. With respect to family dynamics, it is clear that practitioners and researchers must become more attentive to the role of covert abuse in the development of sexually aggressive behaviors. Our review of the literature indicates that this area is relatively ignored when compared with overt abuse but can have just as damaging consequences and lead to sexually abusive behaviors.

The information presented in this chapter also demonstrates that several practitioners are developing typologies of family environments that are conducive to promoting a range of normal sexual behaviors compared with sexually aggressive behaviors. The four typologies reviewed in this chapter were developed by Gil (1993b), Johnson (1993b), Ryan (1991b), and Larson and Maddock (1986). With the exception of Johnson, the four typologies reflected characteristics found in family environments of children already involved in deviant sexual behaviors. Johnson is the only one who discusses a range of family environments that include those that produce healthy, normal sexual behaviors (e.g., natural and healthy homes) to those that produce sexually abusive behaviors (i.e., sexually and emotionally needy homes, homes where sex is an exchange commodity, sexually abusive homes, and multigenerational sexually abusive homes).

Viewing all four typologies together, we grappled with the question of which environments are most likely to produce sexually aggressive children, the group of preadolescents that is the focus of this book. With the exception of perhaps types 1 through 3 in Johnson's (1993b) typology, all others shown in Table 3.1 should be considered risk environments. Those that appear to pose the greatest risks of linking sexual and aggressive behaviors together are those family environments in which covert or overt abuse exists that involves a combination of the following: (a) power imbalances are used to promote abuse; (b) children being used by parents to meet their own needs; (c) siblings using one another to meet their own needs; (d) children being physically or sexually abused or both by parents, other family members, or one another; (e) anger or rage emotions or both accompany physical or sexual abuse processes or both; and (f) intergenerational or polyincestuous abuse or both. This premise receives some support from Friedrich (1990), who reported that many of the sexually aggressive boys he worked with came from families described by Larson and Maddock (1986) as employing an aggression-exchange process. In these families, members expressed sexualized anger in the adult-child incestuous relationship or a rage-exchange process in which rage was a part of the exchange process and may be a part of the pathology of the adult perpetrator.

This premise is also consistent with Johnson's (1993b) observations wherein she indicated that sexually aggressive children are most likely to come from (a) sexually and emotionally needy homes (in which sex is used to meet the unmet needs of the adults, and children may be used to satisfy parental emotional and sexual needs); (b) homes in which sex is an exchange commodity (in which adults use sex as a way to gain material possessions and may involve children in the exchange); (c) sexually abusive homes (in which sexual abuse is perpetuated by one or both parents or another relative); and (d) multigenerational sexually abusive homes (in which sexual abuse simultaneously occurs in several generations across the nuclear and extended families).

In evaluating the role of the family in producing sexually abusive children, it is important to take note of Conte's (1986) critical analysis of the family system approach to the problem of sexual abuse. Although agreeing that to most effectively impact the sexually abusive child's future functioning it is important to understand as much as possible the family of origin, he cautions that the family system approach describes function and not causality. That is, some family dynamics may relate to the developmental history of individuals who become victims or perpetrators, some relate to the roles and interactions that become models for future relationships, and some relate to the system that allows or supports the occurrence of sexually deviant experience or behavior or both. Conte, however, indicates the need for clearly understanding and assessing the pathology of individuals within the family, the pathology of interactions within the family, and the pathology of extrafamilial systems. In doing so, he argues that a distinction must be made between those variables that are *causal* (contributing to development of generation of the problem), *supportive* (allowing or maintaining the problem), and *consequential* (resultant or reactive to the problem). He views the causal variables as basic to the change process of the behaviors or systems, the supportive variables as most relevant to relapse preventions, and the consequential variables as most critical to crisis intervention.

This chapter also demonstrated that sibling incest, a sexual relationship between at least two individuals who share one or both parents, is widespread but commonly ignored, minimized, or underreported even when parents or caretakers are aware of it. For various reasons, the majority of children involved in sibling incest do not tell anyone, and some of those who have disclosed report negative outcomes. These issues are especially important to recognize when preadolescents are the targeted sexually abusive group. Because of the extremely young ages of some sexually aggressive children, siblings may be the only available targets, as noted by Johnson (1993b). Thus, we believe more awareness and research on sibling incest is imperative. Without it, we will be unable to ascertain the extent of sexually aggressive youth who involve their siblings in abusive relationships, and we will lack an understanding of the specific environmental factors and dynamics that contribute to the problem. Furthermore, the degree of knowledge we have has implications for the development of appropriate theory and corresponding prevention, intervention, and treatment programs.

In addition to parents or siblings involvement or both in activities that lead children to becoming sexually aggressive, this chapter demonstrated the importance of being aware and understanding the contributions that intergenerational or polyincestuous families, or both, make to initiating or supporting or both sexually aggressive behaviors in children. As in the case of sibling abuse, the need for this knowledge has theory and practice implications.

Lastly, this chapter discussed the role that extrafamilial environments and situations play in the initiation or facilitation of sexually aggressive behaviors in preadolescent children. As noted by Conte (1986), and as demonstrated in this chapter, knowledge about extrafamilial environments is important to understanding and treating children's sexually abusive behaviors. Adoptive and foster parents, school personnel, parents who employ babysitters, and even professionals who come into contact with these children are in need of accurate and additional information about sexually abusive children. Without such information, too many potential or already acting out sexually abusive children will be placed in settings in which they can initiate or continue their sexual aggression. Without an awareness of what is going on, sexually abusive children will not get the treatment they need, may be continuously moved from one residence to another, and may be placed in situations that are conducive to increasing the populations of victims and potential perpetrators. They can also cause dysfunctions in family systems that may have previously been healthy.

In conclusion, this chapter has demonstrated that sexually abusive behaviors do not occur without cause or in a vacuum, and that familial and extrafamilial environments play a salient role in the development, maintenance, and treatment of such behaviors. Although most current information suggests that the family system is probably the most salient environment to consider in the case of children 12 years of age and younger, this chapter also demonstrated the need for a greater awareness of extrafamilial and situational factors that place children at risk. Without this information, we will be unable to develop appropriate theories and a body of knowledge that underlies prevention, intervention, and treatment programs that can effectively address children's sexually abusive behaviors. These issues are discussed further in Chapters 4, 5, and 6.

Note

1. Because the focus of this book is on sexually abusive and particularly aggressive behavior, the reader is referred to Johnson (1993b) for a breakdown and discussion of family environments of children who display healthy sexual exploration, sexually reactive behaviors, or engage in extensive mutual sexual behaviors. Briefly, Johnson reports that children with healthy sexuality may come from any of these homes but are most likely to come from family environments on the lower end of the continuum, particularly environments 1 through 3. Children with sexually reactive behaviors are likely to be found in family environments 4 through 8, 10, 11, or possibly 3. Extensive mutual sexual behaviors are likely to be found in family environments 6 through 11.

4

Theories Explaining Children's Sexually Abusive and Sexually Aggressive Behaviors

Sharon K. Araji

*It is imperative when working with aggressive and impulsive
children that practitioners understand the theory behind the
behaviors before initiating treatment.*
—Cunningham and MacFarlane (1996, p. 23)

A chapter on theory helps practitioners, researchers, and policymakers
organize ideas and make sense out of why children act sexually abusive
or aggressive toward others. Theory is also important to the development of appropriate prevention, intervention, and treatment programs.
In this chapter, I discuss and critique theories or models that have been
used to explain children's sexually aggressive behaviors and offer new
directions for theory development.

Theories Used to Explain
Children's Sexually Abusive/Aggressive Behaviors

In previous chapters, three levels of variables were identified that, when
linked together, form theories about how children become sexually

aggressive. These included (a) individual characteristics, such as intelligence, age, and sex, as well as physical, cognitive, and emotional development; (b) interactional factors at both the objective (e.g., actual interactions between family members) and the subjective levels (e.g., children's perceptions of the interactions); and (c) societal factors (e.g., cultural, group, or family values and norms, or all three, and other environmental variables) that influence children's patterns of thinking, feeling, and behavior. Although not always mentioned by practitioners or researchers, the variables that were linked together come from four related disciplines: biology, psychology, social psychology, and sociology. This is not surprising because sexual aggression is considered a multidimensional problem.

Developmental Explanations of Behavior

Developmental theory is widely used by practitioners and writers in their explanations of why children act sexually aggressive. As Chapter 1 demonstrated, most practitioners and researchers identify guidelines for what is considered normal sexual development at various ages and use this as a yardstick for measuring behaviors that deviate from these expectations. Using biological and psychological perspectives, children are seen as maturing physically in a relatively uniform sequence and, coinciding with this, engaging in certain normal sexual behaviors that correspond with various biological ages. At the social psychological and sociological levels, developmental theory focuses on the development of factors such as social and familial values, norms, organizational patterns and interactions, and media information that influence children's thinking and behaviors about sex and abuse. These factors are usually discussed in terms of the development of deviations from what society considers normative interactions between parents and children, between children themselves, and within the minds of children—that is, symbolic interaction.

In addition to focusing on stages of normal development patterns, developmental theory also encompasses the notion of disruptions that occur during children's development and how these disruptions help explain sexually aggressive behaviors. The disruptions that are the focus of many theories are framed in the context of traumatic events that include, among others, absent or disrupted attachments, sexual abuse, physical abuse, neglect, and emotional abuse. These experiences are viewed as having the potential to change the normally expected physiological, psychological, or sociological developments, or all three, in children's lives.

William Friedrich (1990, 1991) serves as a good example of a practitioner and researcher who uses developmental theory and the accompanying notion of disruptions in children's lives to guide his practice and research.

Friedrich (1990) contends that the age at which a disruption occurs must be considered because this is the starting point for determining long-term, developmental consequences. In many of his writings, he uses sexual abuse as the disruptive event that can distort the course of children's psychosexual, cognitive, and social development. In his view, disruptive events may predispose children to interpersonal difficulties by damaging their parent-child relationships and inhibiting social contact with their peers.

Friedrich's (1990, 1991) consideration of developmental factors related to sexual abuse begins with a discussion of children's cognitive development and how this is related to the way they appraise and respond to stressful situations. He discusses how children at various cognitive stages are more or less prone to particular coping styles, among which repression, denial, and increased aggression may be present. He also considers the relationship between children's development and the ages at which children tend to attribute blame to external or internal causes.

In addition to individual factors, Friedrich (1990) notes that families contribute to all aspects of the child's development and themselves go through developmental stages of organization and disorganization. Hence, family histories are viewed as an important variable in any analysis of children's behaviors.

Furthermore, Friedrich (1990) notes that the ability of children to manage critical developmental tasks depends heavily on the security provided by their primary caregivers. He refers to research and clinical observations that have shown that children with insecure attachments have an impaired sense of self, are less communicative of their feelings, and frequently form interpersonal networks that reinforce their poor self-images. In discussing family variables that may increase the risk of a child being sexually abused in a family, Friedrich cites research linking a number of family characteristics, including adolescent parenthood, marital instability, and depression in the mother.

When theoretically thinking about the role of the family in the development of children's sexual behavior, Friedrich (1990) stresses that the impact of the family is best described as reciprocal; family characteristics both precede and are influenced by children's sexual behavior. This idea was evident in Chapter 2 and, particularly, in Chapter 3, wherein the importance of the family as a variable in the study of sexually abusive behaviors in children was discussed.

Friedrich (1990) also calls attention to the gender factor, noting that socialization experiences shape the expression and direction of children's sexual interests. Because these experiences are likely to vary by gender, he argues that gender variations must be considered in understanding and treating sexually aggressive children. Although there is a sizable body of literature indicating gender differences among sexually abused populations (e.g., see Finkelhor, 1986; Porter, 1986; Summit, 1983), Young, Bergandi, and Titus (1994) compared the effects of sexual abuse on latency-aged children who had been sexually abused and found no significant gender differences on dependent variables such as aggression, submission, and depression.[1] These authors' findings seem to support research studies reviewed in Chapter 2, which indicated that among very young children males and females were about equally represented in numbers and levels of aggression used in sexually aggressive acts. Hence, it seems important to current theory development to identify ages at which gender begins to make a significant contribution to explaining differences between male and female children's sexually aggressive thinking and behaviors.

Application of some of Friedrich's ideas as they relate to sexually aggressive children is found in a case study about a sexually aggressive boy in his book *Casebook of Sexual Abuse Treatment* (1991). The major theoretical ideas expressed by Friedrich include (a) viewing the sexually abused child as a developing organism within a larger family system; (b) recognizing that abuse at one phase of development, if unresolved, can create new problems at other stages of development, and that children may organize their internal thinking and interpersonal relationships around the traumatic experience wherein the world increasingly becomes viewed as a dangerous place and victimization and victimizing become the norms; (c) assuming the sexual abuse, particularly incestuous abuse, represents a betrayal of a relationship and a disconnection in attachment and, if the disrupted attachment precedes the abuse, it makes the child more vulnerable to abuse; (d) being aware that when basic attachments are disrupted, the risk for psychological disorder significantly increases and, when sexual abuse is added to the disrupted attachment, the likelihood of problems is increased; (e) recognizing that the child and the child's system may carry within themselves the potential for adaptive coping and more positive outcomes; and (f) viewing the parent-child attachment as the paradigm for social development, along with its associated outcomes, including social skills, the capacity for empathy, and the capacity for self-observation.

Another example of the use of developmental theory and the role of disruptive events in the development of sexually abusive behaviors in children is found in the writings of Cunningham and MacFarlane (1991, 1996). These practitioners designed their original and revised manual for treating sexually abusive children around developmental stages in children's lives.

The first chapter of both manuals is devoted to children's sexual development. In fact, my review of existing literature indicates that, like Friedrich (1990, 1991) and Cunningham and MacFarlane (1991, 1996), most practitioners or researchers or both working in the area of sexually abusive children stress the need to consider developmental levels of children when attempting to understand them and develop intervention strategies. Most do not clearly articulate, however, how they apply developmental theory in their practice or research. This will become increasingly apparent in the remainder of this chapter and in Chapter 5, which focuses on intervention programs and practices.

Trauma Models

Because many sexually aggressive children have been victims of sexual abuse, most theories currently used to explain children's sexually aggressive behaviors employ as their central focus the notion that children are reacting to the trauma of being sexually abused. These theories or models cut across the broad psychological perspectives of behaviorism, learning theory, cognitive theories, and psychoanalytic theory, depending on what concepts are used to explain how resolution of traumatic events is processed. For example, if sexual activity is defined as "compulsive repetition," a psychoanalytic concept, behavior is linked to trauma at the unconscious level. When trauma is linked to such phenomena as dissociation, a psychological defense mechanism wherein there is an alteration of the normally integrative function of identity, memory, or consciousness, however, cognitive functions and the conscious level are the primary focus of attention. Most theories or models use an eclectic approach, drawing from many of the broader perspectives noted previously.

Traumagenic Dynamics Model

One trauma model that has been applied to explanations of sexually aggressive children focuses on traumagenic dynamics. This model was developed by Finkelhor and Browne (1985, 1986) as a means of tracing dysfunctional outcomes of child sexual abuse to four dynamics: traumatic sexualization, betrayal, powerlessness, and stigmatization. These researchers surmised that some combination of the four factors occurs in other traumatic experiences, but they contend that it is the coming together of all these dynamics that distinguishes the experience of child sexual abuse from other childhood traumas. The dynamics and long-term psychological consequences of each are (a) traumatic sexualization, which may result in sexual identity problems and aversion to sexual intimacy; (b) betrayal, which can create a lack of trust, fear of intimacy, dependency, anger, and hostility; (c) powerlessness, which might prompt children to dissociate, see themselves as victims in other areas of their lives, identify with the aggressor, and have difficulties with issues of power and control; and (d) stigmatization, which can lead children to experience feelings of isolation, guilt, shame, depression, and lowered self-esteem.

Finkelhor and Browne (1986) argue that for different children and different kinds of abuse, different interrelationships of the traumagenic dynamics are represented, and different psychosocial outcomes may be predicted. What all sexual abuse experiences have in common in this model, however, is distortion in the meaning and function of sexual activity so that for some victims sex becomes a way to satisfy interpersonal needs, whereas for others sex evokes terror, humiliation, pain, or guilt.

In applying the Finkelhor and Browne (1986) theory to understanding preadolescent molesters, Gil (1993c, pp. 55-56) highlights the first dynamic, traumatic sexualization, in discussing how the model is rooted in learning theory. She sees victims of sexual abuse being taught and therefore learning to behave in sexually inappropriate ways through repeated conditioning with positive and negative reinforcements—that is, the "shaping" process. Gil (1993c, p. 55) gives an example of this as an abuser exchanging attention or affection (positive reinforcement) or both for sex with a victim or withholding punishment (negative reinforcement) in exchange for sex. As a concrete case, she describes a child from her practice who was not allowed to sleep or eat unless she initiated and performed oral sex on her parent. Within this model, Gil contends that children learn to respond to specific stimuli in specific ways. In the case of children who molest, if coercion or aggression is part of the victimization conditioning cycle, then this is what we should expect them to learn and repeat as abusers. Gil sees one of the greatest attributes of the traumagenic dynamics model residing in the ability to make specific outcome predictions based on knowledge of a child's specific sexual abuse experiences. Gil's analysis of this process from a learning theory perspective is valuable because it allows researchers and practitioners to see how coercion and aggression can become linked to sexual behaviors.

Cunningham and MacFarlane (1996, pp. 140-141) also use the traumagenic dynamics theory in developing group treatments for addressing the issue of recovery from sexual victimization. The specifics of how this theory is applied, however, are left to the reader's interpretation.

Adaptation Perspective and Coping Theory

Friedrich and Luecke (1988) suggest, from their study of sexually aggressive children and several comparison groups, that the traumatic components of sexual abuse are related to behavioral symptoms noted in the Finkelhor and Browne (1986) model. That is, sexually aggressive children who were victims of sexual abuse did feel powerless and betrayed and were traumatically sexualized. Friedrich and Luecke, however, contend that the sexually abusive experience served primarily to add a sexualized channel to aggressiveness that was already emerging. The authors go on to say that the relationship between the Finkelhor and Browne traumatic elements and the outcome variables is not linear and is modified by what they call buffering or moderator variables. They propose an "adaptation model" as being more useful in understanding the relationship between the stressor of sexual abuse and the behavioral responses. The focus of the adaptation model is on moderator variables that would include both individual factors, such as IQ, cognitive abilities, language abilities, and the absence of psychopathologies, and interpersonal variables, such as parent-child relations, peer relations, and school performance and adjustments.

Within the adaptation perspective, Friedrich (1990) discusses his "coping theory," which is particularly concerned with those whose sexual disturbances are related to being victims of sexual abuse. He favors use of his coping theory in comparison to medical-based models, arguing that the latter are linear, individualistic models that fail to recognize that children differ markedly in their short- and long-term responses to sexual abuse. Explanations of the differences, of course, can be found by applying the adaptation model, which proposes that "buffering variables" affect the outcomes or consequences of children's sexual victimization.

Friedrich (1990, pp. 4-39) argues that his coping theory offers a more systemic approach to explaining the effects of sexual abuse because it attempts to integrate internal and external factors that may affect the impact of sexual abuse on the child. Included in the coping model are the child's individual and family characteristics and resources, patterns of family interaction, their social and physical context, their individual and family appraisals of the event, available coping methods, and the presence of predisposing or ameliorative variables in their environment. Coping theory, according to Friedrich, proposes a more complex approach to understanding the effects of sexual abuse, an approach that emphasizes the active nature of the child's and the family's response to traumatic experiences.

The coping theory discussed by Friedrich (1990) is composed of four sections, each necessarily interrelated but temporally distinct. The first section contains factors relating to functioning prior to abuse. It is the presence of these predisposing characteristics that explains the nonrandom occurrence of sexual abuse across family and income variables.

The second section entails the nature of the trauma, specifically describing the type, source, and number of sexually abusive events. It is assumed that there is wide within-case variability along these dimensions.

The third section, initial response, is viewed as particularly salient because it is argued that the way people initially appraise and respond to stressful events largely determines the emotional distress they feel and their ability to make adaptive responses. Coping theory suggests that these processes extend over time.

Long-term reactions, the fourth and final section of the model, show how the long-term outcome of sexual abuse is dependent on both preceding events and the opportunity for treatment. Friedrich (1990) indicates that the recent growth and attraction to the coping model is based on its intuitive appeal, sound correlational research, and a large body of clinical observations.

The adaptation and coping perspectives outlined by Friedrich and Luecke (1988) are valuable for several reasons. First, they direct attention to the historical nature of the behavioral problem. Second, and extremely important to understanding the process of how aggressive and sexual acts get linked together, is the idea that these children already have problems related to aggressive behavior and sexual abuse serves to add a sexual outlet to the existing aggressive behavior. Third, as attention is focused on both the family environment and the individual child, the systemic nature of the problem is recognized. Fourth, factors that may buffer the effect of abuse are identified that help explain variations in the short- and long-term consequences of sexual abuse. Fifth, the adaptation model has a systemic focus and thus represents a more comprehensive social psychological explanation of the effects of child sexual abuse compared with Finkelhor and Browne's (1986) more restrictive psychological approach.

Because of Friedrich and Luecke's (1988) attention to the family and buffering variables, I believe the adaptation and coping models could be further enhanced by encompassing a sociological model of how families cope with stress. Hill (1958) proposed a simple but powerful model that is widely referred to as the ABCX model of stress. According to this model, A (the event) interacts with B (the family's crisis-meeting resources), which interacts with C (the appraisal or definition the family makes of the event) to produce X (the crisis). This may be represented by $A \rightarrow (B + C) = X$. The two key dimensions in the formula are B and C. If both are adequate, it is hypothesized that the level of stress will be low or nonexistent. If one or both are inadequate, the level of stress will be high. McCubbin and Patterson (1982) and others have attempted to build on the Hill model by proposing a longitudinal model, referred to as the double ABCX model. This model differentiates precrisis and postcrisis variables, with the factor of time differentiating the precrisis from the postcrisis situation. The initial stressor event becomes a double A through separation of changes that occur irrespective of the initial stressor from those changes that result as a consequence of the family's efforts to cope with the crisis. The resources become a double B by differentiating those resources already available to the family from those coping resources strengthened or developed in response to the initial crisis situation. The perception and meaning become a double C by likewise differentiating the precrisis from the postcrisis perceptions of the level of stress. It is predicted that combining the pre- and postcrisis ABC factors leads to family adaptation or maladaptation.[2]

MacFarlane and Cunningham's Use of Four
Related Theories: Posttraumatic Stress Disorder,
the Sexual Abuse Cycle Model, the Addiction Model,
and Finkelhor's (1984) Four Preconditions of Abuse Model

Cunningham and MacFarlane (1996) stress the need for clinicians to be familiar with at least four related theories of human behavior when treating child perpetrators. These include posttraumatic stress disorder (PTSD) theory, the sexual abuse cycle model, the addiction model, and Finkelhor's (1984) four preconditions of abuse model. As can be seen from the descriptions in the following sections, these are also trauma-based models.

Posttraumatic Stress Disorder

Cunningham and MacFarlane (1991, 1996) use PTSD theory as one of the organizational tools for their preadolescent abuser treatment program and materials and note that, when applying the PTSD model to child perpetrators, it relates to children who were traumatized at young ages. In Eth and Pynoos's (1985, p. 14), *Post-Traumatic Stress Disorder in Children*, the authors defined PTSD in children as follows:

1. the existence of a recognizable stressor that would evoke significant symptoms in children. These include physical victimization, observing violence such as homicide, suicide, natural disasters, and war;
2. reexperiencing the trauma in at least one of the following ways: (a) recurrent and intrusive recollections, (b) recurrent dreams or nightmares, and (c) suddenly reexperiencing the traumatic event because of an association with an environmental stimulus;
3. numbing of responsiveness or reduced involvement with the external world—that is, internal or external withdrawal or both; and,
4. the presence of at least two of the following symptoms not present before the trauma: hyperalertness, sleep disturbance, guilt about surviving, trouble concentrating, and avoidance of activities that arouse recollections of the trauma. (p. 14)

Some strengths and weaknesses of the PTSD model have been identified by Finkelhor (1987) and Friedrich (1993b). Finkelhor (1987), although not specifically commenting on the PTSD theory as it relates to sexually aggressive children, supports the model because it locates the problem on an external stressor. He sees this as an opportunity to treat children without a stigmatizing label. On the critical side, he argues that the PTSD model is relevant to only a subset of symptoms in a subsample of sexual abuse survivors. Most important, for this chapter, is his recognition that PTSD represents a diagnostic condition, which is different from a theoretical model.

Friedrich (1993b), in an interview for *Violence Update*, criticized the use of PTSD models in the treatment of sexual victimization, arguing that it masks other factors (e.g., attachment and self issues) that are equally or more salient to understanding sexual victimization issues. I tend to agree with both of these researcher's assessments, although the value of the PTSD model for present purposes is that it directs attention to the fact that the initial trauma, even for sexually aggressive children, is not limited to sexual abuse.

Sexual Abuse Cycle Theory

In addition to using the PTSD theory, Cunningham and MacFarlane (1991, 1996) utilize the sexual abuse cycle theory to guide their understanding and intervention with sexually aggressive children. The notion of a sexual abuse cycle was developed in 1978 at the Closed Adolescent Treatment Center of the Division of Youth Services in Colorado by Lane and Zamora. The model is viewed as a construct representing cognitive and behavioral progressions occurring before, during, and following sexually abusive behavior. The theory describes a cyclical process because the behavior sequence is viewed as repetitive and it is theorized that previous offenses parallel and reinforce subsequent offense patterns.

Lane (1991b) identified several assumptions underlying the sexual abuse cycle, although only an abbreviated discussion is provided here. For a more in-depth discussion, the interested reader is referred to Chapter 8 in Ryan and Lane's (1991) book, *Juvenile Sex Offending*. Lane's assumptions include the following:

1. *Sexual abuse:* Sexually abusive behavior involves violation, exploitation, manipulation, or coercion of another. The behavior is not an impulsive act because the offender thinks about it before acting. The abusive behaviors represent a sexualized expression of nonsexual needs at another's expense.

2. *Power or control aspects:* Sexual abuse represents a need to control or have power over others, and the sexual abuse cycle is viewed as a maladaptive and dysfunctional power-based response to problems. When power or control responses are used as a method of problem solving, it deters the development of self-control or improvement in interpersonal coping skills. The power or control type of response style is easily habituated and interferes with the development of more socially desired coping and social skills. Power or control behaviors and thinking are expressed in both nonsexual and sexual ways, and the behaviors may be expressed in a passive or aggressive manner.

3. *Compensatory aspects:* Sexual abuse is viewed as a compensatory behavior because the sense of being in control or having power decreases anxiety and distress. The need for a compensatory experience is initiated by feelings of helplessness or lack of control associated with a triggering event prior to the offense.

4. *Arousal aspects:* Sexual excitement or arousal occurs prior to the acts while thinking about it or other sexual behavior and recall of prior offenses. Sexual behaviors are supported, and preferences are strengthened, when associated with sexual arousal. Because arousal and orgasm are both psychologically and physiologically pleasurable, they are self-reinforcing. As the associated arousal increases, the urge to engage in offense behaviors intensifies or becomes more frequent. Arousal is strengthened and sexual interest shaped by masturbatory behaviors associated with sexual fantasies. The arousal associated with sexual abuse fantasies or behaviors is viewed as compensatory in that it appears to reduce anxiety and enhance one's self-conception.

5. *Addictive aspects:* Because there is psychological and physiological reinforcement in sexually aggressive behavior, it may become an addictive disorder. Many young offenders demonstrate impulse-control deficits and report that urges or compulsions to engage in sexually abusive behaviors are difficult to manage.

6. *Cognitive aspects:* Adolescent sex offenders exhibit a variety of inaccurate and irrational cognitions or thinking errors. These cognitive distortions arise from inaccurate perceptions, assumptions, and conclusions about the world, and irrational beliefs or thinking errors shape the individual's perceived need for control or power, support cycle progression, and justify abusive sexual behaviors. The individual's thinking errors also influence how he or she appraise or interpret situations. Although there appear

to be common patterns of cognitive distortion that occur prior to sexual abuse, the development of specific distortions is unique for each individual. Through repetition, the individual's thoughts become ingrained and develop into a belief system that supports a habitual response to many situations.

Isaac and Lane (1990) adapted ideas from the sexual abuse cycle to preadolescents, and this adaptation is what Cunningham and MacFarlane used in their 1991 and revised 1996 treatment manual. The sexual assault cycle is shown in Figure 4.1. As can be seen, the cycle begins with a negative experience or feeling (a), then moves to wrong or negative expectations (b), then to a cognitively or behavioral isolation of oneself (c), followed by behaviors that involve feelings of anger and power or control behaviors (d). The next steps involve negative fantasies (e), followed by negative behaviors (f), which again lead to negative feelings (g). Finally, rationalizations or cognitive distortions about the experience are developed (h). Of course, the idea of a cycle is that these processes repeat themselves until effective intervention occurs.

In comparison with other theories previously discussed, this one defines sexually deviant acts similar to the way sexually aggressive behaviors are conceptualized in this book. That is, it employs the concepts of coercion, manipulation, and exploitation, as well as defining the behaviors in terms of power and control rather than impulsive acts. This is understandable, given that the sexual abuse cycle model was originally developed to explain adult males' violent sexual behaviors such as rape.

Another idea the sexual abuse cycle theory contributes to the understanding of sexually abusive behavior is that once the abusive act is repeated, it will continue until something intervenes to stop it. Although these authors do not explicitly identify use of exchange theory, it is clear that this theory is based on the notion that children will continue their sexually abusive behaviors until it is no longer profitable—that is, until the costs outweigh the rewards.

Violence and Fire-Setting Cycles

Cunningham and MacFarlane (1996) included within their chapter on perpetration two additional cyclical models that relate to behaviors associated with sexually abusive behaviors: a cycle of violence and a cycle of fire-setting. The cycle of violence model is shown in Figure 4.2.

SEXUAL ABUSE CYCLE FOR KIDS

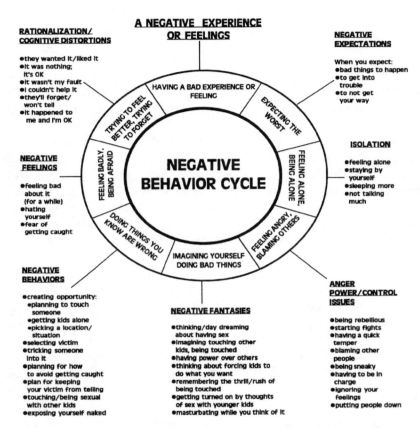

Figure 4.1. Sexual abuse cycle for kids. Reproduced from *When Children Abuse* by Cunningham and MacFarlane, 1996, with permission from the Safer Society Press, P.O. Box 340, Brandon, VT 05733-0340, (802) 247-3132.

As can be seen by comparing the sexual abuse cycle (Figure 4.1) with the cycle of violence (Figure 4.2), all major factors included in the two cycles are the same, with differences found only in the specific content of the negative fantasies, negative behaviors, and rationalization factors. For example, the sexual abuse cycle relates to sexual thoughts (fantasies) and behaviors, whereas the violence cycle relates to issues of power, control, and aggressive or violent fantasies and behaviors.

In contrast to the sexual abuse cycle and violence cycle models, the fire-setting cycle model relates to fantasies and behaviors about fire.

VIOLENCE CYCLE FOR KIDS

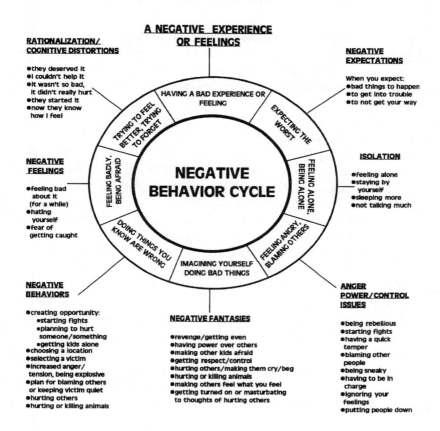

**RATIONALIZATION/
COGNITIVE DISTORTIONS**

●they deserved it
●I couldn't help it
●it wasn't so bad,
 it didn't really hurt
●they started it
●now they know
 how I feel

**A NEGATIVE EXPERIENCE
OR FEELINGS**

**NEGATIVE
EXPECTATIONS**

When you expect:
●bad things to happen
●to get into trouble
●to not get your way

**NEGATIVE
FEELINGS**

●feeling bad
 about it
 (for a while)
●hating
 yourself
●fear of
 getting caught

ISOLATION

●feeling alone
●staying by
 yourself
●sleeping more
●not talking much

TRYING TO FEEL BETTER, TRYING TO FORGET

HAVING A BAD EXPERIENCE OR FEELING

EXPECTING THE WORST

FEELING BADLY, BEING AFRAID

**NEGATIVE
BEHAVIOR CYCLE**

FEELING ALONE, BEING ALONE

DOING THINGS YOU KNOW ARE WRONG

IMAGINING YOURSELF
DOING BAD THINGS

FEELING ANGRY, BLAMING OTHERS

**NEGATIVE
BEHAVIORS**

●creating opportunity:
  ●starting fights
  ●planning to hurt
   someone/something
  ●getting kids alone
●choosing a location
●selecting a victim
●increased anger/
 tension, being explosive
●plan for blaming others
 or keeping victim quiet
●hurting others
●hurting or killing animals

NEGATIVE FANTASIES

●revenge/getting even
●having power over others
●making other kids afraid
●getting respect/control
●hurting others/making them cry/beg
●hurting or killing animals
●making others feel what you feel
●getting turned on or masturbating
 to thoughts of hurting others

**ANGER
POWER/CONTROL
ISSUES**

●being rebellious
●starting fights
●having a quick
 temper
●blaming other
 people
●being sneaky
●having to be in
 charge
●ignoring your
 feelings
●putting people down

Figure 4.2. Violence cycle for kids. Reproduced from *When Children Abuse* by Cunningham and MacFarlane, 1996, with permission from the Safer Society Press, P.O. Box 340, Brandon, VT 05733-0340, (802) 247-3132.

Because Cunningham and MacFarlane (1996) do not discuss how either the violence or the fire-setting cycles guide their theorizing about sexually aggressive children, however, I have chosen not to include a diagram of the fire-setting cycle in this chapter. The reason for including the violence cycle model and excluding the fire-setting model is that the children who are the focus of this book are behaving sexually aggressively. Hence, it makes theoretical sense to use the sexual abuse and violence cycle models together to address both the sexual and the aggressive or violent nature of these children's acts. The comparison can one to assess the extent to which it is the aggressive or violent component or the sexual component of the act that is most salient to the child's involvement in sexually aggressive behaviors or how the two types of behavior are related. I believe this knowledge is important, recalling that Johnson (1993c) found young children were not as likely as older children to use fantasies as part of their sexually abusive acts, but when they did, they focused more on the aggressive than on the sexual component of the act.

The reason for not including the fire-setting cycle diagram is that the theoretical link has yet to be established, although some researchers such as English and Ray (1991) found this behavior associated with young sexually abusive children. Cunningham and MacFarlane (1996, p. 184) also reported that, in one treatment program for abuse-reactive children, approximately 80% of the treatment population were fire starters, and, drawing on the work of Gray, Cunningham, and MacFarlane (1996), indicated that other clinicians and authors have noted the similarities and relationships between the behaviors of individuals who sexually abuse others and those of individuals who set fires. Both behaviors tend to be secretive, compulsive, fantasy bound, and cloaked in denial to others and to self. This denial is usually maintained by an assortment of thinking errors. Currently, however, more research needs to be done on why some children who are sexually aggressive may also be fire setters.

Four Conditions of Abuse Model

Cunningham and MacFarlane (1991, 1996) borrow from Finkelhor's (1984) four preconditions of abuse model the idea that the impulse to perpetrate or the actual perpetration behavior by children may be fostered in a family environment that lacks boundaries and controls that might compensate for children's lack of self-control. The following discussion demonstrates how these practitioners and researchers applied the four preconditions of abuse model to abuse-reactive children.

Considering the first of the four preconditions to abuse, motivation to sexually abuse, Cunningham and MacFarlane (1991, 1996) indicate that this motivation may be a reaction to a child's own abuse, a reaction that may be reinforced sexually during a critical time of sexual development. In addition, the abusive behavior may give the child a feeling of power and control over a victim. Hence, the abusive behavior satisfies a deep emotional need to alleviate feelings of vulnerability.

With respect to the second precondition, overcoming external inhibitors, Cunningham and MacFarlane (1991, 1996) indicate that most children do not sexually victimize others even when they have been victims of sexual abuse. Abuse-reactive children, however, may develop aggressive, sexual, and self-destructive thinking. In addition, many of these children come from families in which there are few role models exhibiting self-control. Thus, development of appropriate moral values is impaired, and they lack empathy.

Regarding the third precondition, overcoming external inhibitors, the family of the abuse-reactive child frequently lacks clearly defined boundaries and external controls that could compensate for the child's lack of internal inhibitors. The family may unconsciously place the abuse-reactive child in situations that encourage sexual acting out or they fail to provide adequate protection for young child victims. Such acts of commission and omission may occur because family members have been victims themselves and need the child to become the "identified patient" for the whole family. This could also explain why some children get singled out as "scapegoats."

Finally, with respect to the fourth precondition, overcoming the victim's resistance, Cunningham and MacFarlane (1991, 1996) state that abuse-reactive children generally pick victims who are younger, smaller, or less powerful. They also use coercion, bribery, or threats to break down the victim's resistance.

In comparison with other theoretical models previously described, this model offers a clearer delineation of both the internal and the external factors, particularly the family, that contribute to a child becoming sexually abusive. The fourth precondition, overcoming the victim's resistance, also speaks to the power-control variable and the aggressive component of sexually aggressive behavior. As with most other trauma-based theories, however, there is the strong implication that these children are reacting to their own sexual victimization. This tends to mask the important role that aggression may play in the development of children's sexually aggressive behavior, unless it is assumed that the initial sexual victimization involved aggressive or violent acts.

Addiction Model

The addiction model can be traced to learning theory and, as previously noted, has also been used by Cunningham and MacFarlane (1991, 1996) as a guide to developing preadolescent sexual molester treatment programs and materials. The authors argue that the addictive behavior model has its place in understanding the dynamics of child sexual offending because sexual preoccupation is one of the common reasons sexually abusive children come to attention in the first place, and family secretivism and massive denial keep many children from getting the help they need.

The addiction model focuses on the idea that sexual orgasm is a powerful reinforcer of sexual acts, and thus the behavior that brings this about may become addictive. To demonstrate why they believe the addiction model has a place in explaining the dynamics of preadolescent sexual offending, Cunningham and MacFarlane (1991, 1996) draw on the works of Carnes (1983), who applied the model directly to sexually related disorders, and Breer (1987), who applied the model to the treatment of adolescents.

Breer (1987) asserts that reinforcers of sexually inappropriate behaviors can occur as a result of specific sexual behaviors or in response to fantasies about molesting behaviors. He also hypothesized that adolescent offenders may use fantasies to work themselves up to the actual molestation behaviors. As shall be shown later in this chapter, Gray and Pithers (1993) include "arousal to abusive fantasy" as one of the compensatory responses of sexually abusive children. As noted earlier, however, Johnson (1993c) found that preadolescents do not engage in substantial use of fantasies, and when they do, they focus more on aggressive than sexual themes. Gil (personal communication, February 1994) generally concurs with Johnson, but notes that some practitioners she knows have found preadolescents who engaged in the use of sexual fantasies.

Carnes (1983) developed indicators of sexual addiction that included (a) preoccupation with sex or sexual thoughts, (b) ritualization, (c) sexual compulsivity, (d) secretivism, (e) sexual behaviors as pain relieving, (f) sexual activity devoid of a caring relationship, (g) despair and shame, (h) progressive addictions, and (i) massive denial. Cunningham and MacFarlane (1991, 1996) indicate that they used the addiction model to guide their development of intervention materials that focus on denial, taking responsibility for one's actions, making amends, scapegoating, and ritualization or compulsivity.

In discussing use of the addiction model, Cunningham and MacFarlane (1991, 1996) note that it has generally been associated with adults and in substance abuse treatment (alcoholism). They view the model, however, as a way of identifying and treating the early stages of repetitive sexually deviant behaviors before they become compulsive or addictive. They indicate that using the word "addictive" versus the psychoanalytic concept of "compulsive" is currently controversial, but they maintain that it is necessary to use some language and ideas from both schools of thought because neither model provides a sufficient framework for understanding preadolescent children's sexually abusive behaviors.

Eroticized Children

Somewhat related to the addiction model is what some call the "eroticized children" theory. For example, Gil (1993c, p. 57) indicates that Yates's (1982, 1987) behavioral theory about "eroticized" children can be useful in understanding very young preadolescent molesters. This theory relates to the conditioning process wherein a physiological response (eroticism) becomes linked to a sexual behavior. Basically, Yates's argument is that sexually molested children become sexually experienced and "highly eroticized" regardless of their age. Because sexual responsiveness does not require cognitive skills, even very young children can become eroticized. Yates, however, also directs attention to the family environments of molested children and asserts that separation anxiety, random physical abuse, or abrupt rejections intensify the importance of the sexual mode. Furthermore, Yates notes that many preschoolers fail to differentiate affectionate relationships from sexual relationships and become aroused by routine physical or psychological closeness. In addition, erotic expression becomes so gratifying that few comparable rewards satisfy this need. These children, she says, are often highly erotic, easily aroused, highly motivated, and readily orgasmic depending on the intensity or duration of the incest they have experienced.

In summary, the eroticized children theory appears useful when explaining sexually abusive behaviors of very young children who have the capacity of becoming sexually stimulated by certain sexual acts through stimulus response conditioning but who are not at the developmental cognitive stage to understand the act. It also draws attention to the role of the family environment in the conditioning process. It remains a rather narrowly focused theory, however, and is subject to some of the same criticisms that have been associated with the PTSD theory. For example, the notion of eroticized children represents more of a diagnostic condition than a theory and may apply to only a subset of children who have been sexually abused.

In combination, the addiction model and the eroticized children theory direct primary attention to the physiological aspects of sexually abusive behavior compared with the more cognitive and behavioral-based models. Nevertheless, cognitive and behavioral models such as Lane's (1991b) sexual abuse cycle theory incorporate these ideas in discussions of the arousal and addictive aspects involved in repetitive behaviors. What Yates's (1982, 1987) theory about eroticized children adds most to models, such as the sexual abuse cycle, is the role that physiological responses play in the earlier stages of sexual conditioning when children are not able to cognitively understand their actions. This is important to remember when attempting to adapt theories and models that have been developed on adolescent or adult populations. Finally, similar to most other theories discussed thus far, the addiction model and the theory of eroticized children may explain how and why deviant sexual behaviors develop, but they provide little insight into how the "aggressive" component of sexually abusive behaviors come about.

Trauma Outcome Process Approach

Rasmussen, Burton, and Christopherson (1992) have applied various sexual assault cycle approaches to their clinical treatment of children ages 4 to 12 who exhibit sexually abusive behavior problems. They also adapt Araji and Finkelhor's (1986) four-factor model that outlines preconditions for adults to be motivated to sexually abuse children. Furthermore, they delineate five factors that they believe are necessary for preadolescent children to sexually abuse others. These include prior traumatization, social inadequacy, lack of empathy, impulsiveness, and lack of accountability. In combination, they refer to this as a trauma outcome process approach. This model is shown in Figure 4.3.

Building on the sexual assault cycle literature, Rasmussen et al. (1992) conclude that having been sexually victimized increases the risk of children developing sexually abusive behavior problems, but this is not seen as a sufficient predictor. Rather, it is proposed that sexual victimization can lead to three possible responses to trauma: (a) Children can express and work through feelings associated with trauma to the point of acceptance (recovery), (b) children can develop self-destructive behaviors (self-victimization), and (c) children can identify with their aggressor and display assaultive behavior against others (assault). These possible trauma responses are viewed as overlapping with a child's level of sexual awareness.

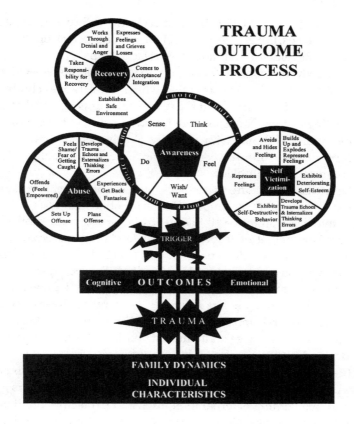

Figure 4.3. Trauma outcome process (Copyright © 1995 by Rasmussen, Burton, Christopherson, Bradshaw, & Brown). Used with permission.

According to Rasmussen et al. (1992), prior traumatization, which may be an actual molestation or other traumatic event, is an essential factor. The authors state that when anger from physical or emotional abuse or both is combined with sexual awareness, this can lead to sexual perpetration.

The second contributing factor identified by the authors is inadequate social skills, defined in terms of children who have problems interacting effectively with peers, who do not have adequate friendship groups or social networks from which they can draw support, or both.

The third contributing factor to children's sexually abusive behaviors is a lack of social empathy. This factor occurs in a relationship when a child uses another for personal gain or encroaches on another's "sense of self." Rasmussen et al. (1992) also discuss the ability to relate well on a superficial basis, but at a deeper level these children feel lonely because they cannot develop or maintain close relationships.

The fourth contributing factor identified by Rasmussen et al. (1992) is impulsivity, above and beyond that which characterizes children age 12 and younger. Fantasies about the sexual act minus factors that would inhibit acting out the fantasies were found in many of the children. For example, many children with sexually abusive behavioral problems were found to lack impulse control in areas such as stealing, attention deficit, and conduct problems.

The fifth contributing factor, lack of accountability, is a denial of personal responsibility for actions. This factor often manifests in the form of cognitive dissolutions or "thinking errors" or rationalization of one's behavior. This denial of responsibility extends to nonsexual types of actions. Rooted within Rasmussen et al.'s (1992) discussion of this contributing factor is a lack of consideration of others' feelings.

In addition to the five contributing factors noted previously that predispose children to engage in sexual perpetration, Rasmussen et al. (1992) note that Araji and Finkelhor's (1986) four preconditions, which are critical for adults to sexually molest children, are also applicable to some degree to children who molest.

These four factors include (a) motivation to sexually abuse, (b) factors predisposing to overcoming internal inhibitors, (c) factors predisposing to overcoming external inhibitors, and (d) factors predisposing to overcome a child's resistance. According to Rasmussen et al. (1992), these four preconditions continue to be valid for sexually reactive children to molest. The five contributing factors interface with the precursors and make children more vulnerable to committing sexually abusive behaviors than if they were not in place.

In Araji and Finkelhor's (1986) model, the first precondition for child molestation to occur by adults was labeled emotional congruence. Rasmussen et al. (1992) believe the concept of emotional congruence is not useful when discussing very young offenders because these children often offend against others with whom they are, by definition, emotionally congruent. Thus, they labeled the precondition "emotional arrest," replacing Finkelhor and Araji's "emotional congruence concept." The authors define this new concept in terms of children who have not moved beyond the experience of prior traumatization.

The second factor, "sexual arousal" of the type that would motivate children to molest, is unlikely to happen, according to Rasmussen et al.

(1992), without prior traumatization. This could include sexual victimization, exposure to explicit sexual stimulation from environmental factors, and other types of trauma.

With respect to the third factor in Araji and Finkelhor's (1986) model, blockage, it was found that children do become blocked in meeting their needs in similar ways as adults. They may become aggressive if they do not know how to meet their needs in acceptable ways. Inadequate social skills and lack of empathy are seen as potential factors leading to blockage in both adults and children.

Internal inhibitors (Precondition II) to offending may be present in young children, dependent in part on the development of appropriate ego boundaries that can be "invisible and symbolic." According to Rasmussen et al. (1992), these boundaries have three purposes: (a) to keep others from coming into one's space for the purpose of abuse, (b) to keep self from going into the space of others and abusing them, and (c) to give self and others a way to express "who we are."

Problems with boundaries are manifest in two ways in dysfunctional families: internally and externally. When families have difficulty relating to the outside world and become socially isolated, their problems with external boundaries may be manifest by inadequate social skills. When boundaries are blurred internally, a lack of intimacy may result. When children are molested at a young age, they grow up relatively confused about personal space. In addition, at early ages there may be an absence of cultural norms that would prevent children from acting on sexual impulses.

Rasmussen et al. (1992) believe that few adaptations to Araji and Finkelhor's (1986) model are needed with respect to the preconditions that relate to overcoming external inhibitors and another child's resistance. Like adults, children who are not closely supervised will have more opportunities to offend. Also, citing a clinical finding by Isaac (1987), these authors report that even young children may choose their victims. Similar to adult offenders, some children assess who is vulnerable and more willing to go along with a molestation without telling. Rasmussen et al. state that children in treatment groups often describe making friends with potential victims to set up offending opportunities. This is synonymous with what is referred to as "grooming" behavior in the adult and adolescent offender literature.

As can be seen in the trauma process model shown in Figure 4.3, Rasmussen et al. (1995) included a "family dynamics" factor. They indicate that this is an important contributor to their theorizing about the dynamics involved in the development of children's sexually abusive behaviors and to their program development (L. Rasmussen, J. Burton, & B. Christopherson, personal correspondence, September and October, 1996).

Considering all the theories discussed thus far, the one by Rasmussen et al. (1992) offers substantial insight into how children become sexually aggressive toward either self or others. First, it incorporates ideas from some of the theories previously described in this chapter such as the sexual abuse cycle theory. Also, like the PTSD model, it highlights traumatic events other than sexual abuse that might set the stage for the later development of sexually aggressive behaviors. The essential condition for sexually abusive behaviors to develop according to the Rasmussen et al. model is sexual awareness, not sexual abuse. The previous two ideas, combined with Friedrich's (1990) theorizing about how sexually aggressive behavior develops, provide important theoretical insights into understanding the processes involved in the development of sexually aggressive behaviors. That is, Friedrich hypothesized that the order in which children learn sexually aggressive behavior is that, first, they are in the process of developing aggressive behaviors and, second, they become exposed to some sexual event (sexual victimization or observation of sexual activities or materials) that provides a sexual channel for developing aggressive behaviors. Hence, aggression and sex became linked together. Further insight as to ordering of the variables is suggested in Rasmussen et al.'s (1992) discussion of how physical or emotional abuse can become linked with anger, and when this is paired with sexual awareness, the outcome can be sexual perpetration. Thus, if the sexual awareness component contains elements of aggression, one would predict sexually aggressive behavior.

Another contribution of the Rasmussen et al. (1992) theory is the focus on more than one outcome of sexual victimization—that is, perpetration. Instead, three outcomes are predicted: The child can (a) work through and recover from the traumatic event, (b) develop self-destructive behaviors, or (c) sexually assault others. These ideas mesh nicely with Friedrich and Luecke's (1988) adaptation model that was previously discussed. Recall that these two authors argued that buffering variables must be considered when predicting outcomes of sexual victimization because these factors influence how children react to being victimized. It also seems possible to attach the sexual abuse and violence cyclical models to the latter two outcomes. This could help determine if the aspects and contents outlined in the cyclical models are the same for self abusers and those who abuse others. Rasmussen et al.'s model could also be used to determine if there is a developmental sequence—that is, if children who abuse themselves later abuse others. Variations by age, gender, and life experiences could also be explored.

Incorporation of the Araji and Finkelhor (1986) model appears to be a good choice because it increases the explanatory power of the model due to the focus on both internal and external factors that deter or increase the risk of children becoming perpetrators. In this model, Rasmussen et al. (1992) suggest replacing Araji and Finkelhor's "emotional congruence" concept with "emotional arrest." Rather than replacing the concept, it might make more sense to modify it with a concept such as "emotional arrest/congruence." That is, when children are very young and choose similar victims and repeat only their own sexual victimization, emotional arrest may accurately describe the situation. It may also explain situations in which older children continue to repeat only their own initial victimization, including choosing a child that represents the age at which the initial victimization occurred and the type of sexual behavior. For children who change their selection of victims as well as initial victimization sexual behaviors, however, it seems that their choice of victims and forms of victimization may be more a function of emotional congruence than emotional arrest.

Finally, when working with very young children, it would seem more appropriate to discuss their perpetrating behaviors in behavioral terms such as "modeling" or "imitating" the perpetrator rather than "identification with the aggressor." The latter concept requires children to have a level of cognitive skills beyond those expected of very young children (e.g., see Mead, 1934; Piaget, 1928).

Balanced Approach

Technically, the balanced approach is a theory for developing an intervention program rather than a theory aimed at explaining children's sexually aggressive behaviors. Nevertheless, I include it in the theory chapter for a number of reasons, which will be discussed after the model is described.

Basically, the balanced approach is a holistic intervention for preadolescent children and is a modification of Relapse Prevention (RP), a theoretical tool developed by William Pithers and others to help adult

sexual offenders control their behavior in various situations and ultimately to change their sexually abusive acts. The model incorporates
affective, cognitive, and behavioral factors and emphasizes self-monitoring or self-control or both by the offender as a means to preventing
relapses.

According to Pithers, Kashima, Cumming, Beal, and Buell (1988), the
earliest signs of increasing danger in the RP model involve affect (feeling
moody or brooding). The second involves fantasies of performing a
deviant act that are later converted to cognitive distortions (e.g., use of
rationalization or minimization or both of contemplated act or attri-
bution of inaccurate perceptions or blame to potential victims). These
two processes culminate in the deviant sexual behavior. Using the RP
model, adult offenders are taught to identify the affective, cognitive, and
situational factors that precede the abusive act. Once these can be identified and controlled, it is reasoned that the deviant sexual act can be
stopped or prevented. The RP model and the sexual abuse cycle theory
previously described share many similarities.

The balanced approach considers the need to address both "victim"
and "perpetrator" issues. It also stresses the importance of both internal
and external variables when identifying at-risk factors or developing
prevention plans. Pithers et al. (1988) indicate that the issues addressed
in the balanced approach apply to both children who are sexually
reactive (victim focus) and children who are sexually abusive (perpetrator focus).

As in most other theories and models, use of the developmental
perspective is implicit in the balanced approach because Pithers et al.
(1988) caution therapists to be aware of the child's competence in attachment, moral reasoning, empathic ability, and autonomy. Also, like most
other theories or models described in this chapter, this one builds on the
notion that children are reacting to some trauma. This may include the
effects of sexual abuse, physical abuse, emotional abuse, neglect, sexualized environments, or role-reversed parenting. The philosophy underlying these practitioners' and authors' treatment plan are that children
have a need to heal from the abuses or situations previously described,
and treatment goals are best served when treatment is balanced across
victim safety, advocacy for personhood, and developmental competency.
Also, children must participate in an empowered way to prevent sexual
abuse, break the abuse chain, and accept an active role in changing
the abuse cycle. Hence, treatment goals are most effective when balanced across community safety and competencies in self-management
(A. Gray, personal communication, October 1996).

In discussing the balanced approach, Gray and Pithers (1993) use the three broad categories of risk factors or precursors to repeating sexual abusive acts that were identified in the RP model: predisposing, precipitating, and perpetuating. According to Gray and Pithers, predisposing risk factors are those occurring during early development or those that fall very early in the abuser's sequence of precursors. Precipitating risk factors generally occur shortly before the sexually abusive behavior and tend to determine that the type of abuse performed will involve coercive sexuality, whereas perpetuating risk factors increase the likelihood that sexually abusive behaviors will continue in the future (Gray & Pithers, 1993).

Four responses are identified that affect the degree to which each of the three risk factor categories influence children's sexually aggressive behaviors. These responses include (a) self-managed responses, (b) trauma-induced responses, (c) compensatory responses, and (d) external supervision. Each of these responses is viewed as leading the child victim or perpetrator to either safe recovery or to the abuse of others. Examples of risk factors and responses are shown in Figure 4.4.

Gray and Pithers (1993) indicate that the four categories interact to increase or decrease concerns about the sexually abusive child's risk factors and abuse deterrents. Over time, the child may progress or regress in one category or another.

Because the balanced approach is considered a prevention-focused model, Gray and Pithers offer four prevention structures to assist in resolution of sexually abusive behaviors. These relate to the four responses described previously and include (a) enhancing children's self-management skills, (b) resolving trauma from the offender's own victimization, (c) addressing compensatory reactions related to exhibiting problematic behaviors that are connected to difficult emotions, and (d) increasing the degree that prevention team members model abuse-prevention beliefs and intervene when abuse-related behaviors are seen (these are discussed further in Chapter 5). In summary, the balanced approach has a prevention focus that emphasizes affective, cognitive, and behavioral characteristics associated with children's sexually reactive or aggressive behaviors. It focuses on controlling behaviors from within the child (self-management skills) and from factors in the environment (the prevention team). Because the balanced approach has its roots in the concept of Relapse Prevention, its focus is on preventing children from repeating sexually abusive behaviors by identifying three sets of risk factors, a set of four related responses, and four preventions connected to the response categories.

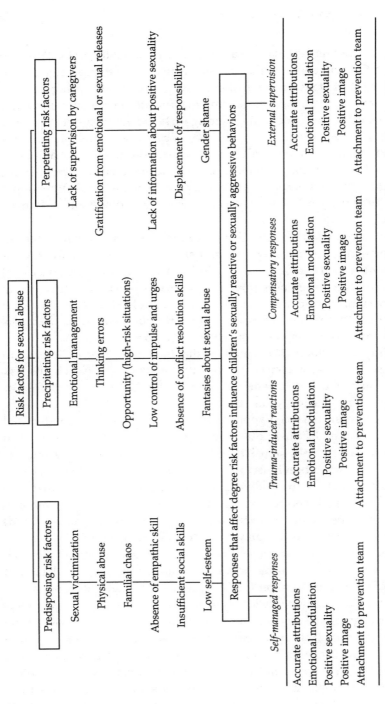

Figure 4.4. Balanced approach's three categories of precursors with four types of responses that can lead to positive or negative outcome. Information derived from Gray and Pithers (1993). Figure reviewed by Gray and Pithers (January 1997).

I return to the reasons the balanced approach was included in this chapter. First, this is the only theory that specifically states it is a prevention-focused model, although prevention in this case is tertiary because its focus is on preventing children from relapsing once abusive behaviors have begun. Second, inclusion of the "prevention team" concept focuses researchers' and practitioners' attention to the role the child's external environment played in introducing the child to sexually abusive behaviors and, hence, the role it must play in intervention of the issues related to victimization and prevention of repeating perpetrating sexual behaviors. The theoretical ideas connoted are that if the problem arose in a system that provided an environment with poor role models and one that was conducive to creating trauma in the child, which in turn led to the development of cognitive and emotional patterns conducive to the child's perpetrating behaviors, then the internal and external environments that prevent these behaviors must replace the dysfunctional ones. Hence, implicit in the balanced approach is the need for a systemic approach to resolve victim issues and prevent sexual perpetration from recurring.

The second contribution of the balanced approach is its recognition that the child is at the stage of being both a perpetrator and a victim. Hence, an understanding of the interaction between these two statuses is necessary.

Third, the prevention team concept was not mentioned in other models, and it is especially important when focusing on very young children, given the model's emphasis on self-monitoring. As a prevention tool, self-monitoring would be restricted to children who have the cognitive skills required to process, reflect, and evaluate their actions and to recognize the danger signals identified in the model. Until these stages are reached, much of the behavioral control would need to come from the external environment—that is, the prevention team.

Linking Sexual Trauma and Sexual Aggression in Preadolescent Children

The current weakness in most theories discussed in this chapter is that they tend to explain children's sexually abusive behaviors as a result of sexual traumatization. How the "sexual" and "aggressive" components become linked together is not specifically addressed, although Gil (1993c) attempted to explain this by applying learning theory to the

"sexual traumatization" factor in Finkelhor and Browne's (1986) traumagenic dynamics model. Rasmussen et al.'s (1992) trauma outcome
process approach was also very informative concerning how sexual and
aggressive behaviors could get linked together. A review of literature,
however, indicates that Friedrich (1990, pp. 251-254) has done the most
groundbreaking research in explaining this linkage. He drew on several
general theories to demonstrate how sexual trauma and children's aggressive behaviors can get connected. First, he applied behavioral research on aggression and delinquency, using Bandura's (1977) work on
"modeling." Basically, Friedrich proposed that children who see aggressive behavior "model" or imitate it. Predisposing variables are being a
male, being less socialized, and coming from punitive families.

Borrowing another behavioral concept, "paired associate learning,"
Friedrich (1990) notes that when aggression is paired with an affective
response that is pleasurable (e.g., release of neurotransmitters) aggression is reinforced. If sexual aggression generates positive affect from both
aggressive and sexual activities, then the reinforcement value is com-
pounded, increasing the likelihood of recurrence.

Next, Friedrich (1990) notes that social learning perspectives can also
contribute to understanding the development of aggression and conduct
problems over time because sexually aggressive children tend to be
oppositional or conduct disordered. He draws on Patterson, DeBaryshe,
and Ramsey's (1989) research to indicate that this antisocial behavior is
frequently related to disrupted family management skills and adds that
parental substance abuse increases risks. Children's antisocial behavior
also increases the risks of academic failures and rejection by peers who
value prosocial behaviors. These factors increase parental rejection and
the child's developing loss of self-esteem. Although Friedrich does not
mention it, his discussion clearly demonstrates his idea about the reciprocal nature of family-child interaction that was discussed earlier in this
chapter (see case study of the sexually aggressive boy).

Drawing from the psychodynamic perspective, Friedrich (1990) discusses how children internalize representations of their external experiences. When confronted with similar situations in the future, these
internalized experiences guide their interaction. Hence, children who are
sexually abused will internalize the experiences into their behavioral
schema and eventually into their sense of self, which serves as a guide
to interactions with others. Friedrich notes that this idea is similar to the
developmental psychology concept of a "functional map of relationships."

The sum total of the child's interactions is seen as being incorporated into the child's emerging self. The degree to which interactions are not overly exciting increases the likelihood of being incorporated into some type of coherent sense of self. If they are overstimulating or overly exciting, however, it is predicted that they will be split off and will not be incorporated but will remain a part of the child's potential behavioral response pattern. Friedrich (1990) indicates that it is at this juncture of information processing that the more traditional formulations of dissociation and primitive defenses come into play. These "split-off" experiences are dissociated or kept out of awareness. This is why some believe that people who act in a dissociative state are unaware of what they are doing. Their understanding of themselves precludes the existence of these behavioral choices. It is viewed as a "not me."

More specific to traditional views of ego defense mechanisms are the processes of undoing and identification with the aggressor. Although the latter concept can be seen from social learning terms as directly related to modeling (the child is abused and thus abuses), Friedrich (1990, p. 252), citing Schafer, views identification with the aggressor as a more likely consequence for children who are temperamentally prone to be active rather than passive.

The next theoretical perspective that Friedrich (1990) draws from is developmental theory, especially affective, cognitive, and social development. First, focusing on affective and cognitive development, he uses the concept of empathy to explain why this may be absent in sexually aggressive children. He notes that empathy has both cognitive and affective components and is one of five core moral emotions. Empathy means reacting to another's feelings with an emotional response, but to react, the child must first accurately recognize the other's feelings—that is, take the role of the other. For young children, the cognitive ability to discern another's feelings is quite limited. Their empathic responses will increase in frequency and scope only as they become more cognitively developed. Friedrich (1990, p. 253), citing Danon, says that empathic dysfunctions can create the conditions for serious antisocial behavior.

With regard to the social development factor (e.g., socialization and peer relationships), Friedrich (1990) notes that lack of socialization and failure to accept rules of normal behavior are common in sexually aggressive children. Because the socialization process begins in a child's first significant relationship with the parents, and most typically the mother, failures in parent-child attachments contribute to the child's failing in relationships with peers. Instead of learning how to negotiate or compromise, the child learns an inconsistent and sometimes explosive pattern of relating. Because the child is frequently criticized and degraded, he or she learns how to criticize and degrade.

In conclusion, Friedrich's (1990) work adds much to our understanding of how the sexual and aggressive components get linked together. In the next section, I examine several articles that demonstrate how aggressive behaviors develop and the role physical abuse plays in this process. These articles are viewed as important because the literature review, as well as conversations with providers, suggests that for sexually aggressive children, physical abuse may be an equally or more important factor than sexual abuse with respect to explaining the aggressive component of their sexually aggressive behaviors. This seems true for both males and females at early ages, and particularly true for males as they become older, due to sex role socialization.

Linking Physical Abuse to Sexually Aggressive Behavior

Fatout (1990)

Fatout (1990) uses developmental and psychoanalytic theory to ground her research, tracing the roots of abnormal levels of aggressive behavior in children to problems in the normal developmental cycle. Focusing specifically on the latency period, she cites research that places this stage at a time when ego functions are being formed in response to social expectations and demands. Some of the specific areas that are modified and reorganized during this time are (a) the defensive structure of the ego and (b) the aggressive drive. Fatout notes that with respect to the defensive structure of the ego, the result should be increasingly calm and controlled behavior. In regard to the aggressive drive, mechanisms of restraint, such as sublimation, symbol and fantasy formation, obsession-compulsion activities, and repression, emerge as the primary defenses developed during the latency stage. Fatout indicates that disturbing or traumatic experiences during latency are incorporated in symbolic stories and fantasies.

Following this discussion, Fatout (1990) cites numerous research studies that link aggression in children to their history of physical abuse. She notes that the environments of these children have not been predictable, and many of their basic needs have not been met—that is, they have been neglected. Several of the areas that are negatively affected by these experiences are the sense of basic trust and a sense of self or identity. The outcome, she argues, is a child who is burdened with many deficits that set the stage for frustrating experiences. These experiences, in turn, lead to aggressive feelings with which the child must cope. Fatout cites a number of studies that demonstrate that physically abused children act significantly more aggressive to peers and self, and their fantasies and play reveal more aggressive themes than comparison groups. Some studies also reported gender differences, with males acting more aggressive, subject to the degree that parents have stressed traditional gender roles.

Green (1985)

Green (1985) has discussed the consequences of children traumatized by physical abuse, which is defined as the repeated infliction of physical injury by a parent and is accompanied by psychological abuse. Similar to trauma theories related to sexual abuse, Green outlines the impact of physical abuse on children, and it is informative to note the similarities.

The findings that form the basis of Green's (1985) writings are derived from clinical studies of approximately 50 abused children and their families. Data were obtained during play therapy and during psychotherapy.

The vast majority of families came from inner cities and only 20% of the children lived in intact families. Demographically, 65% were black, 25% were Hispanic, and 10% were white. Almost half had been removed from the home at one time or another. The profile of families included a parent-child relationship and family environment described as pathological and a climate described as harsh, punitive, and lacking empathy.

In his research, Green (1985) hypothesized that the real or threatened physical and psychological assault creates a state of "traumatic neurosis" that leads to ego disorganization and narcissistic injury and is viewed as activating primitive defense mechanisms and a need to repeat the trauma. Using a case example to demonstrate this progression, Green indicates that severe abuse results in the child feeling helpless and panicky, which results in a severe ego regression that is manifest in (a) loss of ego boundaries, (b) psychotic disorganization, and (c) suspension of reality testing. Other primitive defense mechanisms found associated with physically abused children were avoidance and distancing behaviors, raising of sensory thresholds, denial, projection, and splitting.

In Green's (1985) discussion of avoidance and distancing behavior, he indicates that living in acute physically abusive environments can compromise learning. Noting that a significant percentage (25% of 60 abused children) of children in his sample were found to be mentally retarded and, citing other studies with similar findings, Green indicates that when children's receptor functions used in processing information from the environment are overtaxed by the need to continually identify danger, this conditioning leads to intellectual impairment as well as speech and language disorders.

With respect to repetition of the trauma, Green (1985) indicated that the beatings these children received permeated their dreams, fantasies, play, and object relationships. Sometimes this was demonstrated in the form of being the "victim" of abuse (passiveness), and at other times the children modeled the parent abuser as a way of controlling the painful effects and anxiety created by the abuse. The long-term impact of harsh and punitive child-rearing techniques, scapegoating, and neglect was outlined by Green, and many of the characteristics identified are similar to those found associated with sexually aggressive children's life experiences—for example, scapegoating, neglect, and harsh, punitive physical punishment.

A final concept discussed by Green (1985) is the role of retraumatization. Once a child has been consistently traumatized by some form of abuse, Green indicates that the child remains in constant fear of its recurrence. In this state, the child becomes very sensitive to external stimuli that in any way resembles the abuse. The external signals can trigger old feelings of helplessness or panic and activate defense responses that represent either fight or flight. Green notes that these responses may become overgeneralized to many situations throughout the child's life cycle and indicates that many abused children exhibited symptoms of PTSD.

Although it is obvious that much of Green's (1985) theorizing and observations about the connection of physical abuse to the development of aggressive behavior in children overlap with Fatout's (1990), there is one addition that is important for present purposes. Recalling that most sexually aggressive children also had learning problems, Green adds insight on how these develop and states that they are more a function of living in a punitive, harsh, and dangerous environment than innate characteristics. That is, Green indicates that when children are placed in a position of continually processing information in their environment to identify danger, this leads to an overtaxing of the processing systems and subsequently to intellectual impairment as well as speech and language disorders.

Fraser (1996)

Fraser (1996) uses an ecological development perspective that emphasizes an opportunity structure that provides positive social interactions and skills necessary for prosocial relationships with peers and adults who are committed to conventional normative behaviors. He draws from the research and writing of Maas (1986), who has argued that an ecodevelopmental view emphasizes processes through which people learn to interact competently and responsibly across a variety of situations, recognizing others' as well as self's needs. Maas indicates that the greater the number of contexts with which people can cope, the fewer the situations in which they are overwhelmed by feelings of helplessness and stress. Furthermore, the more they engage in socially responsible interaction, the more they contribute to or sustain a caring and sharing society.

Fraser (1996), citing a number of studies, indicates that confrontation with authority and aggressive behavior have serious consequences from toddlerhood through adolescence. He notes, however, that multicultural studies indicate that the consequences vary by "type of aggression" and age. For example, two types of aggression were identified in these studies and each elicited a different response from children. Reactive aggression involved the defensive use of force. When children were perceived by peers as using force to defend themselves, they were usually viewed positively. Proactive aggression, however, involved the nondefensive use of force. When children initiated proactive aggression, it was viewed negatively by peers who valued prosocial behavior. Children who were proactively aggressive, however, regarded physically coercive acts as socially effective. They considered it normal to employ force to obtain the use of a toy, swing seat, wagon, and so on. They effectively used aggression and coercion to meet instrumental goals. In short, for these children, use of aggression was rewarding.

Fraser (1996) goes on to say that research shows that proactive aggression varies by age. He notes that first graders appear to be more accepting of this type of aggressive behavior than second and third graders. Among the socially accepted children in the latter two groups, problem-solving behavior without physical coercion is expected. Children who continue to use proactive aggression in the second and third grades are likely to be rejected by peers who are beginning to practice and expect "prosocial" social skills.

Fraser (1996) also notes that rejected children are more likely to escalate aggression when they perceive themselves as the object of aggressive acts such as teasing. They are quick to fight and slow to use negotiation, bargaining, and problem-solving skills. For girls as well as boys, the result is increasing rejection by other children. In summary, Fraser indicates that continuing to use proactive aggression has the consequences of isolating children from learning opportunities in socially skilled and prosocial peer groups and increases the risk of subsequent problems in the school and community.

Finally, Fraser (1996) identified a group of social factors such as poverty, which he argues increases stressors that impede effective parenting and problem solving. He also identified individual factors that could contribute to children's aggressive behaviors. These include imbalances of hormones such as testosterone, low IQ, impulsivity, and attention deficit disorders. Because of learning impairments, children may be pushed from early childhood into circumstances that increase the risk of poor school adjustment and achievement, association with aggressive or socially rejected children, and early experimentation with sex and drugs.

On the basis of past research, Fraser (1996) indicates that much individual variation exists in the pathways that lead from early childhood aggressive behavior to violence, but the combination of two factors, (a) adjustment problems and (b) rejection by peers, is sometimes called the "early starter" model.

In summary, from the ecological development perspective, youth aggression is seen as the result of an impoverished opportunity structure, inadequate training in critical social and cognitive skills, and the perception that there are more social and concrete rewards in aggressive behaviors than in prosocial behaviors. Furthermore, based on a review of literature, Fraser (1996) notes that the conditions, processes, and experiences in the family, more than any other social setting, shape children's behaviors. He indicates that research suggests that in some homes children are trained literally, although unintentionally, to respond to authority with hostility. The sequence of events that reinforce aggression in families is inconsistent parental supervision of children, use of harsh punishment, failure to set limits, neglect in rewarding prosocial behavior, and a coercive style of parent-child interaction.

In conclusion, it is evident that Fatout's (1990), Green's (1985), and Fraser's (1996) lines of thinking are very compatible with one another; in addition, Fraser's ecological development perspective increases our understanding of how the aggressive behaviors children learn in the family are carried into peer and school relationships and the negative consequences of the interactions. In addition to the commonalities between the Fatout, Green, and Fraser studies, the thinking of these authors is also very compatible with Friedrich's (1990) theorizing about how sexual and aggressive components can be linked together to produce children who act sexually aggressive. These articles, in combination with other information in this chapter and other chapters in this book, offer insights into the development and linkages of the aggressive and sexual components in children's sexually aggressive behaviors.

Systems Theory: A Proposal

As theories or models were reviewed in this chapter that are used to explain children's sexually aggressive behaviors, common links between them, how they built on or extended one another, and their strengths and weaknesses were discussed. When these theories and models are assessed as a whole, in combination with the literature reviewed in prior chapters, I concluded that a more comprehensive approach to explaining children's sexually aggressive behaviors is necessary. The theory that seems to best address this need is systems theory. Although no researchers or practitioners explicitly cited this as a theory that guided their understanding of sexually aggressive behavior or the development of prevention and treatment plans, it is implicit in their thinking and writings. For example, in discussing the theory that guided his treatment of a sexually aggressive boy, Friedrich (1991) talked about the boy as a developing organism within a larger family system. In Friedrich and Luecke's (1988) adaptation model, they discuss sexual abuse as a systemic problem. Many of the theories and models connect the internal world of the child (affective, cognitive, and behavioral) with the child's external world, generally the family. Some practitioners and researchers, such as Gil (Gil & Briere, 1994), L. Rasmussen (personal communication, September 1996), B. Christopherson (personal communication, October 1996), and A. Gray (personal communication, October 1996), are beginning to refer to systems theory in their workshops as an approach that is needed to provide a comprehensive understanding of children's sexually aggressive behaviors.

Systems theory became less popular with family therapists in the past decade because it was seen as removing the responsibility of the abuse from the offender (Ryan, 1991c, pp. 51-52). I believe, however, the review of theoretical literature on sexually aggressive children in this chapter, in addition to material presented in previous chapters, indicates that it is an important theory to consider. That is, almost all the information I reviewed directly connected the problems sexually aggressive children exhibit to their families and other social groups or institutions (e.g., Cunningham & MacFarlane, 1991, 1996; Friedrich, 1990; Gil, 1993c; Gray & Pithers, 1993; Johnson, 1993c; Rasmussen et al., 1992). Also, unlike adults or many adolescents, many of these young children continue to live in their families and their treatment plans require family participation.

The basic principles of a general systems theory as applied to the family have been offered by Roberts (1994, Chapter 1). Herein, systems theory emphasizes the wholeness of a system in which the whole is seen as more than a sum of the parts. Explanations of individuals' behavior are considered in the context of the whole system because all parts are considered interdependent and related to one another with repeatable patterns. When applied to the family, it is assumed that all family members are tied together in ways that make individual explanations for behavior less than complete. The systems theory assumes that a change in any one family member will affect change in other members.

In addition, this theory views the family as a social group that is governed by rules and norms that are derived from particular cultures and passed down from one generation to another. The rules define such factors as who controls what resources and the division of power. Family rules are also seen as governed by "meta-rules" that take the form of unstated family directives for interpreting or changing rules.

An important concept to system theories is family boundaries. These are viewed as either physical or emotional barriers that distinguish individuals and families and regulate the amount of contact between them. Three types of physical, mental, or emotional boundaries are discussed. These include clear boundaries that allow for adaptation and change, rigid boundaries that restrict adaptation and change, and diffuse boundaries that allow for too much adaptation or change.

Families are further viewed as having a hierarchy, or an organized structure, that dictates who assumes what roles and responsibilities.

These hierarchies can include, among others, such factors as power-control relationships that vary from authoritarian (child has no control) to authoritative (democratic), to laissez-faire (parents provide minimal or no direction or control). The authoritative type is viewed as most healthy.

The concepts of family homeostasis and morphogenesis are considered important to understanding family behavior. On the basis of the assumption that a system attempts to maintain stability or balance, the homeostatic process is viewed as the practices that families use to maintain a sense of well-being when confronted with internal and external changes. Morphogenesis refers to changes that actually take place within a system.

Roberts (1994, pp. 20-21) draws on the writings of such researchers as Boulding (1975), Bertalanffy (1968a, 1968b), and Bronfenbrenner (1979) to argue that the isolation of the family from the larger social network results in placing too much importance on family relationships. Citing statistics such as increasing divorce rates and larger numbers of households being considered nonfamily, Roberts (1994) contends that it is apparent that the family is not the all-encompassing system affecting individual behaviors. The family and the individual cannot be completely understood apart from the society and culture in which they reside. Cultural symbols are viewed as important in analyzing the functional and dysfunctional behaviors of family members.

Bronfenbrenner (1979) developed a model for describing the family in the context of the larger environment and labeled it the human ecological system. The first level of this system is the microsystem, or the interactional relationships within the family. The mesosystem refers to the interactions among various systems, such as the family, workplace, school, peer group, and neighborhood. The third level is the ecosystem, or the major institutions of society (e.g., the family, religions, education, and economic institutions). The fourth level, the macrosystem, is a system of symbols in that behavior is highly influenced by cultural values and expectations.

In conclusion, the previous discussion is obviously a "thumbnail" sketch of systems theory. I believe, however, it is adequate to envision how it could incorporate most of the ideas presented in this chapter and the material reviewed in previous chapters. The major contributions of the systems theory, for present purposes, are that it situates explanations for children's sexually aggressive behaviors within both a micro- and a macrointeractional context and focuses on circular rather than linear causality. As a sociologist, it is, of course, my belief that what is currently known about the factors that contribute to the development of children's sexually aggressive behaviors demands social psychological and socio-logical approaches to the problem rather than continued reliance on primarily psychological theories.

Conclusions

In this chapter, I discussed and critiqued theories and models being used to explain children's sexually abusive behaviors. The first conclusion is that the word theory is used very loosely. Most theories presented in this chapter do not represent theories but only extractions of bits and pieces from general psychological theories or even treatment models that have been developed for adults and adolescents. Thus, the information re-viewed herein represents inductive rather than deductive approaches to explaining children's sexually aggressive behaviors.

Second, many of the theories and models being used to explain children's sexually aggressive behaviors are adaptations of approaches used to explain or treat or both adult or adolescent perpetrators. Al-though theory or model developers caution that children's developmen-tal stages must be considered, it is usually not clear how this is incorpo-rated into their theoretical thinking. Furthermore, the extent to which this practice is valid and reliable remains unclear. Cunningham and MacFarlane (1991, 1996) note, for example, that theoretically derived intervention activities remain virtually untested. Also, with few excep-tions, this means that there is little empirical data to render assurance that appropriate theoretical orientations are being applied to the devel-opment of assessment and treatment tools used with sexually aggressive children.

Third, the primary concept that connects most of the theories and models is that children who are abusive are reacting to the traumatic event of being sexually abused themselves. Hence, the driving force behind most of the theoretical ideas or models is that sexually abusive children are only reacting to their own sexual abuse, although some theories indicate that their models apply to both sexually reactive and other sexually abusive children who may not be victims of sexual abuse.

Fourth, because the theories remain strongly focused on the sexual component, there is little explanation or focus on how the aggressive component develops. Some noted exceptions to this were Friedrich (1990), Gil (1993c), and Rasmussen et al. (1992). Theories that attempt to explain children's sexually aggressive behaviors must demonstrate specifically how the linkage between the sexual and aggressive components occurs.

Fifth, information reviewed in prior chapters raised the question of how abuses, such as physical abuse, neglect, and psychological abuse, fit into the development of sexually abusive and aggressive behavior because it was consistently reported that sexually aggressive children were the object of multiple abuses of greater severity than children who exhibited other sexual behavior problems. This curiosity was heightened by statements from researchers such as Friedrich (1990), who theorized that the first step in the process was that children were already developing aggressive tendencies and exposure to sexual experiences or materials provided a sexual channel for the aggressive behaviors.

As a result of Friedrich's (1990) ideas and those offered by researchers and practitioners such as Gil (1993c) and Rasmussen et al. (1992), I explored the physical abuse-aggressive behavior connection. This led to the review of articles written by Fatout (1990), Green (1985), and Fraser (1996). These articles, similar to literature that focused on sexually aggressive children, stressed the role of harsh, physically abusive families that had other dysfunctions such as substance abuse. This material, combined with the theories and models that focused on sexual abuse and aggression, and the information reviewed for previous chapters, confirmed a growing concern that a more comprehensive theory was needed to explain how children developed sexually aggressive behaviors. As a result, a brief overview of the systems theory was presented.

Finally, the starting point for developing an appropriate theory about children whose acts represent a sexual and an aggressive component is to begin with a concept that specifically describes the behavior. I believe this concept is sexually aggressive, as noted in the Introduction. Continued use of concepts such as sexually reactive, sexually aggressive, sexually abusive, and sexual behavioral problems interchangeably is not conducive to identifying, understanding, and treating young sexually aggressive children. John Hunter (personal communication, June 16, 1994) warns that all sexually aggressive children are not victims of sexual abuse, and reliance on the victimization assumption tends to narrowly focus many theoretical explanations (and treatment programs) on victimization rather than on perpetration issues. Hence, I reiterate the message of Chapter 1—that is, it is important to view children's sexual behaviors on a continuum wherein the wide variety of their behaviors can be studied and appropriately identified and labeled.

Notes

1. Group means were in the expected directions and significant differences between "abused" and "nonabused" groups were found.

2. For more information on the ABCX model of stress and the double ABCX model, the interested reader is referred to Hill (1958), McCubbin and Patterson (1982), and Lavee, McCubbin, and Patterson (1985).

5

Redirecting Children's Sexually Abusive and Sexually Aggressive Behaviors

Programs and Practices

Elizabeth A. Sirles/Sharon K. Araji/Rebecca L. Bosek

The previous chapters demonstrated efforts over the past 10 years to identify a variety of issues surrounding children's sexually abusive behaviors as well as theories or models that have been employed to explain these acts. The past decade also ushered in a growing recognition that some sexually abusive children and their families require intensive intervention. Although the clinical literature, like the theoretical literature, continues to remain limited, programs attempting to provide services for this group of children are emerging. An overview of various programs and practices that are used by therapists who are working with sexually abusive children and their families is the focus of this chapter. Limitations of the overview are also discussed, chapter information is summarized, and a list of factors that can aid in program development and treatment planning is offered.

Overview of Programs, Agencies, and Private Practices

As noted in the Introduction, the Safer Society Program has been conducting nationwide surveys on adult and juvenile treatment programs and models since 1976. They reported no survey responses about available programs or models for sexually abusive children until their 1994 survey. At that time, 390 programs were identified in the United States: 352 were community based and 38 were residential (Freeman-Longo,

Bird, Stevenson, & Fiske, 1994). The number of specialized treatment programs for sexually aggressive children, however, appears to be much smaller. Gil and Briere (1994) and Lane (1991a) estimate that there are approximately 35 programs, whereas Johnson (1993a) proposes only 12 specialized treatment programs currently exist that serve sexually abusive or aggressive children. Whatever the actual number, there is general agreement that sexually aggressive children and their families need services to address dysfunctional and destructive behaviors.

In this chapter, an overview of 10 treatment programs or practices serving sexually aggressive or abusive children under the age of 13 is provided. These programs and practices were identified by searching the available literature, attending workshops, and personal correspondence with providers working with children who are sexually abusing others. Our aim in these descriptions is to provide examples representative of current treatment and practice trends. Although the review is not exhaustive, it offers summaries of small- and large-scale efforts to address the problem of preadolescent sexual abuses. The actual terminology employed by practitioners is used in the program and practice descriptions. This strategy provides an understanding of the various ways therapists view this group of children.

Program summaries identify theories used to guide treatment processes and major goals for intervention. As one would expect from information in previous chapters, there is an attempt to address the complex and interactive nature of children's cognitive thought processes, affective and physiological development, behavioral aggression and sexual acting out, and family dysfunctions associated with children's sexually abusive behaviors. Some treatment modalities are described for target populations.

Programs and Practice Developments

Support Program for Abuse Reactive Kids (Los Angeles, CA)

To the best of our knowledge, the first documented attempts at systematic group treatment began in 1985 when Kee MacFarlane developed the California-based Support Program for Abuse Reactive Kids (SPARK)[1] at the Children's Institute International, a private, nonprofit child abuse treatment agency. The term *abuse-reactive* was used to describe a population of children who had experienced some form of abuse and were reacting to the resulting trauma in a sexually unacceptable manner (Cunningham & MacFarlane, 1996). Group treatment was provided for children between the ages of 4 and 13 who had committed sexual offenses against other children.

In an attempt to share some of the treatment techniques gleaned from working with the first group of children and their parents through the SPARK program, MacFarlane and Cunningham (1988) published *Steps to Healthy Touching*. This publication represented the first manual focusing on treatment techniques for both children who displayed sexually abusive behavior and their families. Subsequent publications, *When Children Molest Children* (Cunningham & MacFarlane, 1991) and *When Children Abuse* (Cunningham & MacFarlane, 1996), updated these practitioners' original work and include valuable information on treatment planning and implementation for sexually abusive children and their families.

The treatment approach used in the SPARK program was derived from theories based on posttraumatic stress disorder, the addiction model, and the sexual abuse cycle (Cunningham & MacFarlane, 1996). The authors report using concepts from the four traumagenic dynamics of child sexual abuse (Finkelhor & Browne, 1986) as well as the four preconditions of abuse (Araji & Finkelhor, 1986). The result of this integration of ideas is a primarily cognitive and behavioral program, blending elements from a variety of theories and concepts into a comprehensive framework.

The SPARK program treats children between the ages of 4 and 13 who have molested other children. Group therapy is the primary treatment modality, with separate groups held for (a) children who molest, (b) siblings with a history of victimization, (c) siblings without a history of victimization, and (d) parents (Johnson & Berry, 1989). Program coordinators Diane Griggs and Frederique Pierre, along with their colleague, supervising psychologist Sandra Ballester, indicate that most children and their parents complete at least 1 or 2 years of treatment (Ballester & Pierre, 1995).

In the SPARK program, group treatment goals for the reactive child relate to the following topics: (a) assessing the specific antecedents to sexual acting out for each child and discussing family dynamics that facilitate or perpetrate acting-out behaviors, (b) developing social skills, (c) increasing self-esteem, (d) developing an internalized locus of control, (e) feeling recognition, (f) addressing a personal history of victimization, (g) decreasing impulsive behaviors, (h) empathy development, (i) gaining mastery over problematic behaviors, and (j) identifying and utilizing resources. The acquisition of new skills is used to decrease sexualized behavior and generalize healthy behaviors in other settings.

For the most part, groups for other family members are held concurrently. Parent groups focus on the same major issues as those identified for their children (Griggs & Boldi, 1995). Topics covered in the group for parents include (a) educating the parents so that they feel empowered while negotiating within the legal, law enforcement, child protective services, school, and child care systems; (b) providing child sexual abuse education to the parents; (c) assisting parents with supervision of the reactive child and victim; (d) providing general child development information; (e) assisting parents in distinguishing between normal versus abuse-reactive behavior; (f) helping parents develop insight into family dynamics and recognizing how these dynamics contribute to the manifestation of reactive behaviors; (g) assisting parents with parenting skills and behavior management issues; (h) assisting parents to normalize fears, shame, and humiliation; (i) strengthening the family's support system and resources; and (j) assisting with the development of appropriate expectations of treatment goals. Parents may use the group format to discuss personal unresolved abuse issues and pertinent issues regarding parenting.

In cases of sibling incest, the group for the victimized siblings places an emphasis on preventing the recurrence of sexual abuse (Johnson & Berry, 1989). The group for siblings who have not been victimized provides support and treats issues relevant to these children. Although the primary focus of the program is on group treatment, individual, couple, and family therapies are offered when clinically indicated.

A major strength of this program is the inclusion of all family members in the treatment process. Clinicians incorporate multiple theoretical perspectives to build a comprehensive approach to treatment. Clever adaptations have been employed to modify treatment strategies for adolescent sexual offenders to the developmental level of abuse-reactive preadolescent children. These efforts represent the beginning treatment services for younger children.

STEP Program, Center for Prevention Services, Underhill Center (Williston, VT)

The STEP program[2] draws information from the fields of cognitive and behavioral, child development, and child sexual abuse theory, and also uses information from theoretical models on sexual offense cycles and relapse prevention (Gray & Pithers, 1993). Relapse prevention is the focus of treatment, with an integrated model for identifying risk factors and teaching internal and external control of behavior. The result is a prevention-focused program with a cognitive and behavioral orientation directly addressing childhood sexual behavior problems. The STEP program staff have modified their Relapse Prevention approach to treating sexual perpetrators so it can address the needs of younger children who exhibit sexually abusive behaviors but who may also be victims of sexually abusive behaviors. This was described in Chapter 4 under the section "The Balanced Approach" to treatment.

Services are provided for children between the ages of 6 and 12 using group therapy as the primary treatment modality. Children are divided into groups by age, taking care to ensure materials are presented within the appropriate cognitive and developmental levels. Groups are held for parents because they are viewed as an integral part of the prevention team and therapy processes. The treatment for children and parents lasts up to 32 weeks.

The STEP program identifies several possible treatment goals for the children's group, with topics relating to (a) forming agreements, (b) improving safety, (c) learning self-management, (d) making healthy decisions, (e) gaining self-esteem, (f) developing sexual attitudes consistent with age, (g) making choices that contribute to abuse prevention, and (h) developing positive friendships. Learning adaptive skills and taking measures to prevent relapse are considered key components of the treatment process. The risk factors associated with the prevention structures were discussed in Chapter 4.

Parents are an important part of treatment in the STEP program and are encouraged to fully participate as members of the prevention team (Gray & Pithers, 1993). Group treatment goals are relevant to issues parents face when dealing with their child's sexual behavior problems. Goals for parents may focus on (a) reducing isolation, (b) gaining support, (c) developing stress-management skills, (d) increasing parenting skills, (e) furthering personal knowledge of childhood sexual behavior problems, and (f) learning to take care of personal needs.

As previously discussed, Gray and Pithers (A. Gray, personal communication, October 16, 1996) are currently conducting research that examines the effectiveness of two different treatment approaches. The first of these is called the sex abuse specific treatment (SAST), which focuses on a modified relapse prevention approach. The second is called abuse prevention treatment (APT). This approach focuses on a variety of topics, including assertiveness, self-esteem, decision making, healthy sexuality, and building positive relationships. Groups are held for 6- to 9-year-old children and those 10 to 12 years of age. Children are randomly assigned to treatment groups.

Children's group goals may include (a) risks and strengths, (b) improving safety, (c) forming agreements, (d) learning self-management, (e) healthy decisions, (f) gaining self-esteem, (g) developing sexual attitudes consistent with age, (h) making choices that contribute to abuse prevention, and (i) developing positive friendships (A. Gray, personal communication, October 16, 1996). Learning adaptive skills and taking measures to prevent relapse are considered key components of the treatment process (see Figure 4.4).

SAST Sexual Abuse Prevention Treatment Curricula

The curricula included in the SAST prevention treatment include the following: (a) Orientation-Introductions/Setting Boundaries/Setting Group Rules; (b) What Is a Sexual Behavior Problem? Part One: Setting Up Sexual Safety Rules, and Part Two: Setting Up Sexual Safety Rules: Rewards and Consequences; (c) Emotional Risk Management; (d) Positive Self Image; (e) Giving Up Sticky Thinking; (f) Cycles and Steps; (g) Managing Risky Factors: Recollections, Urges, Lapses (Slides), and Relapses (Act Outs); (h) Positive Power; (i) Building a Prevention Team; (j) Responding to Body Arousal (Fear, Anger, and Sexual); (k) Nurturing Healthy Sexual Development; (l) Loss and Trauma (History, Effects, Compensatory Behavior); (m) Loss and Trust (Stages of Grief, Practice Good-byes, Self Trust); (n) Respecting Sex Abuse Consequences and Victim Impact, Moral Development and Stages to Empathy, Amends to Others; and (o) Prevention Plans—Where We Started and Where We Are Now, Review Accomplishments and Surprises, Reset Goals, Good-byes.

SAST Children's Group Format

The SAST group format includes a joint weekly review and goal-setting 30-minute session in which children and parents meet together to complete a weekly checklist and report any lapses or relapses from the past week and time is provided for setting goals. The caregiver and child get together with the therapists and pair up with another caregiver and child.

Fifty-five minutes are devoted to the children's group. This is broken down into the following areas and time allotments: Review the last week and report problems or lapses with peers (20 minutes); lesson or activity and homework (20 minutes); snack and clean-up activities (10 minutes); weekly evaluation (5 minutes); and closing circle that involves children and parents. In the closing session, the participants identify "one thing I like; one thing I am thankful for; and one thing I learned."

APT Abuse Prevention Curricula

The curricula for the APT program include the following topics: (a) Introductions/Safety Boundaries/Group Rules/Goals; (b) Touching Rules; (c) Appropriate Sexual Behavior (Definitions and Respectful Language); (d) Emotional Management (Being Brave With Feelings); (e) Sorting Out Effects of Sexual Abuse (Tough Stuff Speak Out); (f) Self-Esteem and Shame (Being My Own Best Friend); (g) Anger Management (Letting Go of Stuffing, Storming, and Cheating); (h) Decision Making (Using Assertiveness in Decision Making); (i) Taking Perspective (How Do I Feel and How Do You Feel?); (j) Choosing Friends (Safe Friends); (k) Healthy Sexual Information I (Getting Clear); (l) Healthy Sexual Information II (Getting Clear); (m) Values and Roles (Brave Beliefs Can Strengthen Safety); (n) Best Safety Problem Solving; (o) Safety Success and Assertiveness; and (p) Celebration and Good-byes.

APT Child Group Format

The group format for the children's groups in the APT program includes therapeutic play and expressive therapies such as puppetry, clay, therapeutic games, and art therapies in workbook form. These therapies are employed to address developmental needs of children. Theme-based weekly activities are designed to build a child's self-esteem, to strengthen their decision-making and problem-solving skills, and to increase their socialization and attachment development. The group opens with self-soothing and interpretive storytelling followed by weekly self-report on sexual safety rules.

APT Parent Group Format

The APT parent group format is designed to provide weekly support to parents in a 1½-hour-long group facilitated by a therapist. The approach is empowerment based and not intended to be "expert focused." Each week, individual goals are set, weekly progress is shared, and problem solving is discussed in an atmosphere of peer support. Targeted change is self-initiated and the therapist facilitator encourages individual and group problem solving.

In the groups, parents learn to identify abuse characteristics and abuse effects and to nurture healthy sexual development. Rule setting for problem sexual behavior is discussed. Nurturing parent experiences in group are considered essential to acquiring healthy reattachment skills. The nature of sexual reactivity in children is described, and relationships with children that build esteem and secure attachments in the face of sexual acting out are encouraged.

In summary, the STEP program offers highly specific interventions that provide a useful guide to formulating a system-based treatment approach to sexually abusive behaviors by young children because it includes the prevention team concept. Also, if needed, children and parents may be referred to individual, couple, and family therapy outside the agency.

William Friedrich (Rochester, MN)

William Friedrich is a theorist, therapist, and leading author on the subject of sexually reactive and sexually aggressive children (e.g., Friedrich, 1990). Over the years, he has worked with many sexually abusive children and their families. His theoretical perspective and pioneering work was extensively reviewed in Chapter 4. As the reader will recall, Friedrich draws from psychodynamic, sexual abuse, developmental, attachment, cognitive, behavioral, and, by implication, systems theories. He blends elements from these theories into an approach that places emphasis on the behavioral management of the child within the system in which he or she developed.

Treatment is provided for children under the age of 13 who display sexually reactive or sexually aggressive behaviors. A combination of individual, group, and family therapies are used as needed. Goals for individual therapy are based on the needs of the child (Friedrich, 1991). Goals might include (a) developing a therapeutic relationship, (b) dealing with a history of personal sexual abuse, (c) eliminating the sexually aggressive behavior, (d) learning alternatives to sexual aggression, (e) dealing with feelings, and (f) developing empathy.

Friedrich (1993a) reports a preference for using pair therapy as an alternative to group therapy. He notes some of the advantages of using this strategy, including (a) a smaller group size, (b) less chance that children may feel overwhelmed, (c) a decreased likelihood that children may be rejected, and (d) an increased benefit for children who do not have the necessary skills to regulate their behavior in a group therapy setting. Pair therapy has been extensively discussed by Selman and Schultz (1990).

Friedrich (1991) reports that several goals and related issues are covered during family therapy sessions. Examples include (a) developing a therapeutic relationship, (b) improving parent-child attachments, (c) increasing positive involvement, (d) developing mutual empathy, (e) conflict resolution, and (f) behavior management.

Friedrich sometimes provides individual therapy for parents. As in other programs, children and parents may be referred to other therapists or agencies for specialized treatment.

The work of Friedrich has been particularly useful in defining the multidimensional, cyclical nature of sexually aggressive behaviors. He is strong in attention to the developmental, cognitive, behavioral, and systemic components of sexually aggressive acts. He is attentive to both the aggressive and the sexual nature of the problem as well as recognizing the recursive, contextual variables involved. Although not specifically defined as a systems approach, Friedrich's work is exemplary in its incorporation of family therapy as a central part of the treatment process. His treatment with rebuilding healthy parent-child attachments, building safe and nurturing environments, and teaching social and coping skills to parents and children represent significant advances in the field.[3]

Eliana Gil (Rockville, MD)

Eliana Gil is a therapist and renowned scholar (e.g., Gil & Johnson, 1993a) currently in private practice in Rockville, Maryland. Gil has worked extensively with sexualized children, children who molest, and their families. She has integrated information from psychodynamic, systems, trauma, attachment, development, cognitive, and behavioral theories. Gil's treatment approach is eclectic, focusing on problematic sexual behavior as well as underlying areas of concern. For children under the age of 13 who display sexualized and molesting behaviors, treatment is provided using a combination of individual, group, family, two-peers, or pair therapies (Gil & Briere, 1994).

Individual therapy is considered an important part of the treatment process and Gil (1993d) divides therapy goals into two groups: primary and secondary. Issues dealt with as primary goals include (a) developing a therapeutic relationship, (b) determining preparedness for group therapy, (c) learning specifics about the problematic sexual behavior, (d) determining risk, (e) eliminating the problematic sexual behavior, (f) assessing personal victimization and other treatment issues, (g) family dynamics, and (h) addressing issues from group therapy.

Issues dealt with as secondary goals include (a) self-concept and self-esteem, (b) helplessness and vulnerability, (c) connectedness to others, (d) social skills, (e) personal needs, (f) developing a realistic expectation of the family, and (g) looking toward the future.

For some children, group therapy is critical. Children are placed in groups by age and characteristics of their problematic sexual behaviors. Highly sexualized children, however, are not placed in the same groups with children who have molested (Gil, 1993d). (A contrast to this practice is found in Gray and Pithers's STEP program previously discussed.) Topics covered in the groups are both offense specific and general. When appropriate, Gil uses two-peers or pair therapy as an alternative to group therapy (Gil & Briere, 1994).

Gil (1993e) describes two different types of groups for parents. The first is an 8- to 10-week psychoeducational group. The issues covered in this group include (a) characteristics of children who molest, (b) problems exhibited by children who molest, (c) definition and description of molesting behaviors, (d) age-appropriate childhood sexual behavior, (e) distinguishing between age-appropriate childhood sexual behavior and sexual abuse, (f) family dynamics, (g) setting external controls, and (h) assisting children to develop internal controls (Gil, 1993e).

In addition to psychoeducational groups, Gil (1993e) holds group therapy sessions for parents. These sessions focus on (a) learning about their child's offense pattern, (b) commitment to using external controls, (c) helping their child use internal controls, (d) assisting their child to deal with high risk factors and situations, (e) using open communication, (f) family dynamics as a contributor to their child molesting, (g) cooperation with therapy, and (h) processing what has happened.

Gil's parent groups' secondary goals include (a) feelings, (b) strengths and weaknesses of the family, (c) strengths and weaknesses of the marriage, (d) conflict resolution, (e) stopping unhealthy patterns of interacting, (f) increasing healthy patterns of interacting, (g) eliminating patterns of interaction conducive to a sexualized family environment, and (h) problem solving and coping (Gil, 1993e).

Family therapy is considered crucial to the treatment process. Emphasis in these sessions is placed on (a) reviewing information covered in individual and group therapy, (b) current perspectives on the problematic sexual behavior, (c) how to avoid future problems, and (d) the contribution of family members to the problem (Gil, 1993d).

The work of Gil and associates has particular value in its attention to building strong and appropriate attachments between children and their parents. The blending of attachment, trauma, and systems theories offers hope for safe, nurturant families who are attentive to risk factors of future aggression and sexual abuse. Using multiple treatment modalities increases the opportunities for positive impact on children and their families.[4]

Harborview Sexual Assault Center (Seattle, WA)

Under the leadership of Lucy Berliner, the Harborview Sexual Assault program has been on the cutting edge of work with sexual behavior problems for many years. The program is the result of a careful literature review, combined with extensive clinical experiences with both children who have sexual behavior problems and their families. The underlying theoretical perspectives in this program assume that inappropriate sexual behaviors are learned, and that treatment must contain a cognitive and behavioral component focusing directly on the behaviors of concern.

Treatment sessions are held for children between the ages of 6 and 12 who display sexual behavior problems. An emphasis is placed on a strong therapeutic relationship as the vehicle through which issues are addressed. To this end, individual therapy is the primary treatment modality.

According to Berliner and Rawlings (1991), treatment goals are offense specific and may relate to areas such as (a) the elimination of the problematic sexual behavior, (b) obtaining sexual information that is developmentally appropriate, (c) learning acceptable sexual behavior, (d) the internalization of healthy values about appropriate sexual behavior, (e) developing strategies that decrease the opportunities to display sexual behavior problems, and (f) understanding the consequences for misbehavior. Further treatment interventions may involve increasing personal responsibility, victim empathy, self-control, and prevention of reoffense.

Whereas children attend individual sessions to increase internal control, sessions for parents revolve around increasing external control over the child. Possible treatment goals for parents relate to increasing supervision, creating a healthy family environment, and limit setting (Berliner & Rawlings, 1991).

Conjoint sessions between the child and parents are the means by which information is shared and integrated. When appropriate, referrals may be made for individual and family therapy so that family members can deal with unresolved issues other than the childhood sexual behavior problems.

The Harborview program targets behavioral change for children with sexual aggression problems. Clinicians are focused on developing prosocial behaviors and minimizing risk for future reoffense, with little attention to the etiology of the problem. This is a strong cognitive and behavioral model of intervention with clear behavioral outcome goals. Berliner and colleagues, however, caution therapists to individualize treatment to include concerns for prior victimization and histories of abuse in the family. Addressing these secondary issues can have significant impact of success of treatment.

As noted in Chapter 2, Berliner has been involved in a 5-year federally funded program from National Center on Child Abuse and Neglect (NCCAN) with Barbara Bonner and Eugene Walker from Oklahoma. Together, these practitioners and researchers are evaluating the efficacy of two treatment approaches—dynamic play and cognitive and behavioral. These approaches were briefly described in Chapter 2. Study results will provide useful empirical information about the effectiveness of these two treatment approaches when applied to children with sexually abusive behaviors and related thinking patterns.[5]

Valley Mental Health Adolescent Residential Treatment Education Center (ARTEC) (Kearns, UT) and Primary Children's Medical Center Child Protection Team (Salt Lake City, UT)

Valley Mental Health and the Primary Children's Medical Center programs offer treatment to children who display sexually abusive behaviors. The two programs incorporate information from several theories, including the four preconditions of abuse as described by Araji and Finkelhor (1986), sexual assault cycles, sexual abuse theory, trauma theory, developmental theory, psychodynamic theory, and cognitive and behavioral theories. The end product emphasizes cognitive and behavioral therapy but incorporates a "systems" approach because parents are viewed as an integral part of the therapy process.

The primary developers of these programs are Lucinda A. Rasmussen, Jan Ellen Burton, and Barbara J. Christopherson. Together, they have extensive clinical experience working in agencies and private practices serving sexually reactive and sexually aggressive children and their families. Despite geographic distance between three western states (California, Oregon, and Utah), they frequently work as a collaborative team.

Rasmussen, Burton, and Christopherson's (1992) approach is called the "trauma outcome process." This is used to plan and guide treatment interventions, as discussed in Chapter 4. The reader may recall that the approach focuses on the history of past trauma as well as developing skills to enable children to avoid self-victimization and sexual offending against others.

Treatment is provided for children ages 4 to 12 who display sexually reactive and sexually abusive behaviors. With few exceptions, treatment groups are divided for 4½- to 8-year-old children and those 8 to 12 years of age. Parents attend parallel group treatment with conjoint sessions held occasionally. Children may attend individual and family sessions as well as their group therapy.

Depending on the age and developmental level of the child, treatment goals may relate to topics such as (a) accountability, (b) empathy, (c) boundaries, (d) social skills, (e) sex education (for older children), (f) anger management, (g) trust, and (h) assertiveness (J. Burton, personal communication, September 2, 1996). Other treatment topics include (a) eliminating sexually abusive behavior, (b) eliminating self-destructive behavior, (c) using the trauma outcome process to assist in recovery from trauma, (d) dealing with feelings related to trauma, (e) improving social skills, (f) establishing empathy with others, (g) impulse control and making healthy choices, and (h) personal accountability (Rasmussen et al., 1992).

Parents are considered an important part of the treatment process. Parenting or family sessions cover topics such as (a) identifying factors that contribute to children's sexually abusive behavior, (b) identifying factors that contribute to children's sexually reactive behavior, (c) setting boundaries, (d) increasing supervision, (e) setting up the environment to decrease opportunities for sexual reoffense, and (f) open communication (Rasmussen et al., 1992).

Redirecting Sexual Aggression, Incorporated (Lakewood, CO)

Redirecting Sexual Aggression, Incorporated (RSA) was founded in 1983 as a community-based outpatient treatment program for adolescent and adult sexual offenders. In 1986, RSA developed a sexual perpetration prevention program. Lane (1991a) reports that the idea for this program came about from information being shared by RSA's adolescent clients who had begun their sexual-offending behavior at the approximate age of 9 or 10. At this point, RSA decided to treat children under the age of 9 to prevent them from initiating sexually abusive behavior. Subsequent information, however, revealed that these children were already engaging in sexually abusive acts. The necessity to treat young children who displayed sexually abusive behavior was apparent, so RSA began providing treatment services to children ages 12 and under.

The RSA staff view sexually abusive behavior as a learned behavior that may begin in early childhood and progress into adolescence and adulthood (e.g., Ryan, Lane, Davis, & Isaac, 1987). The primary theoretical orientation of the program is cognitive and behavioral with treatment interventions targeted to address the problematic sexual behaviors. Sandy Lane (1991b), at RSA, developed the sexual abuse cycle in recognition of the cognitive and behavioral progression occurring before, during, and subsequent to sexually abusive behavior. The RSA treatment program works to assist children in recognizing this cycle and learning new, nonaggressive or sexually abusive methods to cope and relate to others.

For those children between the ages of 7 and 12, group therapy is the primary treatment modality, with children grouped according to age and developmental level. Separate groups are held for children between 7 and 10 years old and for children 11 or 12 years old. Treatment is adjusted to reflect differing levels of emotional, cognitive, and physical development.

According to Lane (1991a), treatment goals are offense specific and relate to areas such as (a) eliminating sexual aggression, (b) changing distorted thought patterns, (c) learning how to manage and control sexual thoughts and arousal associated with sexual aggression, (d) increasing social and coping skills, (e) developing a greater understanding of the effects of sexual abuse on the victim, and (f) gaining an increased awareness of the ramifications of committing sexual offenses. In summary, children are taught how to manage their sexually abusive behaviors and are given new skills to meet their needs in a healthy, age-appropriate manner.

Parents are considered a critical part of the treatment program at RSA (Lane, 1991a). Parents attend 10 to 12 hours of education focusing on (a) increasing knowledge about sexual abusive behavior, (b) understanding forthcoming treatment interventions, and (c) learning ways to assist the treatment process. Parent participants complete weekly risk-monitoring forms, know their child's treatment homework assignments, and assist their child in maintaining treatment gains between sessions.

Individual and family therapy sessions are held within the agency. Outside referrals may be made to therapists or other agencies to deal with other issues that are not directly offense specific.

The delineation of the sexual abuse cycle is the primary contribution of this group to the current literature on sexually aggressive children. The treatment model is strong in addressing the cognitive and behavioral aspects of sexual aggression through group therapy with parents and children.[6]

It's About Childhood: Children Who
Sexually Act and Culpability (Ontario, OR)

Jan Hindman is the clinical director of the It's About Childhood: Children Who Sexually Act and Culpability program. Hindman and a group of practitioners use information from cognitive and behavioral theories, sexual abuse theory, and the perpetrator prevention literature in their treatment program. The result is a cognitive and behavioral program that directly addresses sexually abusive behavior by young children.

Services are provided for children from preschool through age 12, with group therapy as the primary treatment modality. Children are placed in one of four treatment TRACs based on information obtained from the Juvenile Culpability Assessment (JCA) (Hindman, 1994). The program defines culpability as knowledge that a particular sexual act is unacceptable as well as knowledge that there is a consequence for this behavior. Children in TRAC I and TRAC II are termed sex offenders, those in TRAC III are described as sexually acting-out children without criminal culpability, and TRAC IV children are considered "at risk" for becoming sex offenders. Goals are defined to address the understanding of the behavior and its consequences. In addition to the child treatment, parents participate in monthly group sessions.

All clients in this program have treatment contracts outlining expectations for children and their parents. Treatment contracts, plans, and goals are determined by individual issues or the TRAC to which a child has been assigned or both. In general, the two primary goals for all children are (a) to stop the sexually abusive behavior and (b) to learn healthy sexual behavior. Children in TRAC I focus on issues designed to control criminal thinking and behavior, whereas children in TRACs II, III, and IV are required to complete six treatment modules: (a) Society and Sexual Offending, (b) Criminal Thinking, (c) Sexual History, (d) Positive Sexuality, (e) Victim Empathy and Restitution, and (f) Problem-Solving. Additional interventions are based on the particular needs of children and their families.

Parents are considered an important part of the treatment process. They receive an orientation to the program and are given extensive information about their child's contract and how they may assist in increasing their child's chances for successful completion of treatment. In addition, parents participate in monthly group sessions with their child(ren). Goals for parents may relate to topics such as (a) recognizing criminal thinking and behavior, (b) methods to assist their child in eliminating sexually abusive behavior, (c) healthy sexuality, (d) accountability, and (e) limit setting.

Individual, group, and family therapy are conducted at the "It's About Childhood: Children Who Sexually Act and Culpability" program. In some cases, children or their families or both may be referred to other therapists or agencies for treatment issues not dealt with at It's About Childhood.

This group of practitioners have identified an important distinction between children's ability to understand their behavior, the seriousness of the abuse, and the risk factors for future intellectual distortion and behavioral impairment. The JCA assessment tool helps sort out important variables for the treatment planning process and treatment intervention. It is the only program we reviewed that includes the ideas of culpability and criminal intent. These concepts were discussed in Chapter 1.[7]

A Step Forward (Concord, CA)

A Step Forward is a group private practice that specializes in abuse-related treatment. Like most current programs or practices, A Step Forward does not have a separate program for sexually abusive or aggressive children. Individual therapists provide services to this population on demand. Jeffrey Bodmer-Turner, a member of the group practice, combines elements from the assault cycle, relapse prevention, and directed play therapy to create interventions that are primarily cognitive and behavioral but reflect developmental influences. Enid Sanders, also in this group, has done research on normative sexual behavior among 4- to 6-year-old children and assists children toward developing mastery through structured play and group therapy to teach age-appropriate sexuality.

For children between the ages of 4 and 12 who display sexually aggressive behaviors, treatment is provided using individual therapy as the primary treatment modality. When possible, short-term groups of four to six children are formed based on their maturity or cognitive levels or both. Group work is focused on cooperation, containment of aggressive and sexualized behavior, developing interpersonal boundaries, and creating safer interpersonal relationships. Additionally, conjoint sessions are held with children and their parents.

Treatment goals for the child relate to (a) eliminating sexually aggressive behaviors, (b) creating a behavior management plan that emphasizes self-control, (c) learning alternative coping strategies, (d) developing competencies to cope with situations that previously resulted in abusive behavior, and (e) incorporating a sense of healthy sexuality.

Parents participate in conjoint sessions that focus on developing and implementing relapse prevention plans. Treatment goals cover topics such as (a) identifying precursors to abusive behavior, (b) interrupting behavior prior to relapse, and (c) learning to manage the child's overall behavior. Family members may also attend individual, couple, group therapy, or all three to address related issues.

This group of practitioners has combined various models of treatment, blending professional disciplines and talents to approach sexual aggression as a cyclical problem with recognizable precursors and reinforcers that can be addressed. Treatment plans are individualized based on the clinicians' expertise and resources available.[8]

Philly Kids Play It Safe (Philadelphia, PA)

The Philly Kids Play It Safe program is a small program within a larger agency in which prevention and intervention services are provided for children and their foster parents. This program is unique in helping children to build strong and safe relationships with foster parents subsequent to being removed from severely dysfunctional families. This is a proactive approach to preventing further sexual aggression and supporting foster parents while children with such problems live in their homes.

Like most programs, this one does not ascribe to a single theoretical orientation; rather, it blends elements of cognitive, behavioral, and psychodynamic theories. Cognitive work is typically tied in with some form of play, art, music, or other medium that provides an opportunity for movement.

Treatment services are provided for children ages 3 to 12 who have been placed in a foster home. Group therapy is the primary treatment modality with groups for 3- or 4-year-olds, 5- or 6-year-olds, and 7- to 11-year-olds. These groups are formed when caseloads permit. Twelve-year-old children participate in groups for adolescents. Groups meet for 2 hours per week for up to 30 weeks.

Group treatment goals are written to reflect the developmental levels of the children and include the following topics: (a) eradicating abuse-reactive or sexually aggressive behavior, (b) preventing sexual reoffense, (c) learning to set boundaries, (d) increasing empathy, (e) dealing with family of origin issues, (f) resolving personal victimization, (g) expressing grief and loss, (h) developing trust, (i) building a sense of self, and (j) gaining hope for future families. The latter is accomplished through exercises designed to examine past, present, and possible future families. For very young children, group treatment goals include the ability to respond to group limits and a behavior management program. All children are taught a variety of skills to increase adaptive functioning.

A separate group is held for foster parents. Group goals focus on (a) developing an understanding of sexual abuse and the assault cycle, (b) examining personal histories to understand how foster children trigger old issues, (c) decreasing the tendency to self-victimize, (d) strengthening parenting skills, (e) learning to set healthy boundaries and rules in the foster home, and (f) improving overall communication.

Within the agency, children are sometimes seen for individual counseling or limited family work. Referrals are made when children or foster parents require in-depth individual and family therapy.

The Philly Kids Play It Safe program is a good example of adapting knowledge of sexually abusive children to a special needs group: foster families who have accepted placement of multiproblem cases. Treatment goals validate the new family constellation and work with both the children and the foster parents to support the process of placement and adaptation to a new family system. Foster family placements frequently fail with reactive and aggressive children because of sexual acting out, behavioral problems, and victimization of other foster children by the sexually aggressive youth. Foster parents need support with managing abusive children and developing healthy and safe families.[9]

Limitations

In the previous section, we provided an overview of a variety of treatment programs, agencies, and therapists in private practice who serve sexually reactive and sexually abusive or aggressive children and their families. This overview highlighted treatment providers that ranged from the individual private practitioner to large-scale programs with multiple clinicians and services. Programs summarized included a relapse-based prevention program as well as services that focused on individual, group, pair, and family therapy. Although most of the approaches described have not been empirically demonstrated as effective models for intervention, the Bonner et al. and Gray and Pithers studies are attempting to provide such information. These comprehensive studies have been federally funded (NCCAN), and initial findings from both were presented in Chapter 2. Relevant to this chapter is Gray and Pithers's (A. Gray, personal communication, October 16, 1996) preliminary conclusions from their evaluation and comparison of the two treatment modalities described previously. They indicate that their earliest data analysis indicates it is absolutely evident that treatment for children with sexual behavior problems must involve their caregivers, given the extensive data that suggest parental characteristics act as mediating variables in the sexual behavior problems of their children. They also note that they are about to begin analyzing data pertaining to treatment efficacy. Their hypothesis is that the less intensive APT may be a more effective program with the least intrusive subtype of children with sexual behavior problems, whereas children who engage in more playful and intrusive sexual misbehavior might derive greater benefit from the more structured treatment condition—the SAST. For most programs, however, experience and clinical judgment remain the standard for evaluating the merits of the programs described herein.

As a concluding note to this section, we are unable to include all the specialized services currently available. Some individuals within programs or agencies could not, for various reasons, share information at the current time, and many other programs are simply unknown to us. Despite these obstacles, we hope the previous section has given the reader a useful overview of programs, agencies, and private practitioners who provide treatment to sexually abusive or aggressive children and their families.

Summary of Programs

The treatment approaches described in this chapter have many similarities as well as some differences. An overview of this is shown in Table 5.1, which presents a list of the providers reviewed, enumerating the terminology, theories, and modalities identified.

As evident from Table 5.1, the language employed ranges from "sex-abuse reactive" to "sexually aggressive" to "sex offender," although the latter is used only under specific conditions involving the criminal justice system. As noted in previous chapters, this reflects a hesitation on the part of some professionals to use terms that may negatively label young children and even carry into adolescence or adulthood. In addition, some professionals are reluctant to use a descriptive term that carries pejorative connotations and that may be incorrectly associated with the criminal justice system.

All the programs reviewed developed interventions based on the child development literature and reflect differences in age, cognitive, or maturity levels. Unfortunately, details regarding the specific developmental theories used and applications of the theories are primarily absent from program descriptions.

Most programs incorporated information about sexual abuse in their treatment formulations. As noted in Chapter 4 and this chapter, some programs used Finkelhor and Browne's (1985) four traumagenic dynamics of sexual abuse or Araji and Finkelhor's (1986) four-factor model of child sexual abuse as partial explanations for children's sexually abusive or aggressive behaviors. Many professionals incorporated information from what is known about perpetrator prevention, and some borrowed from adolescent and adult models to design interventions that focus on personal accountability, the sexual abuse cycle, and relapse prevention.

The majority of professionals prefer a cognitive and behavioral orientation, wherein sexual aggression is viewed as learned behavior. Professionals who operate under this premise support the idea that a

TABLE 5.1 Summary of Programs Reviewed

Specific Program	Ages Served	Theories Utilized	Modalities Offered
Support for Abuse Reactive Kids (SPARK) (Los Angeles, CA)	4-12	PTSD/addiction/sexual abuse/cognitive and behavioral	Group/parental group/sibling group/family
STEP program (VT)	6-12	Cognitive and behavioral/sexual abuse/relapse prevention	Group/parental group
William Friedrich (Rochester, MN)	Under 13	Psychodynamic/sexual abuse/attachment/cognitive and behavioral	Individual/family/group/pair
Eliana Gil (Rockville, MD)	Under 13	Psychodynamic/systems/trauma/attachment/cognitive and behavioral	Individual/family/group/pair/parental group
Harborview Sexual Assault Center (Seattle, WA)	6-12	Cognitive and behavioral	Individual child and parents/conjoint child and parents
Valley Mental Health (Kearns, UT) and Primary Children's Medical Center, Child Protection Team (Salt Lake City, UT)	4-12	Assault cycle/sexual abuse/trauma/cognitive and behavioral	Individual/family/group
Redirecting Sexual Aggression (RSA) (Lakewood, CO)	6-12	Cognitive and behavioral	Group/parental group
It's About Childhood (Ontario, OR)	Preschool-12	Cognitive and behavioral/sexual abuse theory/perpetrator prevention	Group/parental group
A Step Forward (Concord, CA)	4-12	Cognitive and behavioral/assault cycle/relapse prevention/play	Individual/group/conjoint parental
Philly Kids Play It Safe (Philadelphia, PA)	3-12	Cognitive and behavioral/psychodynamic	Group/parental group

child who engages in sexually aggressive behaviors must have learned them somewhere. In theory, this learning results in a progression of behaviors with the end result being sexually abusive behaviors directed against other children or individuals viewed as vulnerable.

Combining cognitive and behavioral theories of human psychology provides for working with specific thought processes as well as teaching age-appropriate behaviors. Most of the programs and providers described in this chapter recognize a need to resocialize sexually reactive or sexually aggressive children to prosocial behaviors. Therefore, treatment includes positive reinforcement for acquisition of good coping skills, age-appropriate sexual conduct, internalized mechanisms for problem solving, and a myriad of prevention strategies.

Although a cognitive and behavioral orientation appears dominant, many professionals from these programs, agencies, or private practices blend elements from other theories, resulting in treatment interventions with multiple features. Most programs incorporate a biopsychosocial orientation, drawing from theories addressing the physiological and psychological development of the child, the relationships influencing the child's development, and societal forces impinging on personal growth and development. As discussed in Chapter 4 and demonstrated in this chapter, no single theory has been proven to address the complexities of preadolescent sexual aggression. Hence, the combining of theories and treatment methods offers the potential for a more holistic impact on the child and his or her family or caretakers.

Individual, peer, pair, and group work are used to work with sexually abusive or aggressive children, depending on each child's level of maturity and ability to benefit from working with other children. The primary treatment modality for the child who sexually abuses is group therapy. Groups are often structured as psychoeducational experiences for children, teaching a variety of cognitive and behavioral skills. Children are divided into small groups reflecting age and developmental differences. Both Friedrich and Gil recommend the use of pair therapy, helping to avoid rejections, decrease anxieties, and maximize controlled peer contacts.

Most professionals believe sexually abusing children require offense-specific treatment goals that stress the elimination of the sexually abusive behaviors. At the same time, interventions are aimed at replacing maladaptive behavior with sexual feelings, thoughts, and behaviors that are age appropriate. Many professionals teach some type of skills related to self-management, self-control, or relapse prevention. This appears to be indicative of a tendency to teach these children to gain some measure of internal control over their behavior. As a general treatment strategy, providers teach prosocial and adaptive skills.

In all the programs, agencies, or private practices reviewed in this chapter, parents are considered important to the treatment process. Although parents most often attend some type of group, some receive individual and family services. Treatment goals for parents may be specific to either the issue of childhood sexual aggression or other related concerns. Often, there is an attempt to increase knowledge about prior sexual abuse. In some instances, parents are taught specific techniques that are used to assist children in preventing reoffense. Other treatment goals relate to increasing supervision, improving parenting skills, and creating a healthy family environment. Less common are treatment goals focusing on grief, coping, or self-care.

There does not appear to be complete agreement as to the range of family problems that should be included in treatment. Some professionals treat the family unit as a whole, covering multiple problem areas and providing a variety of services. In other cases, therapists may choose to remain focused on the childhood sexual abuse and directly related family issues. In these instances, referrals are made to specialized programs, other agencies, or other therapists.

Likewise, the degree to which the child receives treatment for a personal history of sexual abuse varies as a function of clinical preference, available resources, or how treatment services are designed. Professionals acknowledge the role of abuse or trauma in the development of sexual aggression for some children. Some therapists choose to treat a history of sexual abuse as part of the basic treatment program, whereas others make referrals for this issue.

The programs reviewed demonstrate the creativity that is being brought to the clinical arena. Each program reflects the expertise of the providers, biases associated with professional and theoretical orientations, a multiplicity of treatment modalities, utilization of resources, and collaboration with colleagues both locally and nationally.

Clearly, large programs, such as the Harborview Sexual Assault Center in Seattle and SPARK in Los Angeles, can provide highly specialized groups and a variety of services. Their staffs are composed of multidisciplinary teams and they are capable of embarking in research endeavors. These programs, based in major metropolitan centers, have the advantage of large caseloads, multiple funding sources, and a diversity of staff expertise. In comparison, private practitioners in rural or

isolated areas are limited in their resources, their ability to accept multiproblem cases, and their ability to provide specialized groups and
services. These limitations appear to have resulted in collaborative activities with colleagues outside their practices. In either case, therapists
are breaking new ground by experimenting with various theories and
methods of intervention. Practitioners are working to maximize their
impact within the resources available.

As demonstrated in this book, sexually abusing behavior by children
is a complex phenomenon presented by multiproblem youth and, frequently, multiproblem families. It is important to recognize, as identified
in previous chapters, that many children who are sexually abusive or
aggressive are also involved in other antisocial activities. Substance
abuse, violence, gang activities, and other criminal behaviors can also be
present in these cases, although there is little research or information
specifically relating to these activities and sexually abusive or aggressive
children.

The programs, agencies, and practices reviewed in this chapter all
recognize the importance of developing individualized treatment plans.
These plans may require the assistance of collateral resources in the
community, including residential treatment, hospitalization, multisite
treatment teams, and comprehensive case management. In all cases,
establishing a healthy environmental context for the child is central to
the success of treatment.

Program Development and Treatment Planning

Although a relatively new area of practice and research, the knowledge
and experiences of professionals throughout the country can be helpful
in identifying common themes and issues in service provision for sexually abusive or aggressive youth. This chapter has described the diversity
of approaches being used by pioneers in this field, which can be a
valuable shortcut to successful program development.

As information provided in previous chapters and this chapter
demonstrates, therapists attempting to design treatment programs or
practices that work with sexually abusive or aggressive youth face a
variety of challenges. Questions arise as to the most important factors to
take into consideration in developing specialized services. What theories
should be used in formulating interventions strategies? What treatment
modality is most effective? Who should be involved? What goals should

be used? How flexible should providers be in addressing issues other than sexual aggression? These and other questions need to be answered in the program development phase. The answers and availability of resources will mold and shape the treatment to be provided.

On the basis of the review of the programs described, and the extensive clinical and research experience of the authors, a list of 10 factors that can aid in program development and treatment planning is presented in Table 5.2. We believe this list will be useful for designing programs that serve children who are engaged in sexually aggressive behaviors.

Factor 1

Chapter 4 provided a review of numerous theories used to make sense out of why children act sexually aggressive and why they molest others. General psychological, social psychological, and sociological theories permeate beliefs about the origins and maintenance of sexual aggression by young children. Among others, learning theory, coping theory, and systems theory can be used to describe and understand factors associated with how children grow and learn. Different theories provide different explanations for why a child might become violent, act out sexually, and abuse other children, and no single theory has been identified as the answer for why children become sexually abusive. Therefore, a working knowledge of multiple theories will be beneficial in gaining a comprehensive perspective on the problem.

Factor 2

Experienced practitioners are incorporating a variety of theoretical perspectives in their treatment plans. Many use theories specific to child development (e.g., Friedrich, 1991; Gil, 1993c); trauma models (Finkelhor & Browne, 1986; Gil, 1993c); sexual abuse (e.g., Finkelhor, 1984); cyclical explanations of sexual aggression such as the cycle of violence (Isaac & Lane, 1990), and the sexual abuse cycle (Lane, 1991b); the trauma outcome process (Rasmussen et al., 1992); and the balanced approach (e.g., Gray & Pithers, 1993). Each of these inclusions in treatment planning represents a significant step in tailoring therapy to the specific problem of childhood sexual aggression.

TABLE 5.2 Ten Factors for Program Development and Treatment
Planning

1. The treatment of preadolescent sexual aggression requires a comprehensive knowledge of biopsychosocial theories of sexuality and aggression to guide in the development of intervention models.

2. A treatment model should incorporate theories of child development, sexual abuse, trauma, reciprocal cycles of abuse, learning, relapse prevention, and systems theories.

3. The treatment should incorporate cognitive and behavioral interventions that place responsibility for behavior with the child and address sexual aggression as a learned behavior that is changeable.

4. Family systems theory and therapy need to be integrated into treatment models to address dysfunctional family dynamics.

5. Group,, peer,, or pair therapy are useful methods for working with sexually aggressive youth. Children are best managed and treated in developmentally divided age groups.

6. Treatment that is individually tailored and offense specific offers the greatest likelihood for success.

7. Treatment goals should target eliminating sexually abusive and aggressive behavior, increasing behavioral controls, and developing competencies for coping with precursors to sexual aggression.

8. When appropriate, treatment needs to address the history of sexual abuse of the perpetrator—that is, victimization issue.

9. Parental groups are an effective means for teaching parents the skills necessary to prevent further aggression and abuse by themselves and their children.

10. When needed, referrals should be made to specialized programs, agencies, or therapists to facilitate as comprehensive a treatment approach as local services allow.

Chapter 4 summarized the applicability of these and other models that have been helpful in conceptualizing treatment. Clinicians are cautioned to select theories and models that address both sexual abuse and violence as interactive components of sexual aggression. Recognizing the recursive nature of the problem, including antecedents, variables related to offense, and reinforcers subsequent to offense patterns is important for treatment and program planning.

Factor 3

Cognitive and behavioral theories are useful for their explanatory power with sexual aggression. They describe thoughts and behaviors as learned activities, capable of being changed with active intervention. These theories allow for interpreting sexual aggression as maladaptive responses to inappropriate stimuli in a child's life.

Targeting cognitive aspects of sexual aggression involves attention to thinking errors, distortions, inaccurate perceptions, false assumptions, and irrational beliefs that justify antisocial behavior (Ryan & Lane, 1991). Developing insight about thought processes that perpetuate these misperceptions aids in empathy development, understanding of consequences, and assumption of responsibility for destructive behaviors.

Similarly, targeting behavioral aspects of sexual aggression involves identifying negative behaviors and teaching and reinforcing prosocial behaviors. Practitioners are reminded that sexually aggressive youth may exhibit multiple behavioral problems such as conduct disorder and fire-setting. Teaching impulse control and providing external supervision are important to treatment success.

Every program and practice described in this chapter incorporated cognitive and behavioral theories in its work (e.g., Berliner & Rawlings, 1991; Cunningham & MacFarlane, 1996). With cognitive and behavioral interventions, children can learn new ways of thinking about their behavior and gain mastery over their conduct.

Factor 4

As evident from previous chapters in this book, the family is universally recognized as the primary social influence on young children who sexually aggress. Research and practice knowledge have repeatedly documented the impact of family and environmental disorganization, physical abuse, domestic violence, incest, substance abuse, neglect, and isolation as contributing factors to the etiology of sexual aggression (e.g., Friedrich, 1990; Gil, 1993c). Families provide the learning environment and are the most important source of nurturance and guidance for children. Helping families to create safe, predictable, and growth-promoting relationships among family members is key to helping the sexually reactive and sexually aggressive child.

Family systems theory is useful for treatment planning because of the inclusion of parents, siblings, and extended family members and other relevant social systems. The theory directs attention to the roles other significant people can play in the development of abusive behaviors and the role they can play in creating change. Isolating sexually aggressive children from the context of their primary relationships can result in serious problems, including scapegoating, victimization, and family disruption. Including family members can lead to protecting members from abuse; establishing age-appropriate rules and roles; developing safe personal, sibling, parental, and family boundaries; and building support systems for members.

Factor 5

Whenever possible, groups should be used as a method of intervening with sexual aggression. Children can benefit from exposure to peers who are experiencing the same or similar problems. Meeting other children who have been sexually aggressive can help with (a) learning new skills from each other, (b) understanding common misperceptions they have about their behavior, (c) confronting denial about the consequences of their actions, (d) normalizing responses to maladaptive stimuli, and (e) reducing isolation for these children. Group therapy is the modality of choice for most practitioners because of the power of group process as an intervention tool for seriously maladaptive behaviors. In addition, group therapy maximizes resources by being cost and time efficient.

Preschool (ages 3-5), latency (ages 6-9), and preadolescent (ages 10-12) age groupings serve as helpful developmental divisions for groups. Age-specific groups allow for using age-appropriate techniques such as guided play, art projects, written tasks, and video productions. Children can learn behaviors acceptable within their age group without being exposed to concepts they are not developmentally ready to address.

Age groupings also allow for variability of gender inclusion or exclusion. Preschool-age girls and boys may be amenable to coeducational groups, whereas preadolescent children might be inhibited by the presence of cross-gender peers. Therapists need to consider the impact of having mixed groups versus boy or girl groups. The gender of the participants can positively or negatively affect the group dynamics.

Factor 6

Children can be sexually aggressive in many different ways. Therefore, treatment programs need to recognize differences and intervene accordingly. The nature of the abuse, duration, frequency, relationship of the perpetrator to the victim, type of coercion used, and etiology of the abuse need to be considered when making decisions about treatment goals and strategies for intervention. Individualizing the treatment to the specifics of the case respects differences in need and allows for flexibility in treatment planning. Sexually aggressive children may be experiencing a myriad of other problems that need professional intervention. Practitioners are cautioned to conduct full diagnostic and psychosocial assessments before treatment planning.

Factor 7

Children need to learn about the conditions that lead to their sexually aggressive behaviors and learn strategies for changing their response to internal and external stimuli. Examining their thoughts, feelings, and behaviors, as well as those of others, and situations that resulted in sexual aggression can help with recognizing cues that set off abusive events. Teaching age-appropriate sexuality and rewarding positive gains with sufficient reinforcement to establish stable changes in behavior can result in positive treatment outcomes.

Factor 8

Not all children who are sexually aggressive have been sexually abused in their past. Many, however, have been abused and may need to address victimization experiences as part of their therapy. It is important to determine if incest has occurred and to intervene accordingly. Establishing a safe home environment is critical to treatment success. Children who have been, or who are being, sexually abused by a parent or other family member need the protection of professionals involved in their lives. Neglecting this dimension of sexually aggressive behavior can result in further victimization and negate the impact of treatment. Working with parents on incest issues can help establish appropriate personal and parental boundaries and address sexual misconduct within the family. This can avoid scapegoating the sexually aggressive child and focus on family dysfunction that is contributing to the child's behavior. Working with children separate from their parents may be only minimally successful if they return to abusive or dysfunctional family systems.

The different programs and practices reviewed varied in their responsiveness to prior sexual abuse. Whereas some incorporated specific treatment goals into their treatment plans, others ignored or referred out for issues related to prior victimization. Theoretical perspective, expertise, and resources may drive the decision for clinicians. Many therapists are reluctant to address victimization issues because of a belief that it detracts from the primary treatment goals related to sexual aggression—a perpetrator issue. Others may believe addressing a personal history of abuse is central to a positive outcome. In the absence of empirical data to support one position or the other, practitioners are left to decide the best approach to this issue. Clinicians agree, however, that whatever the background, children need to learn they are responsible for their own behavior and need to learn prosocial sexual conduct. If the children are victims of abuse, however, this issue must be included in the overall treatment if treatment is to be effective.

Factor 9

Many of the programs reviewed used parental groups concurrent with children's groups (e.g., Cunningham & MacFarlane, 1996; Gray & Pithers, 1993; Griggs & Boldi, 1995; Rasmussen et al., 1992). There were numerous goals for parents that were primarily focused on reinforcing gains made by their children in treatment. Parents may be taught about (a) childhood sexual behavior problems, (b) parenting skills for managing sexual aggression, (c) setting boundaries and supervising their child, (d) identifying familial conditions that might have contributed to the sexually aggressive behavior, and (e) stress management and self-care.

Parent groups provide opportunities for parents to develop peer relationships, establish support systems, and gain understanding of their children in a safe environment. The adults can deal with their own histories as they relate to sexual aggression, their own sexuality, and their roles and responsibilities as parents with multiproblem children. Groups are helpful with confronting denial, self-examination, and learning new skills as adults and parents.

Factor 10

Recognizing the complexity of these cases and using collateral resources can help prevent burnout and maximize the effectiveness of services provided. Practitioners are cautioned to work within the limits of their expertise and to seek consultation and supervision while working with sexually aggressive youth. Multidisciplinary treatment teams are useful for dividing tasks, providing balance and peer support and preventing triangulation, manipulation, and boundary problems. Clear assignments of roles and tasks can protect against problems with confidentiality, role confusion, overextension, and maltreatment. Professional affiliations, legal regulations, and well-defined policies and procedures will prevent programs and practitioners from making serious mistakes that result in treatment failures and further abuse of children in treatment.

Conclusions

This chapter has presented overviews of 10 programs, agencies, and practices that have specialized in the treatment of sexually abusive or aggressive children. Summaries of each program were provided with recommendations for treatment planning and program development.

We conclude this chapter by recommending more empirical testing and program evaluations of all services provided to sexually reactive and sexually abusive or aggressive children and their families. The Bonner et al. and Gray and Pithers longitudinal comparative program evaluation studies are an important step in this direction. It is not sufficient to conduct practice based on the collective wisdom of experts, theoreticians, or blind faith. Each case needs to be closely scrutinized for goal attainment as well as for areas that need further development or changes. As this chapter and Chapter 4 demonstrate, multiple theoretical approaches and treatment modalities have been found useful for intervening with sexually abusive or aggressive children. We are now at the threshold of knowledge development that requires systematic inquiry and validation.

Notes

1. Information about the SPARK program was provided by Frederique Pierre and associates.

2. Information on the STEP program was obtained from written materials and published information about the program as well as verbal, written, and personal communications with Alison Gray (October 1996).

3. The previous information was reviewed by William Friedrich.

4. This information was reviewed and revised by Eliana Gil.

5. This information was reviewed by Lucy Berliner.

6. Information about RSA, Inc., was provided by Christopher Labanov-Rostovsky.

7. Written information about this program was provided by Jan Hindman.

8. Information about A Step Forward was provided by Jeffrey Bodmer-Turner.

9. Information about this program was provided by Arlene Skversky.

6

Closing the Cracks

Systemwide Response Needed

Sharon K. Araji

In several chapters of this book, I discussed the reasons sexually abusive children 12 years of age and younger remain largely unidentified (e.g., lack of awareness and resistance to believing children can engage in abusive and aggressive sexual behaviors) or untreated. This chapter elaborates on the consequences of these problems for parents, educators, child protective workers, clinicians, policymakers, and legal professionals who encounter a social system largely unprepared to cope with young children who are sexually abusing others. The chapter begins by arguing that closing the awareness, definitional, descriptive, treatment, and policy gaps are the first steps toward preventing sexually abusive and aggressive children from dropping through the system's cracks.

In addition to the previously mentioned problems, information in previous chapters demonstrated that the issue of children acting sexually abusive is a social problem, not a psychological one associated with only a few children. Because social problems require social solutions, this chapter provides examples of how some communities and states have responded or are attempting to develop system responses that are directly or indirectly related to sexually abusive children. A discussion and assessment of this information is the second focus of the chapter. The chapter concludes with a discussion of the need to combine theory and practice as part of a communitywide systems approach to the social problem of children sexually abusing others.

Awareness, Definition, and Labeling Issues

Previous chapters covered the lack of public awareness that children 12 years and younger could engage in sexually abusive activities, especially aggressive and violent behaviors traditionally associated with adults and adolescents. Coupled with this lack of awareness is the denial and minimization that occur when parents and the public are exposed to the problem. Also, closely related to parents' and the public's lack of awareness, denial, and minimization is a resistance by some professionals in the field to view young children as capable of initiating harmful sexual behaviors that involve threats, coercion, and force. The end result is a "culture of denial," wherein children's sexually abusive behaviors become characterized as exploratory and harmless or merely "reactions" to sexual victimization.

As noted in previous chapters, many of these sexually abusive behaviors are not harmless and, as other professionals and researchers have argued, views such as that described previously excuse children's sexually abusive behaviors rather than holding young sexual aggressors accountable. All sexually aggressive children are not victims of sexual abuse and thus must be viewed as initiators of abusive behaviors and not merely as reactors. Even if they are reactors, the offending behaviors must be the ones initially addressed. Furthermore, based on material reviewed in this book and discussions with therapists, I have reached the conclusion that physical abuse and other related abuses are probably more important than sexual abuse in explaining the "aggressive" component of children whose sexually abusive behaviors include violence.

Another problem that corresponds with the reluctance to correctly describe sexually aggressive behaviors by children is the resistance of some providers to label children "sexually aggressive," "molester," "perpetrator," or "offender." These professionals prefer more inclusive terms such as "children with sexual behavior problems." Although this approach is definitely applicable to some sexually abusive children, it has the potential of masking the seriousness of the sexually aggressive acts and, as a consequence, preventing this group of children from getting appropriate treatment and services. Additionally, this practice places others at a risk of being victimized by sexually aggressive children.

From a scientific perspective, failure to accurately describe and label the variety of children's sexually abusive behaviors prevents the development of knowledge, including the gathering of statistics necessary to generate prevalence and incidence rates about the number of children who exhibit the varying types of sexual misbehaviors, including those that have a sexual and an aggressive component. As was evident from previous discussions, this is an area in which a paucity of information exists.

From a prevention perspective, failure to appropriately recognize, label, and treat children with sexually abusive behaviors represents a "missed opportunity." That is, given the young ages of this abusive population, one might expect greater success at stopping their deviant behaviors than has been shown with adolescent and adult offenders because these children have generally had a shorter time frame for patterns of sexually abusive behaviors to develop and become reinforced.

In summary, closing the awareness, definitional, descriptive, and treatment gaps is the first step toward preventing sexually aggressive and other sexually abusive children from dropping through the cracks in the social, judicial, and legislative systems. For example, as stated in the Introduction, I believe the concept "sexually aggressive" is the one that best describes abusive behaviors by children that have a sexual and an aggressive component. It clearly describes the behavior, and both components are measurable. This term can also be used to differentiate children who are engaged in these types of abusive behaviors from those engaged in other normal and sexual misbehaviors that do not include aggressive or violent components, as discussed in Chapter 1. The practice of clearly differentiating children's sexual misbehaviors will do much to ensure the choice of appropriate treatment methods.

How Laws View Children

Some state laws related to children and crime have contributed to the awareness, definitional, policy, and treatment problems surrounding sexually abusive children. For example, one of the problems that parents, providers, and members of the social and justice systems have encountered when attempting to find solutions for children who are involved in sexually abusing behaviors is that, legally, young children are conceptualized as incapable of committing crimes.

State laws and the conditions under which a child may be considered and treated as a criminal and juvenile penal codes vary across states. With respect to the age individuals can be considered capable of committing a crime, the youngest age is eight in the states of Washington and

Utah; the oldest is 18 in states such as Wyoming. The most popular age is 14, which probably reflects the continued use of "common law doctrine."

States such as Alabama maintain the common law doctrine, which means that children under the age of 7 are conclusively presumed incapable of committing a crime and those between ages 7 and 14 are merely presumed to be incapable of crime; incompetency is conclusive. Hence, in Alabama and other states that follow the common law doctrine, prosecution is barred if the alleged offense is committed when a person is less than 14 years of age.

When a crime has a sexual component, some laws tend to reflect the "protection paradigm" of child sexuality. This is the idea that a properly raised child should not see, hear, or participate in sexual activity (Martinson, 1994, p. 121). This paradigm was predicated on the notion that children are innocent and inappropriate sex objects for adults and was a reaction to the "children as property" paradigm popular in the Western world until the introduction of Christianity (Martinson, 1994, Chapter 8). When made into laws, the protection paradigm came to include ages defined as minority (child) and majority (adult). These two concepts rest on the assumption that a child or minor is incapable of self-management, which includes managing his or her own sexuality (Martinson, 1994, p. 121). The protection paradigm reflected the notion that children, when involved in crimes, including sexual crimes, were victims rather than perpetrators. Hence, children came to be viewed as incapable of sexual acts and certainly not those defined as criminal. Information covered in this chapter and previous chapters indicates that the protection paradigm rationale continues to influence thinking about children and sexual behavior—that is, that children are incapable of sexual abuse, particularly sexual acts that include aggressive, coercive, or violent components.

Some Laws Change the View of Children

In response to an increasing number of young children involved in violent behaviors that would be considered criminal if enacted by adolescents or adults, some states have introduced legislation wherein a child below the age of majority can be considered competent. One of the concepts associated with such legislation is "variable competence," wherein it is assumed that there are determining factors other than chronological age that should be considered in deciding whether children are competent to make decisions. These factors include whether the perpetrators are normal and rational and clearly know what they are doing at the time they commit a crime. The program reviewed in this book that is currently most reflective of this idea is Jan Hindman's, It's About Childhood, located in Ontario, Oregon. As discussed in Chapter 1, this program is based on the notion that children who are engaging in what I call sexually aggressive behaviors are committing a crime and should be treated as criminals if they are culpable. Culpability refers to the knowledge of inappropriateness of the behavior and knowledge that a consequence (e.g., punishment) for the behavior exists. It is assumed that children who rank high on culpability have criminal intent and should be charged with a sexual crime.

Another indication of a shift in public attitudes away from both the common law doctrine and the protection paradigm comes from Colorado. According to Cantwell (1995), Colorado amended its Child Protection Law in 1991 to mandate reporting of children under 10 years old who were acting sexually aggressive toward other children. Cantwell cites several reasons why amendments such as these are occurring. First, the law recognizes that sexually imitative or aggressive behavior is a common signal of a child's own sexual victimization, and it is assumed that the younger the child, the stronger the connection between the two. Second, although most states have provisions for criminal prosecution after a child has turned 10 years of age, it does not make sense to allow a child to sexually abuse another until the abusive child reaches an age when he or she can be defined as criminal. A better solution is to determine what can be done to alter the aggressive behavior as soon as it is observed or is reported for treatment. Third, it has been clearly shown that treatment of adult sexual offenders is not particularly successful. Finally, because a significant number of children are victimized by adult perpetrators, it is assumed that the earlier these perpetrators (adults) are discovered and stopped, the fewer potential perpetrators will be created.

Minnesota has an antisexual harassment law that covers all children, including those who are of kindergarten age. In discussing a publication from the Minnesota Department of Education (MDE) regarding what types of sexual harassment school supervisors were looking for on playgrounds, Martinson (1994, p. 137) provided several examples. Acts defined as sexual harassment included sexual gestures such as boys' grabbing their groin when a girl passes them or males bragging about their penis size.

Martinson (1994) further reported that proponents of Minnesota law argue that tough penalties for offenses such as those described previously are what the future holds. He noted that Minnesota is viewed as a national leader in fighting sexual harassment, and he provides a case study of what the MDE regarded as an open-and-shut case. This case involved a 5-year-old boy leading a 5-year-old girl into a resource room, pulling her pants down, pulling his own pants down, getting on top of her, and simulating sexual intercourse. Martinson (1994, p. 137) reported that a specialist from the MDE responded to the case by saying that "something very, very serious was going to happen to that little boy."

Although it is important to identify children's sexually abusive behavior as early as possible, there were several cases in 1996 that indicated that policies such as those in Minnesota must be approached with caution. One such case is that of Johnathan Prevette, a 6-year-old, first grader in Lexington, North Carolina. Johnathan was barred from his class for 1 day because he kissed a classmate on the cheek. He said he did it because "he liked her and she asked him to." A teacher saw the incident and reported that the girl complained. As a result, school officials said Johnathan had broken written school rules against sexual harassment. They later lowered the charge to violation of a general school rule that prohibited "unwarranted and unwelcome touching of one student by another." Later still, the superintendent gave a statement that he had met with Johnathan's parents and in response to their request was working on an age-appropriate revision of the school's policy.

This is an important case to analyze for several reasons. First, although I do not have all the information, the behavior exhibited by Johnathan would fit into what I describe as "normal" sexual behaviors for this age group (see Chapter 1). Second, Johnathan's mother indicated that they were a very affectionate, outgoing, friendly family, and that Johnathan's behavior was "natural" given their family's interaction. Third, there is no indication that Johnathan has been in trouble before— that is, he has no record. Fourth, and perhaps most important, is what Johnathan learned from this event. To begin with, he found out he received a lot of attention for engaging in a behavior that his school had labeled deviant—probably more attention than he received when he obeyed the rules. Did he like the attention? If so, this could lead him to repeat the behavior, and he will get into trouble again. Has he become labeled as a "sexual harasser"? If so, how will this affect his interactions with his peers and his family and his view of self? Fifth, this incident not only involved the child, his family, and the school, but also made Johnathan into an overnight international celebrity. The case of the "smooching six-year-old" (Zoglin, 1996) was headlined on the *Today* show and even on the front page of the London *Times*. Johnathan's parents said they had been offered $100,000 for movie rights (Zoglin, 1996).

This case serves as a caution that extreme reactions and labels to what would be considered normal sexual or perhaps just normative interpersonal attraction behavior have the potential for negative short- and long-term effects on children and the people with whom they interact—family and friends. Thus, it is important to provide appropriate education and training to educators, professionals, and lawmakers who are in positions to design and enact policies and laws relating to children's sexual behaviors. Within the education and training, several ideas need to be emphasized and reemphasized. On the one hand, it must be clear that the use of "soft" labels or language to describe sexually abusive behaviors by children 12 and under can mask the seriousness of sexually abusive behaviors. On the other hand, one must guard against a "rush to judgment" by labeling all children's sexual behaviors and misbehaviors as sexually abusive and aggressive. As noted in Chapter 1, the category of sexual aggressive behaviors by children 12 years of age and younger represent only a subset within a continuum of children's sexual behaviors. A. Gray and W. Pithers (personal communication, February 1997) have offered new empirical support for this view. In summary, it is important not to "overdiagnose" or "underdiagnose" children's sexual behaviors. Rather, care must be taken to correctly describe and label sexual behaviors so that children can obtain appropriate intervention and treatment.

Second, as demonstrated in this chapter, there is a national trend toward lowering the age that adolescents may be remanded to adult court as well as advancing the notion that children may be adjudicated for a crime. A. Gray (personal written correspondence, January 1997) views this as a potentially dangerous trend and sees it as slowly eroding the foundation of the juvenile justice system—that is, to provide families an opportunity for involvement in the correction of juvenile development and behavior. Gray views the trend toward "accountability of the individual child" as demonstrating a narrowing of the intervention focus to a single individual rather than expanding intervention to include a wider sense of community and restorative justice. Gray's caution serves to alert communities and states of the need to carefully evaluate these two intervention approaches when making or changing laws that concern children age 12 and under. It is important that children do not become victimized by policies and laws that are designed to protect them.

Alaska Says Prevention Must Be
Priority: Not Tougher Laws

In September 1996, the state of Alaska's Department of Law, Office of the Attorney General, completed a final report on the Governor's 1995 Conference on Youth and Justice. The conference had been initiated to address the growing concern in Alaska that the juvenile justice system was no longer adequate to respond to today's delinquents. The study concluded that (a) the state was trying to do too much with too little; (b) communities must assume a greater role in addressing juvenile issues in terms of conceiving, developing, and implementing their own local efforts to maintain and improve the well-being of their children, families, neighborhoods, and communities; and (c) the process must be supported by the state with collaborative efforts and technical assistance achieved by developing local and state partnerships.

A second general perception underlying the formation of the governor's conference was that Alaska has a growing number of juveniles who are committing violent crimes at younger ages. Although the accuracy of this perception has not been determined, Alaska does have a rapidly growing population of juveniles, much greater than the juvenile population in the United States as a whole. That is, between 1980 and 1990, the juvenile population in the United States as a whole increased 1% compared with 40% in Alaska.

The rapid growth in the juvenile population is translating into a noticeably increasing number of juvenile offenders. With respect to violent crimes by juveniles, however, Alaska ranks 37th in the nation; for each 100,000 juveniles, 458 are arrested annually for a violent offense. Regardless of its relatively low ranking in its percentage of serious violent juvenile offenders, Alaska ranks second in terms of both the percentage of juveniles it commits to secure facilities and the length of the time they are committed. The conclusion drawn from these findings was that Alaska is already "tough" on juvenile crime and does not need tougher laws.

Another factor that influenced decision making concerning what to do with the theoretically increasing number of juvenile offenders was cost. In Alaska, the geographic remoteness of its cities and the higher costs of living considerably increase the costs of incarcerating juveniles. Compared with the national average of $35,000, it costs Alaskans $50,000 to $100,000 a year, depending on the location of the facility. This is one of the most expensive services the state provides for individuals.

The governor's conference and subsequent task forces concluded that the state must consider alternatives to simply increasing the number of juveniles who are locked up or increasing the length of time that they are kept in detention. This course of action would be too costly. It was proposed that a more effective alternative was suggested by the statistic that most young people who come in contact with the juvenile justice system do so only once. This means that the vast majority of violent juvenile offenses are committed by a small group of chronic, serious offenders. Given this situation, it was concluded that the state can have the biggest impact on reducing serious violent juvenile offenses in Alaska not by indiscriminantly toughening all laws relating to juvenile offenders but by targeting those few individuals who are at risk of becoming chronic serious offenders. Thus, a conference recommendation was to create "community justice action teams" composed of representatives from social services, law enforcement agencies, and members of the community. It was assumed that these people would be able to identify the juveniles most at risk of becoming serious, repeat offenders in their communities and help divert them from a life of crime.

Another recommendation targeting this population was that Alaska should adopt a "dual-sentencing" scheme whereby those juvenile offenders whose records show them to be at risk of becoming chronic serious offenders would be given both a juvenile and an adult sentence. If the offender complies with the juvenile sentence and conditions of probation, then he or she would be given the full benefit of that disposition, including the possibility of having his or her juvenile record sealed sometime after the age of majority is reached. If, however, the offender does not comply with the court's sentence or reoffends before reaching the age of majority, then the district attorney would have the authority to seek imposition of the adult sentence. The responsibility for the ultimate disposition would rest with the juvenile (i.e., hold the juvenile accountable), who accordingly should feel a strong motivation for complying with the court's probation terms, including paying full restitution. Although this proposal will not be acceptable to all, it seems worthy of exploration.

The governor's conference report concluded that prevention must be made a priority in Alaska. Also, many of the recommendations set out in the report related to promoting healthy families.

One of the report recommendations directly related to children who are the topic of this book was that the governor create a juvenile sex offender task force. Several of the topics included in this recommendation were to focus attention on young sex offenders 12 years of age and younger; sex offenders who are institutionalized and reach 19 years of age without having completed their court-ordered treatment; the lack of any sex offender day treatment programs; the need for specialized foster care; the lack of enough social workers to address the needs of sexual abuse victims (who are at risk of becoming offenders); and to study whether juvenile sex offenders should be required to register as do adult offenders.

Utah's Statewide Coordination of Services for Juveniles and Sexually Abusive Children

Whereas Alaska is in the planning stages of what to do with juvenile sex offenders, a model program has already been developed by The Utah Network on Juveniles Offending Sexually (NOJOS). In 1995, the Utah state legislators authorized the creation of the Utah State Master Plan for sexually offending juveniles. The plan called for and designated agency population responsibilities, professional qualifications, and a sex offender-specific continuum of services needed to provide effective and efficient community protections and professional interventions. An outgrowth of the mandate was the third edition of *Protocols and Standards* (Utah NOJOS, 1996) that designates and represents the best practices for professionals and services delivered to juvenile sex offenders. The guidelines represented the work of NOJOS and The Utah Juvenile Sex Offender Authority and are consistent with those developed by the National Taskforce on Juvenile Sexual Offending.

According to Dave Fowers (personal communication, August 1996), Utah Division of Youth Corrections, the document was an outgrowth of more than 10 years of work by a multidisciplinary team of professionals concerned with abusive and criminal behavior by children and juveniles. Members of the team had come together in recognition of the increases in the number of sex offenders perpetrated by juveniles in Utah and in recognition that these children needed a variety of services and guidelines that were not available. The section that focuses on juvenile sex offender-specific protocols and standards for children ages 4 to 11 with sexually abusive behavior problems was developed by Lucinda Rasmussen, Barbara Christopherson, Connie Mendez, and Jan Ellen Burton (Utah NOJOS, 1996). The focus of the section was on treatment and placement of these children. Each of the juvenile sex offender-specific protocols for the treatment or placement of children (ages 4-11) with sexually abusive behavior problems includes the following seven separate levels of service delivery: Level 1, Outpatient/In-Home-Psychoeducational; Level 2, Outpatient/In-Home-Psychotherapy; Level 3, Day Treatment/In-Home; Level 4, "Enriched" Group Home/Therapeutic Foster Home; Level 5, Inpatient/Assessment and Stabilization; Level 6, Residential Treatment; and Level 7, State Hospital/Psychiatric Treatment Enhanced. Each of these levels is divided into six sections: client profile, assessment, treatment goals, treatment modalities and frequency, monitoring, and criteria for discharge. Samples of Level 1 and Level 3 protocols for children with sexually abusive problems are shown in Table 6.1. As can be seen in the table under Monitoring, professional qualifications for those who treat children ages 4 to 11 who exhibit sexually abusive behavior are mentioned, although these are found in a separate section of the *Protocols and Standards Manual*. Basically, the qualifications indicate that those who treat children with sexually abusive behavior problems must have specialized training, which includes expertise in play therapy and other treatment techniques for young children. Considerable training and expertise in intervention with both sexual abuse victims and children who sexually abuse others (i.e., knowledge in victim and offender intervention) is also recommended.

With respect to treating juvenile sex offenders, overall, networking with other professionals is viewed as an essential component of providing treatment services. Statewide networks provide opportunities for consultation and coordination of treatment services. Membership in national organizations of professionals who work with sex offenders is also highly desirable. Examples of such national organizations are the Association for the Treatment of Sexual Abusers, the American Professional Society on the Abuse of Children, and the National Adolescent Perpetrator Network.

Currently, there is no specialized national certification or sex-specific licensure for clinicians and service providers, although the National Task Force on Juvenile Sexual Offending has defined specific guidelines for professionals working with juvenile sex offenders. These guidelines are outlined by the National Adolescent Perpetrator Network (1993). As will be apparent, however, these guidelines refer to adolescent offenders.

Because the Utah NOJOS (1994) *Protocol and Standards Manual* represents a statewide comprehensive network of services and agencies involved in intervening with juvenile offenders, it includes protocols on (a) Investigations for Law Enforcement and Child Protective Services

TABLE 6.1 A Comparison of Level 1 Outpatient, In-Home, and Psychoeducational and Level 3 Day Treatment, In-Home, and Out of the Services Protocol for Sexually Abusive Children

	Level 1	Level 3
Client profile	Outpatient psychoeducational intervention is most appropriate for young children (ages 4-7) who are sexually curious and impulsive. These children may be victims of some type of abuse. Short-term educationally focused outpatient intervention may be adequate to address their sexually inappropriate behavior.	Children who display severe and repetitive patterns of self-destructive behavior usually require more intensive intervention than is typically provided in outpatient programs. These children lack empathy, may be opportunistic and aggressive toward others, and may show predatory behavior patterns. They have frequently experienced significant abuse or neglect resulting in severe attachment problems. Many exhibit severe psychiatric problems (e.g., thought disorders or dissociation). Others exhibit several oppositional defiant behavior and appear uncontrolled when angry. These children are at high risk for reoffending sexually and often require intervention in a structured and restrictive treatment setting.
Assessed	Level B: sex offender specific assessment	Level A: line worker assessment (if adjudicated) Level B: sex offender specific assessment Level C: comprehensive sex offender specific
Treatment goals	Educate the child about sexual behavior problems. Ensure that he or she understands what is appropriate versus inappropriate sexual behavior. Help parent(s) establish appropriate supervision to deter recurrence of sexual acting out. Treatment should also focus on identification and expression of feelings related to any prior abuse, social skill development, and teaching assertiveness and self-protection skills.	Treatment should focus on management of all significant problem behaviors (e.g., aggression, impulsiveness, or compulsive patterns of sexually assaultive behavior). Parents must provide vigilant supervision to help child accomplish the following goals: increase accountability for sexually inappropriate and other victimizing behaviors; increase responsible thinking and develop understanding of own behaviors; improve ability to identify and express feelings; develop empathy for feelings to others; address personal victimization or loss skills or both; demonstrate ability to manage sexual feelings and thoughts; and develop a workable relapse prevention plan.

	Level 1	Level 3
Treatment modalities	Individual and family therapy are the primary treatment modalities, but modalities can include referral to a psychoeducational group. The group should address self-protection and prevention of further sexually-inappropriate behavior. In most cases, treatment is weekly and short term.	In day treatment, the child receives daily supervision and clinical intervention in a structured program. Intervention is educational, and therapeutic contact should focus specifically on issues related to the child's sexually abusive behavior problems. The child should be seen at least weekly in group therapy that addresses perpetration issues. If client population is insufficient to create groups, children may be seen in individual and family therapy by clinicians who specialize in treating sexually abusive children. The Professional Qualifications Protocol, described in a later section of the manual, outlines the specific expertise needed.
Monitoring	All cases should be investigated by Child Protection Services (CPS) of the Division of Child and Family Services (DCFS). Investigation can help protect children involved in the inappropriate sexual behavior and assist the families to obtain treatment. Some cases may require ongoing monitoring by the DCFS through protective supervision. Due to the young age of Level 1 children, the juvenile court should not be involved.	All cases should be investigated by CPS of DCFS and, if appropriate, by law enforcement. Investigation can help protect the victim(s) of the sexually abusive child, assist the victim(s) to obtain therapy, encourage the parents of the sexually abusive child to seek treatment, and determine if the child should be adjudicated.
	The therapist is responsible for monitoring the treatment process. Clinicians must have specialized expertise to treat children with sexually abusive behavior problems and should receive specific training. The Professional Qualifications Protocol is described in a later section of the book.	In most cases, the therapist and day treatment staff monitor compliance to treatment. With older children (ages 8-11), there may be adjudication and thus monitoring by the juvenile justice system. If children have been placed in the custody or protective supervision of the DCFS, the DCFS caseworker also monitors compliance.
Criteria for discharge	To be discharged from treatment, children must understand that sexually inappropriate behavior is unacceptable. They must cease to display sexually abusive behavior. Additionally, parents must understand their child's problem and implement adequate super-vision. Clinicians should make parents aware of treatment resources in case sexually abusive behavior problems recur.	A child must leave day treatment when the assigned therapist, parent(s), and day treatment staff determine that the child's problem behaviors are manageable in a less restrictive setting. Transfer of therapy in an outpatient treatment program allows the child and his or her parents to continue to address treatment goals related to sexually abusive behavior problems.
		If the child has been adjudicated or is receiving supervision by the juvenile court or both, the juvenile monitoring authority must approve discharge of a child placed in custody or protective supervision of the DCFS. Parents must demonstrate they can provide adequate supervision before a child is returned to their care. Treatment professionals in both day treatment and outpatient psychotherapy settings should be careful to coordinate the transfer of treatment services and keep parents adequately informed.

SOURCE: Utah NOJOS (1996). Used with permission.

(CPS); (b) Child and Family Services; (c) Prosecution, Juvenile Court; (d) Assessment Guidelines; (e) Treatment/Placement (for juveniles not in the 4-11 age groups); (f) Mental Health; (g) Services for Disability Population; (h) Youth Correction; (i) Education; (j) Professional Qualifications; (k) Agency Responsibility; and (l) Specific Regional Resources. Overall, this manual could serve as a model for states wishing to coordinate services for juvenile sex offenders, including the emerging group of children 12 years of age and younger.

In conclusion, and similar to the Alaska report, information provided in the NOJOS manual indicates that families and environments that facilitate the development of sexually abusive behaviors are the places to begin resolution of the problem. Waiting until children are identified by social service systems and punished by the legal system may be too late.

Models for Community Response

Gil and Johnson (1993b)

Gil and Johnson (1993b, pp. 131-135) have also recognized the need for developing a community response to the social problem of children who are sexually abusing others, and they have outlined several recommendations. The recommendations focus on agencies and clinical responses as well as responses related to the legal area and schools.

Agency and Clinical Responses

With respect to agency and clinical responses, Gil and Johnson (1993b) indicate that there is a need to identify policies for intake assessment of children referred with sexual behavior problems; develop tools for interviewing children with sexual behavior problems; determine a set of criteria for assessing sexually abusive children and for assessing risk factors associated with sexually aggressive children; identify protective service policies for providing in- and outreach services to sexually abusive children and their families; determine community resources that provide services to child victims, as well as specialized programs for children who offend, and identify places that provide diagnostic or treatment services; combine agency or clinical interviews or both with police where possible, avoiding duplication; and design (a) criteria for filing dependency petitions for sexually abusive children, (b) criteria for removal, and (c) a system for selecting the most appropriate placements.

Legal Actions

Gil and Johnson (1993b, p. 132) offer several recommendations for developing legal responses, including determining which laws pertain to sexually abusive behaviors by children; developing and using an interview protocol with these children; establishing a working relationship with probation departments regarding services to sexually abusive children; establishing joint interviews with child protective service workers whenever possible (avoiding multiple interviews); determining the circumstances in which prosecution or referral to probation or diversion programs, and removal from the home, are appropriate or necessary; identifying the most effective way of using the authority of the legal system to mandate necessary treatment for sexually abusive children and their families; identifying community resources that specialize in the treatment of sexually abusive children; and identifying the out-of-home care settings providing diagnostic or treatment services to sexually abusive children.

School Responses

Gil and Johnson (1993b, p. 132) view schools as playing an integral role in attacking the social problem of children sexually abusing others. They recommend the following responses: First, school personnel need to understand the duty to report suspected abuse by any person, including young children. Second, there is a need to establish criteria for differentiating between normal childhood sexual play and abusive sexual behavior. (This would have helped in the Johnathan Prevette case discussed previously.) Third, schools need to cooperate with treatment specialists in providing a safe and appropriate school setting for sexually abusive children. Where necessary, school policies should be flexible to provide needed monitoring of these children. Fourth, there is a need to identify and use community resources and maintain a list of therapeutic services available for children with sexual behavior problems.

In conclusion, Gil and Johnson (1993b, pp. 133-134) add that when following reports of children who have been victimized by other children, problems may emerge in the system because child protective agencies are available to respond to victims but not to the sexually abusive child—that is, the perpetrator. They caution that investigatory agencies must make sure that both the victim and the perpetrator are provided the necessary services.

Finally, Gil and Johnson (1993b) address the need for families of sexually abusing children to be mandated into treatment. They emphasize that family involvement is a critical component of treatment for this age group of sexual offenders, noting the relationship between the sexually abusive child's behavior and the child's influences and interactions within the family. The authors stress that without cooperative parents, children at these young ages will not even get to treatment unless they are removed from the home.

Anchorage Juvenile Sex Offenders Continuum Group Report

In the early 1990s, recognition of an increasing number of sexually aggressive juveniles in Alaska led to the development of a committee to study the juvenile sexual offender population. The committee called itself the Anchorage Juvenile Sex Offenders Continuum Group (AJSOCG). In 1991, AJSOCG completed a report on existing services, gaps, and recommendations concerning the juvenile sex offender population. One subcommittee report within this document focused on young child perpetrators under the age of 12 who exhibit sexual behavior toward another that is unlawful or harmful due to intimidation, coercion, or force. In this subcommittee report, McBee (1991) suggested several programs that would be necessary to bring these children to the attention of the public. Her suggestions, as well as ideas derived from doing research for this book, are presented in the following list. As will be apparent, some of these recommendations overlap with those suggested by Gil and Johnson (1993b) in the Utah model. In the following list, however, there are new ideas that are not included in the other proposals and model:

1. *Public awareness:* McBee (1991) argues that public awareness is necessary to educate professionals and parents about the characteristics and the behaviors of sexually abusive children. (Material provided in this book should prove useful in accomplishing this recommendation.)

2. *Training educators and service providers:* McBee (1991) notes that there exists a need to train educators and service providers to identify and confront early sexually offending behaviors, report

signs of victimization, and counter inappropriate sexual messages that children are exposed to. (Again, information provided
in the previous chapters of this book should prove useful in
accomplishing this goal.)

3. *Evaluation of media messages:* McBee (1991) discusses the need for
   public awareness and research to evaluate media messages that
   give children ideas that society condones exploitive and aggressive sexuality. She suggests replacing these types of messages
   with portrayals of positive sexuality. (This recommendation
   is especially timely with the increase of, and accessibility to,
   sexually explicit and pornographic material such as adult videos
   and access to the Internet. It is also important to call the media's
   attention to the potentially negative consequences of creating
   "titillating" news out of cases such as Johnathan Prevette's,
   which was discussed earlier in this chapter.)

4. *Perpetration prevention programs:* McBee (1991) notes that many
   schools have personal safety and sexual abuse programs that
   teach children how to protect themselves from becoming sexual
   abuse victims. She suggests that perpetration prevention—the
   notion that children can be perpetrators as well as victims—
   needs to be added to the curriculum (as editor of this book,
   however, I encountered resistance from school administrators
   when the idea of incorporating the "children as perpetrators"
   concept into existing personal safety or sexual abuse prevention
   programs offered in a school district was proposed. This was not
   because the administrators were opposed to the idea but because of anticipated pressure by a variety of groups that were
   opposed to any type of sex education in schools. Because changes to existing programs needed to go through reviews by
   school boards, teachers, principals, and parents, the administrators were concerned that those opposed to existing sex education prevention programs might try to eliminate the program if
   given the opportunity. Although acknowledging the need to add
   the perpetration education component, they were more willing
   to continue the existing program rather than risk losing it if it
   was subjected to new reviews).

5. McBee (1991) offers a definition and label for children who are
   behaving in a sexually aggressive way. Although it is obvious
   from previous chapters in this book that everyone will not accept
   her label of "young child perpetrator," her definition is similar
   to those used by practitioners and researchers who use the terms
   sexually aggressive children, children molesting children, child
   perpetrators, and child sex offenders. She describes young child
   perpetrators as children who are 12 years of age or younger who

exhibit sexual behaviors toward others that are harmful or unlawful due to intimidation, coercion, or force. (Although I prefer
the term sexually aggressive children, it may be that labels such
as molesters, offenders, and perpetrators need to be applied to
these children to get them the appropriate treatment, despite the
potential dangers associated with negative labels. Perpetrator
and offender labels are also more familiar to those who work in
the justice system, in which one of the current gaps exists for
coping with sexually aggressive children.) In addition to an
appropriate definition or label, I believe the use of a continuum
of sexual behaviors, such as that proposed by Johnson and
Feldmeth (1993) in Chapter 1, is necessary to include in awareness and training programs. Tools such as this provide markers
that differentiate normal from reactive from sexually aggressive
or molesting behaviors by children.

6. *Legal education on consequences of sexual perpetration:* McBee (1991)
   contends that children need to be educated on the legal consequences of behaviors that are abusive or exploitative. (With
   changes in laws and policies occurring throughout the country,
   this recommendation will become increasingly important.)

I add a seventh recommendation to McBee's (1991) list, which is
the following:

7. *Research component necessary for program development and assessment:* A research component should be built into program development. System models can be tested before and after each stage
   of implementation using computer simulations, and an evaluation component is also essential. These research aspects are
   necessary to avoid building systems with missing parts and to
   redirect programs that are not achieving objectives or goals.
   Given the decreasing federal and state funds for service-oriented
   programs, the research component, although not always popular, is important and necessary.

Coordinating and Training Target
Audiences in Communities

In addition to the previously discussed recommendations, the
AJSOCG (1991) report identified specific target audiences in the community that need training with respect to juvenile sex offenders. Many

of these were included in Gil and Johnson's (1993b) list, although the AJSOCG committee also included medical professionals and legislators.

Recommendations were also made in the report that focused on specific community training modules. An "awareness training" module for in-servicing school administrators, state agencies that serve children and families, and legislators was suggested. For psychologists, medical professionals, counselors, social workers, clinicians, law enforcement personnel, probation officers, residential care providers, foster parents, and the Division of Family and Youth Services, AJSOCG (1991) suggested the development of a "technical training" module. They also outlined the content of in-service training. This included sex offender profiles, awareness and strategies for dealing with thinking errors associated with these youthful sex offenders, treatment issues, and methods for working effectively with manipulative deviant behaviors. They recommended addressing offender issues from a generic behavioral approach, and recommended that training be done on a continuous basis and repeated a minimum of once every 2 years.

Other recommendations offered by the AJSOCG (1991) committee for developing a comprehensive community-based sex offender program were (a) coordination of tasks by the various agencies and providers in the community; (b) establishment of a clearinghouse for in-service training and sharing of materials across agencies, departments, and community groups; and (c) quarterly meetings and information-sharing activities of the AJSOCG training subcommittee. As can be seen, many of these recommendations overlap with the model developed by the Utah NOJOS team.

Department of Social and Health Services
Children's Administration, State of Washington:
Two Program Reports

Two studies by Washington State's Department of Social and Health Services (DSHS) are important because they highlight the need for research and continuous monitoring of programs once they are established. Both of the studies reported here were an outgrowth of the 1989 Washington state legislature passing a bill referred to as the Community Protection Act (CPA). This act increased the penalty for sexual-offending behaviors and provided resources for treating high-risk sexually aggressive youth. The resources made available were $1.196 million for specialized treatment of youth currently being treated by the Division of Child and Family Service (DCFS). To be eligible for these special funds, children had to have committed a sexually aggressive act, have been a victim of abuse, and be in the custody and care of DSHS.

On the basis of studies of the youth and a program developed by English and Ray (1991) and Ray and English (1991), a report by DSHS (1992b) concluded that the service system did not have appropriate placements for children who were frequently removed from their homes for their own protection (most were victims as well as perpetrators) as well as the protection of others. Furthermore, the DSHS concluded that it was unclear whether the traditional services available were appropriate for sexually aggressive children. They suggested a reexamination of how all sexually aggressive youth were handled in the areas of risk assessment and case planning, treatment methods, placement resources, and training of staff and alternate care providers. The recommendations follow.

Risk Assessment and
Case Planning

First, a standardized model for assessing the probability of reoffending for sexually aggressive children should be adopted by DCFS. This would allow appropriate case planning and victim protection.

This recommendation was based on several study findings. Many treatment cases had plans that demonstrated good practice in coupling risk assessment with case planning using a family-focused approach. Many plans, however, lacked basic components for a thorough treatment plan or did not address identified risk factors or both.

Second, available DCFS staff statewide should have more training or consultation on outside available resources to assist in the day-to-day management of sexually aggressive youth (e.g., electronic monitoring devices, respite care, etc.).

Although DCFS workers were identifying younger sexually aggressive youth, it was found that a tendency existed to characterize the acts of these youth as playful sexual experimentation. Furthermore, younger children were assessed by caseworkers as less likely to recommit sexually aggressive behaviors when in reality they reoffended as often as the older youth. These problems, relating to identification, labeling, and assessment, needed correction.

Treatment Methodologies

Treatment issues of accountability, consequences, and supervision must be developed for DCFS case management and contracted treatment services. It was noted that in the past, DCFS may have counted on the juvenile justice system for these services.

This recommendation was based on study findings that most youth in the study were referred to victim-oriented treatment, regardless of the current trend in sex-offender treatment that stresses the need for dealing with offending behaviors before the perpetrator's own victimization. Less than half of the children under age 12 received offender-specific assessments. Few of the sexually aggressive youth in DCFS were held accountable by the justice system, DCFS, or the treatment community.

Placement Treatment Resources

DCFS should consider strategies to develop new resources for sexually aggressive youth. These strategies should include recruitment and training for specialized foster and group care, expanded and specialized contract services, utilization of contracted certified clinicians for treatment oversight, and consultation and foster care training.

Study findings revealed that DCFS social workers statewide identified a shortage of placement resources and evaluation or treatment resources as barriers to effective case management with sexually aggressive children. Inefficient utilization of CPA treatment funds was found because of service resource shortages. Nearly 50% of all the youth were not in the placement of choice but rather in the only placement available. Older children were often returned to their own homes while awaiting an opening in foster or group care. In some cases, previous victims of the perpetrators were still in the home.

Training of Staff and Alternate Care Providers

First, DCFS should consider specialized training for at least some, if not all, their social work staff. The study reported that the information necessary to work with this specialized population of youth far exceeded what was currently provided in DCFS core training.

In an earlier DSHS (1992a) report, another set of recommendations related to the need for a community-based response was set forth by the DSHS's Division of Management Services. Again, these recommendations were based on study findings that most of the youth in the agency were referred to victim-oriented treatment, regardless of the trend in sex-offender treatment. The agency report concluded that few of the sexually aggressive youth in DCFS, the justice system, or the treatment community were being held accountable for their behaviors. They speculated that this problem was due to policies, lack of knowledge and understanding of the problem, lack of resources, or all three. Whatever the explanation, they argued for an assessment of all social systems associated with these youth—social services, juvenile justice prosecutors, probation and parole, and community providers. The following recommendations were set forth in January 1992 (DSHS, 1992a):

1. DCFS should take the lead in establishing an advisory council for the purpose of examining current issues associated with sexually aggressive children. It was suggested that at a minimum the review include the following:
   a. It should include law enforcement policies regarding the arrest of juveniles because statewide standards existed that were uniformly applied in cases of suspected sexual abuse cases.
   b. It should include prosecutorial policies regarding prosecution of sexually aggressive children because it was found that, currently, this was a discretionary decision within state guidelines and varied widely across counties.
   c. It should include DCFS policies and procedures related to reporting to law enforcement and prosecutors suspected sexual offenses by children in out-of-home care.
   d. It should include availability, adequacy, and consistency of offender treatment specialists because study findings indicated there was no current requirement for certified providers for sexually aggressive children. The certification requirement applied only to providers who were seeing adjudicated youth.
   e. It should include availability and adequacy of placement resources for these youth because there existed current needs assessment research on group care facilities, but there were no specialized receiving homes or foster homes for sexually aggressive children.

2. The advisory group develop comprehensive recommendations for coordinating public and private responses to these children.

3. DCFS should consider specialized training staff in the area of sexually aggressive children. It was proposed that there should be at least one specially trained staff within each DCFS.

4. A sexually aggressive child treatment or case management model should be developed and adopted. The model should specify standards for investigation and assessment of risk, evaluation, treatment, monitoring and supervision, and so on. The model should incorporate agency standards—that is, family focused, least restrictive, and culturally responsive.

5. DCFS should not simply assume that credentialing sex-offender evaluators would ensure adequate evaluations and treatment. The case management model should specify exactly what is expected in evaluations, treatment, and foster care milieu for incorporation into contract specifications.

Valuable Reference

In addition to the plans and studies discussed previously, another resource that should prove valuable to states and communities that are in the planning or evaluation stages of programs or policies associated with sexually aggressive children and juveniles is Fay Honey Knopp's 1991 revision of her 1985 booklet titled *The Youthful Sex Offender: The Rationale and Goals of Early Intervention and Treatment*. Although the booklet was aimed at adolescents, I believe it provides a good reference for use in developing a community response to preadolescent sex offenders. It is approximately only 30 pages in length and has five applicable sections: rationale for early intervention, some guidelines for determining normal and inappropriate behavior, criteria for assessing risk, goals and treatment methods, and state planning.

Combining Theory and Practice

Another important step in preventing sexually abusive and aggressive children from dropping through the system's cracks is the development and utilization of two types of theories. The first type involves well-developed theories that explain why children become sexually abusive and aggressive, as discussed in Chapter 4. Currently, most practitioners readily admit that their treatment programs are primarily atheoretically driven or adopted from theories previously used to explain adult and adolescent sex-offending behaviors or behaviors that represent a reaction to the offender's own victimization history or both. Currently, there is little substantial evidence that these approaches work with sexually abusing children, although several longitudinal studies by Bonner et al. and Gray and Pithers are in the beginning stages of data analysis and should provide valuable information. The information that is available from these studies was discussed in Chapters 2 and 5.

The second type of theories that are necessary are those that summarize the state-of-the-art intervention and prevention knowledge about what seems to be the most effective community approaches to working with sexually abusive children. As evidenced in this chapter, clinicians, researchers, social service agencies, and members of the justice system are only at the beginning stages of sharing information with respect to identifying, treating, and adjudication of these children. As we are developing community responses to the problem of sexually abusive children, it is important to recognize the need to match interventions to the local community and organizational contexts. What works in a large, multiethnic municipality such as Los Angeles may not be effective in a small rural community that has little ethnic diversity. I believe partnerships such as those discussed in the Alaska intervention plan will be a useful starting point.

Finally, as proposed in Chapter 4 that a systems theory approach was needed to fully explain children's sexually aggressive behaviors, an ecological systems planning approach offers a model appropriate for community planning. The following stages are necessary:

1. An understanding of the psychological and sociological factors that relate to the problem and the interrelationships that interact at various levels of analysis must be developed—for example, the individual, family, community, and society.
2. Information about various interventions and their effectiveness with various cultures, populations, and urban and rural settings must be gathered.
3. Knowledge about the organizational structures within the community and state and how they will interact and function to prevent or treat or both sexually aggressive behaviors by children must be gained.

4. Identification and sharing information must be done with communities and states working on issues related to sexually aggressive youth. This can avoid "reinventing the wheel," which is neither cost nor time efficient.
5. The "turf barriers" that prevent or slow down a much-needed systemic response to children and families involved in sexually abusive behaviors must be broken down.
6. The media must be engaged in attempts to address this social problem. It is relatively clear that they are an active player.
7. A research design and evaluation component at all phases of program development must be included.

Conclusions

This chapter demonstrates that a comprehensive-based effort is necessary if sexually abusive behaviors by children 12 years of age and younger are to be recognized and addressed. It is clear that these types of behavior cannot be left to subjective assessments of isolated individuals, agencies, schools, and departments in urban and rural communities across the nation. Rather, there needs to be a carefully planned and coordinated community, state, and even national response that might be based on some of the suggestions, programs, and studies discussed in this chapter. I hope much of the information presented in this chapter and previous chapters of this book will prove useful in developing appropriate responses to defining, identifying, treating, and preventing young children and their families from continuing sexually abusive behaviors.

Although there still exist relatively few researchers and providers who are heavily involved in gathering information or developing materials and programs for these children, most would agree that treating and preventing further victimizations by these young sexual abusers may offer the best hope to mitigating the growth of sexual victimization by all age groups.

In conclusion, any systemwide response that addresses the problem of children acting sexually abusively must begin, first, with public awareness and acceptance that children age 12 and younger are capable of sexual abuse against others that involves threats, coercion, and violence. Second, a continuum of sexual behaviors must be used as a guide to ensure that appropriate terms or labels are used to describe children's diverse sexual behaviors and misbehaviors. This practice will do much to increase the probability that children receive appropriate treatment and services. Third, it must be recognized that sexual behaviors, like other behaviors, are frequently learned in the home, and thus families must be a part of treatment or prevention plans. Fourth, it must also be recognized that children's sexually abusive behaviors are influenced by social institutions other than the family—for example, the media—and also influence other social institutions and agencies—for example, the school and social and legal services. Fifth, all solutions, treatments, and prevention plans must be cost and time effective and involve an evaluation research component. Finally, although still in its infancy, information in this book should prove useful in guiding efforts to achieve these goals. A consequence of such efforts will, it is hoped, begin to close the system cracks that allow young children with sexual behavior problems and their families to move through society unnoticed and untreated or inappropriately labeled and treated.

References

Achenbach, T. M., & Edelbrook, C. (1983). *Manual for the Child Behavior Checklist and Revised Child Behavior Profile.* Burlington: University of Vermont, Department of Psychiatry.

Ageton, S. S. (1983). *Sexual assault among adolescents.* Lexington, MA: D. C. Heath.

American Association of University Women. (1993). *Hostile hallways: The AAUW survey on sexual harassment in America's schools.* Washington, DC: Harris Scholastic Research.

American Psychiatric Association. (1980). *Diagnostic and statistical manual of mental disorders* (3rd ed.). Washington, DC: Author.

The Anchorage Juvenile Sex Offender Continuum Group. (1991). *Data on existing services, gaps, and recommendations.* Unpublished report.

Araji, S., & Finkelhor, D. (1986). Abusers: A review of the research. In D. Finkelhor and Associates (Eds.), *A sourcebook on child sexual abuse* (pp. 89-118). Newbury Park, CA: Sage.

Araji, S., Jache, A., Pfeiffer, K., & Smith, B. (1993). *Survey results describing sexually aggressive children.* Unpublished report, University of Alaska at Anchorage.

Araji, S., Jache, A., Tyrrell, C., & Field, C. (1992). *An analysis of case records of children who molest.* Unpublished report, University of Alaska at Anchorage.

Bagley, C., & Shewchuk-Dann, D. (1991). Characteristics of 60 children and adolescents who have a history of sexual assault against others: Evidence from a controlled study [Special issue]. *Journal of Child and Youth Care,* 43-52.

Ballester, S., & Pierre, F. (1995). Monster therapy: The use of metaphor in psychotherapy with abuse reactive children. In M. Hunter (Ed.), *Child survivors and perpetrators of sexual abuse: Treatment innovations* (pp. 125-146). Thousand Oaks, CA: Sage.

Bandura, A. (1977). *Social learning theory.* Englewood Cliffs, NJ: Prentice Hall.

Bank, S. P., & Kahn, M. D. (1982). *The sibling bond.* New York: Basic Books.

Barringer, F. (1989, May 30). Children as sexual prey and predators. *New York Times,* pp. A1, A16.

Barth, R. P., & Berry, M. (1988). *Adoption and disruption: Rates, risks, and responses.* Hawthorn, NY: Aldine.

Barth, R. P., Berry, M., Carson, M. L., Goodfield, R., & Feinberg, B. (1986). Contributors to disruption and dissolution of older-child adoptions. *Child Welfare, 65*(4), 359-371.

Barth, R. P., Berry, M., Yoshikami, R., Goodfield, R. K., & Carson, M. L. (1988). Predicting adoption disruption. *Journal of the National Association of Social Workers, 33*(3), 227-233.

Becker, J., Kaplan, M., Cunningham-Rathner, J., & Kovoussi, R. (1986). Characteristics of adolescent incest sexual perpetrators: Preliminary findings. *Journal of Family Violence, 1*(1), 85-97.

Beitchman, J., Zucker, K., Hood, J., DaCosta, G. A., & Akman, A. (1991). A review of the short-term effects of child sexual abuse. *Child Abuse & Neglect, 15,* 537-556.

Berliner, L., Manaois, O., & Monastersky, C. (1986). *Child sexual behavior disturbance: An assessment and treatment model.* Seattle, WA: Harborview Sexual Assault Center.

Berliner, L., & Rawlings, L. (1991). *A treatment manual: Children with sexual behavior problems.* Seattle, WA: Harborview Sexual Assault Center.

Berry, M. (1990). Preparing and supporting special needs of adoptive families: A review of the literature. *Child and Adolescent Social Work, 7*(5), 403-418.

Berry, M., & Barth, R. P. (1989). Behavior problems of children adopted when older. *Children and Youth Services Review, 11,* 221-238.

Bertalanffy, L. von. (1968a). *General systems therapy: Foundation, development, applications.* New York: Braziller.

Bertalanffy, L. von. (1968b). General systems theory: A critical review. In W. Buckley (Ed.), *Modern systems research for the behavioral scientist* (pp. 11-30). Chicago: Aldine.

Bonner, B., Walker, E., & Berliner, L. (1991-1996). Unpublished raw data.

Boulding, K. E. (1975). General systems theory: The skeleton of science. In B. D. Ruben & J. Y. Kim (Eds.), *General systems theory and human communication.* Rochelle Park, NJ: Hayden.

Brant, R. S., & Tisza, V. B. (1977). The sexually misused child. *American Journal of Orthopsychiatry, 47*(1), 80-90.

Breer, W. (1987). *The adolescent molester.* Springfield, IL: Charles C Thomas.

Bronfenbrenner, U. (1979). *The ecology of human development.* Cambridge, MA: Harvard University Press.

Burton, J., Rasmussen, L., Christopherson, B., Bradshaw, J., & Huke, S. (1997). *Treating sexually abusive behavior problems: A clinician's guide for child and parent intervention.* Unpublished manuscript.

Canavan, M. M., Meyer, W. J., & Higgs, D. C. (1992). The female experience of sibling incest. *Journal of Marital and Family Therapy, 18*(2), 129-142.

Cantwell, H. B. (1988). Child sexual abuse: Very young perpetrators. *Child Abuse & Neglect, 12,* 579-582.

Cantwell, H. B. (1995). Sexually aggressive children and societal response. In M. Hunter (Ed.), *Child survivors and perpetrators of sexual abuse: Treatment innovations* (pp. 79-107). Thousand Oaks, CA: Sage.

Carlo, P. (1985). The children's residential treatment center as a living laboratory for family members: A review of the literature and its implications for practice. *Child Care Quarterly, 14*(3), 156-170.

Carnes, P. (1983). *Out of the shadows: Understanding sexual addiction.* Minneapolis, MN: CompCare.

Cicchetti, D., & Toth, S. (1995). A developmental psychopathology perspective on child abuse and neglect. *Journal of the American Academy of Child and Adolescent Psychiatry, 34,* 541-565.

Cole, E. (1982). Sibling incest: The myth of benign sibling incest. *Women and Therapy, 5,* 79-89.

Cole, E. S., & Donley, K. S. (1990). History, values, and placement policy issues in adoption. In D. M. Brodzinsky & M. D. Schechter (Eds.), *The psychology of adoption* (pp. 273-294). New York: Oxford University Press.

Conte, J. (1986). Sexual abuse and the family: A critical analysis. In T. Trepper & M. Barrett (Eds.), *Treating incest: A multimodal systems perspective.* New York: Hawthorn.

Conte, J., & Schuerman, J. (1987). Factors associated with an increased impact of child sexual abuse. *Child Abuse & Neglect, 11,* 201-211.

Cooper, C. S., Peterson, N. L., & Meier, J. H. (1987). Variables associated with disrupted placement in a select sample of abused and neglected children. *Child Abuse & Neglect, 11,* 75-86.

Courtois, C. A. (1988). *Healing the incest wound.* New York: Norton.

Crenshaw, D. A. (1988). Responding to sexual acting-out. In C. E. Schaefer & A. J. Swanson (Eds.), *Children in residential care: Critical issues in treatment* (pp. 50-76). New York: Van Nostrand Reinhold.

Cunningham, C., & MacFarlane, L. (1991). *When children molest children: Group treatment strategies for young sexual offenders.* Orwell, VT: Safer Society Press.

Cunningham, C., & MacFarlane, L. (1996). *When children abuse.* Brandon, VT: Safer Society Press.

Daie, N., Witztum, E., & Eleff, M. (1989). Long-term effects of sibling incest. *Journal of Clinical Psychiatry, 50,*(11), 428-431.

De Jong, A. R. (1989). Sexual interactions among siblings and cousins: Experimentation or exploitation? *Child Abuse & Neglect, 13,* 271-279.

de Young, M. (1982). *The sexual victimization of children.* Jefferson, NC: McFarland.

English, D. J., & Ray, J. A. (1991). *Children with sexual behavior problems: A behavioral comparison.* Olympia, WA: Department of Social and Health Services.

Eth, S., & Pynoos, R. (1985). *Post-traumatic stress disorder in children.* Washington, DC: American Psychiatric Press.

Everstine, D. S., & Everstine, L. (1989). *Sexual trauma in children and adolescents: Dynamics and treatment.* New York: Brunner/Mazel.

Faller, K. C. (1990). *Understanding child sexual maltreatment.* Newbury Park, CA: Sage.

Faller, K. C. (1991). Polyincestuous families: An exploratory study. *Journal of Interpersonal Violence, 6*(3), 310-322.

Fatout, M. F. (1990). Aggression: A characteristic of physically abused latency-aged children. *Child Adolescent Social Work, 7*(5), 365-376.

Federal Bureau of Investigation. (1990). *1990 report of age specific arrest rates and race specific arrest rates for selected offenses between 1985 and 1988.* Washington, DC: United States Department of Justice.

Fehrenback, P. A., Smith, W., Monastersky, C., & Deisher, R. W. (1986). Adolescent sexual offenders: Offender and offense characteristics. *American Journal of Orthopsychiatry, 56*(2), 225-233.

Finkelhor, D. (1973). *Childhood sexual experiences: A retrospective survey.* Durham: University of New Hampshire.

Finkelhor, D. (1980). Sex among siblings: A survey on prevalence, variety and effects. *Archives of Sexual Behavior, 9*(3), 171-194.

Finkelhor, D. (1984). *Child sexual abuse: New theory and research.* New York: Free Press.

Finkelhor, D. (with Araji, S., Baron, L., Browne, A., Doyle Peters, S., & Wyatt, G. E.). (1986). *A sourcebook on child sexual abuse.* Newbury Park, CA: Sage.

Finkelhor, D. (1987). The trauma of child sexual abuse: Two models. In G. E. Wyatt & G. Johnson Powell (Eds.), *Lasting effects of child sexual abuse* (pp. 61-82). Newbury Park, CA: Sage.

Finkelhor, D., & Browne, A. (1985). The traumatic impact of child sexual abuse: A conceptualization. *American Journal of Orthopsychiatry, 55*(4), 530-541.

Finkelhor, D., & Browne, A. (1986). Initial and long-term effects: A conceptual framework. In D. Finkelhor & Associates (Eds.), *A sourcebook on child sexual abuse.* Newbury Park, CA: Sage.

Finkelhor, D., Hotaling, G. T., Lewis, I. A., & Smith, C. (1990). Sexual abuse in a national survey of adult men and women: Prevalence characteristics and risk factors. *Child Abuse & Neglect, 14,* 19-28.

Fortenberry, J. D., & Hill, R. F. (1986). Sister-sister incest as a manifestation of multigenerational sexual abuse. *Journal of Adolescent Health Care, 7*(3), 202-204.

Forward, S., & Buck, C. (1978). *Betrayal of innocence: Incest and its devastation.* New York: St. Martin's.

Fraser, M. W. (1996). Aggressive behavior in childhood and early adolescence: An ecological-development perspective on youth violence. *Social Work: Journal of the National Association of Social Workers, 41*(4), 347-361.

Freeman-Longo, R. E., Bird, S., Stevenson, W. F., & Fiske, J. A. (1994). *1991 nationwide survey of treatment programs.* Brandon, VT: Safer Society Program & Press.

Friedrich, W. N. (1990). *Psychotherapy of sexually abused children and their families.* New York: Norton.

Friedrich, W. N. (1991). *Casebook of sexual abuse treatment.* New York: Norton.

Friedrich, W. N. (1993a). Foreword. In E. Gil & C. Johnson (Eds.), *Sexualized children: Assessment and treatment of sexualized children and children who molest* (pp. ix-xii). Rockville, MD: Launch Press.

Friedrich, W. N. (1993b, January). Sexual behavior in sexually abused children. *Violence Update,* 7-11.

Friedrich, W. N. (1995). *Psychotherapy with sexually abused boys.* Thousand Oaks, CA: Sage.

Friedrich, W. N., & Gerber, P. (1996). *Multiple methods to assess dissociation in adolescent sex offenders.* Paper presented at the biannual meeting of the International Society for the Prevention of Child Abuse and Neglect, Dublin, Ireland.

Friedrich, W. N., Grambsch, P., Broughton, D., Kuiper, J., & Bielke, R. L. (1991). Normative sexual behavior in children. *Pediatrics, 88*(3), 456-464.

Friedrich, W. N., & Luecke, W. J. (1988). Young school-age sexually aggressive children. *Professional Psychology: Research and Practice, 19*(2), 155-164.

Friedrich, W. N., Urquiza, A. J., & Beilke, R. (1986). Behavior problems in sexually abused young children. *Journal of Pediatric Psychology, 11,* 47-57.

Gallo, A. M. (1979). Early childhood masturbation: A developmental approach. *Pediatric Nursing, 12,* 47-49.

Gelinas, D. (1988). Family therapy: Characteristic family constellation and basic therapeutic stance. In S. M. Sgroi (Ed.), *Vulnerable populations, Volume 2, evaluation and treatment of sexually abused children and adult survivors.* Lexington, MA: Lexington.

Gelman, G., Gordon, J., Christian, N., Talbot, M., & Snow, K. (1992, March). When kids molest kids. *Newsweek,* 68-70.

Gil, E. (1987). *Children who molest: A guide for parents of young sex offenders.* Walnut Creek, CA: Launch Press.

Gil, E. (1993a). Age-appropriate sex play versus problematic sexual behaviors. In E. Gil & T. C. Johnson (Eds.), *Sexualized children: Assessment and treatment of sexualized children and children who molest* (pp. 21-40). Rockville, MD: Launch Press.

Gil, E. (1993b). Family dynamics. In E. Gil & T. C. Johnson (Eds.), *Sexualized children: Assessment and treatment of sexualized children and children who molest* (pp. 101-120). Rockville, MD: Launch Press.

Gil, E. (1993c). Etiological theories. In E. Gil & T. C. Johnson (Eds.), *Sexualized children: Assessment and treatment of sexualized children and children who molest* (pp. 53-66). Rockville, MD: Launch Press.

Gil, E. (1993d). Individual therapy. In E. Gil & T. C. Johnson (Eds.), *Sexualized children: Assessment and treatment of sexualized children and children who molest* (pp. 179-210). Rockville, MD: Launch Press.

Gil, E. (1993e). Family treatment. In E. Gil & T. C. Johnson (Eds.), *Sexualized children: Assessment and treatment of sexualized children and children who molest* (pp. 275-302). Rockville, MD: Launch Press.

Gil, E., & Briere, J. (1994, February). *Assessment and treatment of sexualized children and children who molest and dissociation, repressed memories, and false memory syndrome: Working with survivors in the age of denial.* Workshop presentation, Tacoma, WA.

Gil, E., & Johnson, T. C. (1993a). *Sexualized children: Assessment and treatment of sexualized children who molest children.* Rockville, MD: Launch Press.

Gil, E., & Johnson, T. C. (1993b). Current and proposed community response. In E. Gil & T. C. Johnson (Eds.), *Sexualized children: Assessment and treatment of sexualized children and children who molest* (pp. 121-135). Rockville, MD: Launch Press.

Gray, A., & Friedrich, W. N. (1996). *Precursors to sexual aggression, research implications for changing treatment of sexual misbehavior in young children.* Paper presented at the annual meeting of the Association for the Treatment of Sexual Aggression, Chicago.

Gray, A. S., & Pithers, W. D. (1992). *A balanced approach with sexually aggressive and sexually reactive children: Frameworks and strategies.* Paper presented at the meeting of the Association for the Behavioral Treatment of Sexual Abusers, Portland, OR.

Gray, A. S., & Pithers, W. D. (1993). Relapse prevention with sex offenders. In H. E. Barbaree, W. L. Marshall, & S. M. Hudson (Eds.), *The juvenile sex offender* (pp. 289-319). New York: Guilford.

Green, A. (1985). Children traumatized by physical abuse. In S. Eth & R. Pynoos (Eds.), *Post traumatic disorder in children.* Washington, DC: American Psychiatric Press.

Green, A. H. (1988). Special issues in child sexual abuse. In D. Schetky & A. H. Green (Eds.), *Child sexual abuse: A handbook for health care and legal professionals* (pp. 125-135). New York: Brunner/Mazel.

Greenwald, E., & Leitenberg, H. (1989). Long-term effects of sexual experiences with siblings and nonsiblings during childhood. *Archives of Sexual Behavior, 18*(5), 389-399.

Griggs, D. R., & Boldi, A. (1995). Parallel treatment of parents of abuse reactive children. In M. Hunter (Ed.), *Child survivors and perpetrators of sexual abuse: Treatment innovations.* Thousand Oaks, CA: Sage.

Groth, A. N., & Loredo, C. (1981). Juvenile sexual offenders: Guidelines for assessment. *International Journal of Offender Therapy and Comparative Criminology, 25,* 31-39.

Haugaard, J., & Tilly, C. (1988). Characteristics predicting children's responses to sexual encounters with other children. *Child Abuse & Neglect, 12,* 209-218.

Henderson, J. E., English, D. J., & MacKenzie, W. R. (1989). Family centered casework practice with sexually aggressive children. *Journal of Social Work and Human Sexuality, 7,* 89-108.

Henry, D., Cossett, D., Auletta, T., & Egan, E. (1991). Needed services for foster parents of sexually abused children. *Child and Adolescent Social Work, 8*(2), 127-140.

Hill, R. (1958). Social stresses on the family. *Social Casework, 39,* 139-150.

Hindman, J. (1989). *Just before dawn.* Boise, ID: Northwest.

Hindman, J. (1994). *JCA—Juvenile Culpability Assessment* (2nd rev. ed.). Ontario, OR: Alexandria.

Hochstadt, N. J., Jaudes, P. K., Zimo, D. A., & Schachter, J. (1987). The medical and psychosocial needs of children entering foster care. *Child Abuse & Neglect, 11,* 53-62.

Isaac, C: (1987, May). *Identification and interruption of sexually offending behaviors in prepubescent children.* Paper presented at the Proceedings of the Sixteenth Annual Child Abuse and Neglect Symposium, Keystone, CO.

Isaac, C., & Lane, S. (1990). *The sexual abuse cycle in the treatment of adolescent sexual abusers.* Shorham, VT: Safer Society Program & Press.

James, B. (1989). *Treating traumatized children: New insights and creative interventions.* Lexington, MA: Lexington Books.

Johnson, T. C. (1988). Child perpetrators—Children who molest other children: Preliminary findings. *Child Abuse & Neglect, 12,* 219-229.

Johnson, T. C. (1989). Female child perpetrators: Children who molest other children. *Child Abuse & Neglect, 13,* 571-585.

Johnson, T. C. (1990). Children who act out sexually. In J. McNamara & B. H. McNamara (Eds.), *Adoption and the sexually abused child* (pp. 63-73). Portland: University of Southern Maine, Human Services Development Institute.

Johnson, T. C. (1991, August/September). *Understanding the sexual behaviors of young children.* SEICUS report, pp. 8-15.

Johnson, T. C. (1993a). Assessment of sexual behavior problems in preschool-aged and latency aged children. *Child and Adolescent Psychiatric Clinics of North America, 2*(3), 431-449.

Johnson, T. C. (1993b). Childhood sexuality. In E. Gil & T. C. Johnson (Eds.), *Sexualized children: Assessment and treatment of sexualized children and children who molest* (pp. 1-20). Rockville, MD: Launch Press.

Johnson, T. C. (1993c). Preliminary findings. In E. Gil & T. C. Johnson (Eds.), *Sexualized children: Assessment and treatment of sexualized children and children who molest* (pp. 63-89). Rockville, MD: Launch Press.

Johnson, T. C., & Aoki, W. T. (1993). *Sexual behaviors of latency age children in residential treatment* (pp. 1-22). New York: Haworth.

Johnson, T. C., & Berry, C. (1989). Children who molest: A treatment program. *Journal of Interpersonal Violence, 4*(2), 185-203.

Johnson, T. C., & Feldmeth, J. R. (1993). Sexual behaviors: A continuum. In E. Gil & T. C. Johnson (Eds.), *Sexualized children: Assessment and treatment of sexualized children and children who molest* (pp. 39-52). Rockville, MD: Launch Press.

Justice, B., & Justice, R. (1979). *The broken taboo: Sex in the family*. New York: Human Sciences Press.

Kadushin, A., & Seidl, F. W. (1971). Adoption failure: A social work postmortem. *Social Work, 16*(3), 32-38.

Kaslow, F., Haupt, D., Arce, A., & Werblowsky, J. (1981). Homosexual incest. *Psychiatric Quarterly, 53*(3), 184-193.

Katz, L. (1977). Older child adoptive placement: A time of family crisis. *Child Welfare, 56*(3), 165-171.

Kehoe, P. (1988). *Helping abused children: A book for those who work with sexually abused children*. Seattle, WA: Parenting Press.

Kempe, C. H., Silverman, F. H., Steele, B. F., Droegmueller, W., & Silver, H. K. (1962). The battered child syndrome. *Journal of the American Medical Association, 181*, 17-24.

Kempe, R. S., & Kempe, C. H. (1978). *Child abuse*. Cambridge, MA: Harvard University Press.

Kendall-Tackett, K. A., Williams, L. M., & Finkelhor, D. (1993). Impact of sexual abuse on children: A review and synthesis of recent empirical studies. *Psychological Bulletin, 113*(1), 164-180.

Kikuchi, J. J. (1995). When the offender is a child: Identifying and responding to juvenile sexual abuse offenders. In M. Hunter (Ed.), *Child survivors and perpetrators of sexual abuse: Treatment innovations* (pp. 108-124). Thousand Oaks, CA: Sage.

Kilpatrick, A. (1992). *Long range effects of child and adolescent sexual experiences*. Hillsdale, NJ: Lawrence Erlbaum.

Kinsey, A. C., Pomeroy, W. B., & Martin, C. E. (1948). *Sexual behavior in the human male*. Philadelphia: W. B. Saunders.

Kinsey, A. C., Pomeroy, W. B., Martin, C. E., & Gebhard, P. (1953). *Sexual behavior in the human female*. Philadelphia: W. B. Saunders.

Kirschner, S., Kirschner, D. A., & Rappaport, R. L. (1993). *Working with adult incest survivors: The healing journey*. New York: Brunner/Mazel.

Kizza, T. (1993, October 1). Homer police want charges of rape against three boys. *Anchorage Daily News*, pp. A1, A10.

Klee, L., & Halfon, N. (1987). Mental health care for foster children in California. *Child Abuse & Neglect, 11,* 63-74.

Knopp, F. H. (1982). *Remedial intervention in adolescent sex offenses: Nine program descriptions.* Orwell, VT: Safer Society Program & Press.

Knopp, F. H. (1991). *The youthful sex offender: The rationale and goals of early intervention and treatment.* Orwell, VT: Safer Society Press.

Kohan, M. J., Pothier, P., & Norbeck, J. S. (1987). Hospitalized children with history of sexual abuse: Incidence and care issues. *American Journal of Orthopsychiatry, 57*(2), 258-264.

Krona, D. A. (1980). Parents as treatment partners in residential care. *Child Welfare, 59*(2), 91-96.

Lambert, P. (1976). Memo to child care workers: Notes on the management of sex and stealing. *Child Welfare, 55*(5), 329-334.

Lambert, P. (1977). *The ABC's of child care work in residential care: The Linden Hill manual.* New York: Child Welfare League of America.

Lane, S. (1991a). Special offender populations. In G. D. Ryan & S. L. Lane (Eds.), *Juvenile sexual offending: Causes, consequences, and correction* (pp. 299-332). Lexington, MA: Lexington Books.

Lane, S. (1991b). The sexual abuse cycle. In G. D. Ryan & S. L. Lane (Eds.), *Juvenile sexual offending: Causes, consequences, and correction* (pp. 103-141). Lexington, MA: Lexington Books.

Larson, N. R., & Maddock, J. W. (1986). Structural and functional variables in incest family systems: Implications for assessment and treatment. In T. S. Trepper & M. J. Barrett (Eds.), *Treating incest: A multiple systems perspective* (pp. 27-44). New York: Haworth.

Lavee, Y., McCubbin, H. I., & Patterson, J. M. (1985). The double ABCX model of family stress and adaptation: An empirical test by analysis of structural equations with latent variables. *Journal of Marriage and the Family, 47,* 811-825.

Laviola, M. (1989). Effects of older brother-younger sister incest: A review of four cases. *Journal of Family Violence, 4*(3), 259-274.

Laviola, M. (1992). Effects of older brother-younger sister incest: A study of the dynamics of 17 cases. *Child Abuse & Neglect, 16,* 409-421.

LeCroy, C. W. (1984). Residential treatment services: A review of some current trends. *Child Care Quarterly, 13*(2), 83-97.

Lewis, D. O., Shanok, S. S., & Pincus, J. H. (1979). Juvenile male sexual assaulters. *American Journal of Psychiatry, 139*(9), 1194-1196.

Longo, R. E., & Groth, A. N. (1983). Juvenile sexual offenses in the histories of adult rapists and child molesters. *International Journal of Offender Therapy and Comparative Criminology, 27,* 150-155.

Loredo, C. M. (1982). Sibling incest. In S. M. Sgroi (Ed.), *Handbook of clinical intervention in child sexual abuse* (pp. 177-189). Lexington, MA: Lexington Books.

Maas, H. S. (1986). *From crib to crypt: Social development and responsive environments as professional focus.* New Brunswick, NJ: Rutgers University Press.

MacFarlane, K., & Cunningham, C. (1988). *Steps to healthy touching*. Mount Dora, CA: Kidrights.

Magnus, R. A. (1974). Teaching parents to parent: Parent involvement in residential treatment programs. *Children Today, 3*(1), 25-27.

Maluccio, A. N., & Fein, E. (1983). Permanency planning: A redefinition. *Child Welfare, 62*(3), 195-201.

Maluccio, A. N., Fein, E., Hamilton, J., Ward, D., & Sutton, M. (1982). Permanency planning and residential child care. *Child Care Quarterly, 11*(2), 97-107.

Martinson, F. M. (1976). Eroticism in infancy and childhood. *Journal of Sex Research, 12,* 251-262.

Martinson, F. M. (1981). Preadolescent sexuality: Latent or manifest? In L. Constantine & F. Martinson (Eds.), *Children and sex: New findings, new perspectives* (pp. 83-94). Boston: Little, Brown.

Martinson, F. M. (1991). Normal sexual development in infancy and early childhood. In G. D. Ryan & S. L. Lane (Eds.), *Juvenile sex offending: Causes, consequences, and correction* (pp. 57-82). Lexington, MA: Lexington Books.

Martinson, F. M. (1994). *The sexual life of children*. Westport, CT: Bergin & Garvey.

Mathews, R., Mathews, J., & Speltz, K. (1990). Female sexual offenders. In M. Hunter (Ed.), *The sexually abused male: Prevalence, impact, and treatment* (Vol. 1, pp. 275-294). Lexington, MA: Lexington Books.

Matsuda, B., & Rasmussen, L. A. (1990, November). *Comprehensive plan for juvenile sex offenders: Preliminary report*. Salt Lake City: The Utah Governor's Council on Juvenile Sex Offenders.

McBee, D. (1991). *Anchorage Juvenile Sex Offender Continuum Group* (Prevention Subcommittee Report). Anchorage: Anchorage Juvenile Sex Offender Continuum Group.

McCubbin, H. I., & Patterson, J. M. (1982). Family adaptation to crisis. In H. I. McCubbin, A. E. Cauble, & J. M. Patterson (Eds.), *Family stress, coping, and social support* (pp. 44-46). Springfield, IL: Charles C Thomas.

McFadden, E. J. (1989). The sexually abused child in specialized foster care. *Child and Youth Services, 12*(1/2), 91-105.

McFadden, E. J., & Ryan, P. (1991). Maltreatment in family foster homes: Dynamics and dimensions. *Child and Youth Services, 15*(2), 209-231.

McNamara, J. (1988). *Tangled feelings: Sexual abuse and adoption*. Greensboro, NC: Family Resources.

McNamara, J. (1990). Structure for safety: Parenting adoptive children who were sexually abused. In J. McNamara & B. H. McNamara (Eds.), *Adoption and the sexually abused child* (pp. 47-61). Portland: University of Southern Maine, Human Services Development Institute.

McNeil, E. B., & Morse, W. C. (1964). The institutional management of sex in emotionally disturbed children. *American Journal of Orthopsychiatry, 34,* 115-124.

Mead, G. (1934). *Mind, self, and society*. Chicago: University of Chicago Press.

Meiselman, K. (1978). *Incest*. San Francisco: Jossey-Bass.

Meyer-Bahlberg, H., Wasserman, G., Dolesal, C. L., & Bueno, Y. (1996). *Predictors of sexual behavior in boys age 7-12 years*. Paper presented at the annual meeting of the Society for the Scientific Study of Sex, Houston, TX.

Mian, M., Wehrspann, W., Klajner-Diamond, K., LeBaron, D., & Winder, C. (1986). Review of 125 children six years of age and under who were sexually abused. *Child Abuse & Neglect, 10*, 223-229.

Money, J., & Ehrhardt, A. A. (1972). *Man & woman, boy & girl*. Baltimore, MD: Johns Hopkins University Press.

National Adolescent Perpetrator Network. (1988). Preliminary report from the national task force on juvenile sexual offending. *Juvenile and Family Court Journal, 39*(2), 41-43.

National Adolescent Perpetrator Network. (1993). Revised report from the national task force on juvenile sexual offending. *Juvenile and Family Court Journal, 44*(4), 5-120.

Nielson, G., Young, D., & Latham, S. (1982). Multiple acting out adolescents: Developmental correlates and response to secure treatment. *International Journal of Offender Therapy and Comparative Criminology, 26*(3), 195-206.

O'Brien, M. J. (1991). Taking sibling incest seriously. In M. Q. Patton (Ed.), *Family sexual abuse: Frontline research and evaluation* (pp. 75-93). Newbury Park, CA: Sage.

Okami, P. (1992). Child perpetrators of sexual abuse: The emergence of a problematic deviant category. *Journal of Sex Research, 29*(1), 109-140.

Patterson, G. (1982). *Coercive family processes*. Eugene, OR: Castalia.

Patterson, G. R., DeBaryshe, B. D., & Ramsey, E. (1989). A developmental perspective on antisocial behavior. *American Psychologist, 44*, 329-335.

Piaget, J. (1928). *Judgement and reasoning in the child*. London: Routledge Kegan Paul.

Pierce, L. H., & Pierce, R. L. (1990). Adolescent/sibling perpetrators. In A. L. Horton, B. L. Johnson, L. M. Roundy, & D. Williams (Eds.), *The incest perpetrator: A family member no one wants to treat* (pp. 99-108). Newbury Park, CA: Sage.

Pithers, W., Gray, A. S., Cunningham, C., & Lane, S. (1993). *From trauma to understanding*. Brandon, VT: Safer Society Program & Press.

Pithers, W. D., Kashima, K. M., Cumming, G. F., Beal, L. S., & Buell, M. (1988). Relapse prevention: A method of enhancing maintenance of change in sex offenders. In A. Salter (Ed.), *Treating child sex offenders and victims* (pp. 131-170). Newbury Park, CA: Sage.

Pittman, F. S. (1987). *Turning points: Treating families in transition and crisis*. New York: Norton.

Plach, T. A. (1993). *Residential treatment and the sexually abused child.* Springfield, IL: Charles C Thomas.

Pomeroy, J. C., Behar, D., & Stewart, M. (1981). Abnormal sexual behavior in pre-pubescent children. *British Journal of Psychiatry, 138,* 119-125.

Porter, E. (1986). *Treating the young male victim of sexual assault: Issues and intervention strategies.* Orwell, VT: Safer Society Press.

Price, S. (1993, September 30). Boys charged in rape of 5 year old. *Homer News,* pp. 1, 17.

Radbill, S. X. (1968). A history of child abuse and infanticide. In R. E. Helfer & C. H. Kempe (Eds.), *The battered child.* Chicago: University of Chicago Press.

Rasmussen, L. A., Burton, J. E., & Christopherson, B. J. (1992). Precursors to offending and the trauma outcome process in sexually reactive children. *Journal of Child Sexual Abuse, 1*(1), 33-48.

Ray, J. A., & English, D. J. (1991). *Children with sexual behavior problems: A behavioral comparison.* Olympia, WA: Department of Social and Health Services, Office of Children's Administration Research.

Roberts, J. (1986). Fostering the sexually abused child. *Adoption & Fostering, 10*(1), 8-11.

Roberts, T. W. (1994). *A systems perspective of parenting: The individual, the family, and the social network.* Pacific Grove, CA: Brooks/Cole.

Rogers, C. M., & Tremain, T. (1984). Clinical intervention with boy victims of sexual abuse. In I. R. Stuart & J. G. Greer (Eds.), *Victims of sexual aggression: Treatment of children, women, and men* (pp. 91-104). New York: Van Nostrand Reinhold.

Rushton, A. (1989). Annotation: Post-placement services for foster and adoptive parents-support, counseling or therapy? *Journal of Child Psychology and Psychiatry, 30*(2), 197-204.

Russell, D. (1983). The incidence and prevalence of intrafamilial and extra familial sexual abuse of female children. *Child Abuse & Neglect, 7,* 133-146.

Russell, D. E. (1986). *The secret trauma: Incest in the lives of girls and women.* New York: Basic Books.

Ryan, G. (1987). Getting the facts. *Interchange: National Adolescent Perpetrator Network.* Denver, CO: Kempe National Center.

Ryan, G. (1989). Victim to victimizer: Rethinking victim treatment. *Journal of Interpersonal Violence, 4*(3), 325-341.

Ryan, G. (1990). Sexual behavior in childhood. In J. McNamara & B. H. McNamara (Eds.), *Adoption and the sexually abused child* (pp. 27-45). Portland: University of Southern Maine, Human Services Development Institute.

Ryan, G. (1991a). Perpetration prevention: Primary and secondary. In G. D. Ryan & S. L. Lane (Eds.), *Juvenile sex offending: Causes, consequences, and correction* (pp. 393-408). Lexington, MA: Lexington Books.

Ryan, G. (1991b). The juvenile sex offender's family. In G. D. Ryan & S. L. Lane (Eds.), *Juvenile sex offending: Causes, consequences, and correction* (pp. 143-160). Lexington, MA: Lexington Books.

Ryan, G. (1991c). Theories of etiology. In G. D. Ryan & S. L. Lane (Eds.), *Juvenile sex offending: Causes, consequences, and correction* (pp. 41-55). Lexington, MA: Lexington Books.

Ryan, G., & Blum, J. (1993). *Understanding and responding to the sexual behavior of children: A primary perpetration prevention project, revised curriculum.* Denver: Kempe Children's Center, University of Colorado Health Sciences Center.

Ryan, G., & Blum, J. (1994). *Childhood sexuality: A guide for parents.* Denver: Kempe Children's Center, University of Colorado Health Sciences Center.

Ryan, G., Blum, J., Sandau-Christopher, D., Law, S., Weher, F., Sundine, C., Astler, L., Teske, J., & Dale, J. (1993). *Understanding and responding to the sexual behavior of children: Trainer's manual.* Denver: Kempe Children's Center, University of Colorado Health Sciences Center.

Ryan, G., Lane, L., Davis, J., & Isaac, C. (1987). Juvenile sex offenders: Development and correction. *Child Abuse & Neglect, 11,* 385-395.

Ryan, G. D., & Lane, S. L. (Eds.). (1991). *Juvenile sex offending: Causes, consequences, and correction.* Lexington, MA: Lexington Books.

Sanford, L. T. (1980). *The silent children: A parent's guide to the prevention of child sexual abuse.* New York: McGraw-Hill.

Selman, R. L., & Schultz, L. H. (1990). *Making a friend in youth: Developmental theory and pair therapy.* Chicago: University of Chicago Press.

Sgroi, S. (1978). Child sexual assault: Some guidelines for intervention and assessment. In A. W. Burgess, N. A. Groth, L. L. Holmstrom, & S. M. Sgroi (Eds.), *Sexual assault of children and adolescents* (pp. 129-143). Lexington, MA: Lexington Books.

Sgroi, S. M., Bunk, B. S., & Wabrek, C. J. (1988). Children's sexual behaviors and their relationship to sexual abuse. In S. M. Sgroi (Ed.), *Vulnerable populations and treatment of sexually abused children and adult survivors* (Vol. 1, pp. 1-24). Lexington, MA: Lexington Books.

Smith, H., & Israel, E. (1987). Sibling incest: A study of the dynamics of 25 cases. *Child Abuse & Neglect, 11,* 101-108.

Sorrenti-Little, L., Bagley, C., & Robertson, S. (1984). An operational definition of the long-term harmfulness of sexual relations with peers and adults by young children. *Canada's Children, 9,* 46-57.

Steinhauer, P. D. (1991). *The least detrimental alternative: A systematic guide to case planning and decision making for children in care.* Toronto: University of Toronto Press.

Summit, R. (1983). The child sexual abuse accommodations syndrome. *Child Abuse & Neglect, 7*(2), 177-193.

Treacy, E. C., & Fisher, C. B. (1993). Foster parenting the sexually abused: A family life education program. *Journal of Child Sexual Abuse, 2*(1), 47-63.

Utah Task Force of the Utah Network on Juveniles Offending Sexually. (1996). *The Utah report on juvenile sex offenders.* Salt Lake City: Author.

Valentine, D., Conway, P., & Randolph, J. (1988). Placement disruptions: Perspectives of adoptive parents. *Journal of Social Work and Human Sexuality, 6,* 133-153.

Washington State Department of Social and Health Services. (1992a, January). *A comparison of sexually aggressive youth on open/active DCFS caseloads referred for Child Protection Act treatment compared to youth eligible for treatment but not referred.* Olympia: Washington State Department of Social and Health Services, Division of Management Services.

Washington State Department of Social and Health Services. (1992b, June). *A comparison of sexually aggressive youth on open/active caseloads, comparing youth under and over the age of 12.* Olympia: Washington State Department of Social and Health Services, Office of Children's Administration.

Wiehe, V. R. (1990). *Sibling abuse: Hidden physical, emotional, and sexual trauma.* Lexington, MA: Lexington Books.

Wiehe, V. R. (1991). *Perilous rivalry: When siblings become abusive.* Lexington, MA: Lexington Books.

Winkler, R. C., Brown, D. W., Van Keppel, M., & Blanchard, A. (1988). *Clinical practice in adoption.* Elmsford, NY: Pergamon.

Yates, A. (1982). Children eroticized by incest. *American Journal of Psychiatry, 139*(4), 482-485.

Yates, A. (1987). Psychological damage associated with extreme eroticism in young children. *Psychiatric Annals, 17,* 257-261.

Young, R. E., Bergandi, T. A., & Titus, T. G. (1994). Comparison of the effects of sexual abuse on male and female latency-aged children. *Journal of Interpersonal Violence, 9*(3), 291-306.

Zoglin, R. (1996, October 6). A kiss isn't just a kiss. *Time, 148.*

Index

About the Author

Sharon K. Araji is Professor of Sociology at the University of Alaska Anchorage. She has an MA and a PhD in sociology from Washington State University and an MEd from the University of Idaho. She first became interested in the topic of child sexual abuse when she was a National Institute of Mental Health postdoctoral fellow at the Family Research Laboratory at the University of New Hampshire. During this time, she worked with David Finkelhor and Murray Straus. She has authored and coauthored articles in the areas of sexual abuse of children and domestic violence and teaches courses and conducts workshops on these topics.

About the Contributors

Rebecca L. Bosek, MS, LMFT, is a licensed marital and family therapist in Alaska. She received her MS in counseling psychology from the University of Alaska at Anchorage in 1990. She has done clinical work with sex abuse-reactive and sexually aggressive children and their families. She is an interdisciplinary PhD candidate in clinical psychology at the University of Alaska at Fairbanks.

Elizabeth A. Sirles is Associate Professor of Social Work at the University of Alaska at Anchorage and is also department chair. She has an MSW from the University of Kansas and a PhD in social work from Washington University (St. Louis, MO). She was formerly the director of the Child Sexual Abuse Treatment Program in the Division of Child Psychiatry at the Washington University Medical School. She has authored and coauthored articles in the areas of incest and domestic violence.